YEOMAN SERVICE

YEOMAN SERVICE

A Short History of the Kent Yeomanry
1939—1945

by

LT.-COLONEL FRANKLIN LUSHINGTON

The Naval & Military Press Ltd

Published by

The Naval & Military Press Ltd
Unit 10 Ridgewood Industrial Park,
Uckfield, East Sussex,
TN22 5QE England

Tel: +44 (0) 1825 749494
Fax: +44 (0) 1825 765701

www.naval-military-press.com
www.military-genealogy.com

In reprinting in facsimile from the original, any imperfections are inevitably reproduced and the quality may fall short of modern type and cartographic standards.

Dedicated by permission
to
Kent's foremost Citizen
THE RIGHT HON. WINSTON S. CHURCHILL, O.M.
Warden of the Cinque Ports

"History with its flickering lamp stumbles along the trail of the past trying to reconstruct its scenes, to revive its echoes, and kindle with pale gleams the passions of former days. What is the worth of all this? The only guide to a man is his conscience; the only shield to his memory is the rectitude and sincerity of his actions. It is very imprudent to walk through life without this shield, because we are so often mocked by the failure of our hopes and the upsetting of our calculations; but with this shield, however the fates may play, we march always in the ranks of honour."

WINSTON CHURCHILL.

CONTENTS

		PAGE
AUTHOR'S FOREWORD		vii
INTRODUCTION		1
CHAPTER		
I	France, September 1939–June 1940	9
II	France, continued	30
III	Interlude between battles, June 1940–June 1942	60
IV	The Western Desert, June 1942–December 1942	81
V	The Western Desert, continued	108
VI	Second Interlude between battles, December 1942–March 1944	143
VII	Italy, March 1944–May 1945	157
VIII	143rd Field Regiment R.A.	186
	Epilogue	194
	Appendices	201

MAPS AND ILLUSTRATIONS

Kent Yeomen, Past and Present	Frontispiece
Map of France	facing 14
Flag Signal, Desert Formation	82
Flag Signal, Column of Route	85
Flag Signal, Halt or Go On	87
Flag Signal, Action	109
Map of Western Desert	facing 134
Map of Syria and Palestine	149
Map of Italy	159
Map of Middle East	End paper

AUTHOR'S FOREWORD

A GOOD regiment is like a large family in which all the members have their own pet stories about each other as well as their own views about the important part they themselves play, have played, and will always continue to play, in the family life. In compiling a family history one knows that Aunt Emily is bound to be offended if you leave out the story about the broken teapot while Uncle John will doubtless regard the omission of any account of his early struggles in the office as an unforgivable affront. So in presenting this short history of the Kent Yeomanry I feel I must begin by apologizing to all those whose individual deeds in the late war, although obviously of great interest, have through some oversight been omitted, and add by way of further excuse that, owing to the present paper shortage, it was found necessary to confine this particular history to one volume.

There are, however, other and perhaps more important charges to which I am aware I have laid myself open. Among these are the accusation of devoting too much space to the history of the regiment up to and including the battle of Alamein, in comparison with the period from Alamein to the end of the war, and too much space to the history of the first line, the 97th Field Regiment R.A. with that given to the second line, the 143rd Field Regiment R.A. Apart, however, from the fact that I myself served with the 97th, and had the honour to command it for the first three and a half years of the war, and that it is always easier to write about events of which one has personal knowledge, there are good reasons for this which I should like to submit to my would-be critics. First from the point of view of the reader of history by far the most interesting and exciting part of the war was the early period, the period of survival, when the British Empire and Commonwealth was fighting alone and all that we held most dear was at stake. Nearly all the great British epics took place then, Dunkirk and St. Valery, the Battle of Britain, the Battle of the Atlantic, Wavell's victories in the desert, the siege of Tobruk, Crete, the defence of Malta, the terrible retreat from Gazala to Alamein and finally and lastly Alamein itself, the turning point of the purely British side of the war. After Alamein the atmosphere of the war changed. We were no longer fighting alone; the period of our greatest danger was over; we had changed over from a defensive war, in which we were fighting for our very existence as a nation, to an offensive war in which our identity was merged with the great mass movements of our Allies. It seems to me only natural that the ordinary British reader should find more interest in the early period than the later.

Secondly, the compiler of history is largely dependent on the sources available. The story of the 97th has been drawn from a number of different accounts, to the authors of which my grateful acknowledgements are due, that of the 143rd from one account only written by Major E. R. H. Bowring, M.C., and a very excellent account it is too, but of necessity shorter and more concise than the other.

Thirdly, this is in no sense an official history based on official records but rather a collection of personal stories taken down while the events described are still fresh in the minds of those who wrote them. It is my belief that this method of writing history gains in authenticity of atmosphere what it loses in accuracy of detail. In time of war the tempo of men's lives moves at a faster pace. The feelings and the passions engendered by battle are not the prerogative of one man alone but, being common to all, are shared in a comradeship which takes no account of rank. Grief and fear, loneliness and exaltation and despair lie closer to the surface of everyday life and the sum total of all this is a spiritual entity which has little or nothing to do with dates and place names. It is the business of the regimental historian to catch this spirit, as it were, on the wing, to reveal it for what it was, a living breathing thing and not to bury it in the grave clothes of official language.

To conclude, it seems to me that a history of this kind only fulfills half its object if it is read solely by those members of the regiment who took part in the events described. It is my earnest hope that in spite of its shortcomings it will also appeal to a wider audience, to the wives and mothers

AUTHOR'S FOREWORD

who should be proud to know what their menfolk have done, to the people of the county of Kent, who should be proud to read of the historic deeds of one of their county regiments and, last but not least, to the coming generation of Kent Yeomen, who may gain inspiration and pride from these tales of their fathers and their fathers' fathers so that as long as the regiment remains in being their story will be handed down from one generation to another.

ACKNOWLEDGEMENTS

I HAVE to express my most grateful thanks to all those who have helped me to produce this book. The names of the authors of the various accounts already appear in the text. To them must be added Gunner F. H. Roberts of the 97th Field Regiment Survey Section who is responsible for the excellent maps, Gunner Lindrop of 387 Battery who is responsible for the four illustrations showing flag signals in the desert, and Major R. A. L. Hartman for the illustration depicting a Kent Yeoman, Past and Present.

I have also to acknowledge my indebtedness to *A Miniature History of the War* by R. C. K. Ensor, published by the Oxford University Press, from which I have drawn most of my facts about the history of the war as a whole.

Finally I should like to acknowledge my debt to Gunner Holdstock. For the purposes of my story I was anxious to include someone who should represent the opinions and views of the rank and file of the Regiment. I hope therefore that my friends and batmen Gunners Webb, Sullivan, Cole and Walker will forgive me for combining all four of them in one composite character under this purely fictitious name. I like to think that Gunner Holdstock is typical of the ordinary Yeoman Gunner, a person whose courage, constancy, and cheerfulness under all conditions were my inspiration and comfort during six long years.

INTRODUCTION

IN the spring of 1793 France declared war upon England. Fears for the safety of our coasts and particularly of the coasts of Kent, gave rise to the formation of various volunteer defence units. Among these the most notable were certain Volunteer Corps of Horse for a few years called Fencibles which later became known as Yeomanry Cavalry. Each member of the Corps was expected to provide himself with his own horse and such arms and accoutrements as might be required.

From these early beginnings the East Kent Yeomanry came into being in 1793 and the West Kent Yeomanry the following year. Five years later in the summer of 1799 King George III reviewed both regiments in the Mote Park, Maidstone. An account of this event states that "The crowds that thronged in from all round Maidstone to see the review were such that the roads were rendered almost impassible. The town itself was so full the previous evening that many visitors were unable to obtain accommodation. The Volunteers, about 5,000 in number, provided their own transport and distinguished themselves by wearing oak boughs in their hats. On the conclusion of the review Lord Romney entertained the company to dinner which was laid for 6,000 people."

It is interesting to record in these times of austerity that the dishes included sixty lambs, 700 fowls, 300 hams, 300 tongues, 220 dishes of boiled beef and 230 dishes of roast beef as well as quantities of meat and fruit pies.

In 1827, owing to one of those fits of mistaken economy to which, in times of peace, even the best of governments is subject, the two regiments were disbanded, only to be reformed again three years later. From the point of view of the Kent Yeomanry this break of three years was unfortunate as it resulted in a considerable loss of precedence. Their date of formation was only allowed officially from 1830, and instead of occupying places among the first five Yeomanry regiments, they now number nineteen and thirty-two respectively.

In 1856 the East Kent Regiment of Yeomanry Cavalry were armed with rifles, and changed their title to the

"East Kent Mounted Rifles". Two years later they were granted the prefix "Royal" by Queen Victoria.

In 1864 the West Kent Yeomanry Cavalry, in recognition of the number of occasions on which they had served as escort to Her Majesty, received the additional prefix of "The Queen's Own".

In 1873 the Duke of Connaught became Honorary Colonel of the Royal East Kent Mounted Rifles. Since then the regiment, and the two batteries which succeeded it, have borne the title of "Duke of Connaught's Own".

During the Boer War, 1900–1902, both regiments served with distinction in South Africa as mounted infantry.

During the 1914–18 war both regiments served first in Gallipoli and then in North Africa. It is interesting to note that the actual amalgamation of the two regiments first took place at Sollum in 1917, a place only too well-known to their successors in 1942. From North Africa the combined regiments under the title of the 10th (East and West Kent Yeomanry) Battalion the Buffs moved to Palestine and played its part in General Allenby's successful campaign against the Turks. In the spring of 1918 they moved once more to France and took part in the final battles which resulted in the capture of the Hindenburg Line, the retreat of the invading German armies, and the end of the war. Again it is interesting to note that the day before the armistice in November, 1918, the battalion were the leading troops of the brigade to enter Tournai, a place that became known under very different circumstances to their successors in May, 1940.

The following account of the West Kent Yeomanry in 1914–16 and of the combined regiments in 1917–18 is by the present Honorary Colonel of the Kent Yeomany, Col. C. E. Ponsonby, O.B.E., T.D.

"In the summer of 1914 the Regiment had only just completed its annual training when on the 5th August its members were recalled to the colours and mobilized at Maidstone. Shortly after its mobilization the Regiment proceeded to its war station near Canterbury, where it formed part of the South Coast Defences. For the space of a year training was carried on under war conditions until in September, 1915, the Regiment received its orders for service abroad, and left in the S.S. 'Olympic' for Gallipoli. The Regiment arrived on the Peninsula only to see the last three months of that phase of the campaign, but it had an interesting experience of trench warfare under the worst possible conditions. Officers and men obtained an insight into the difficulties and uncertainties surrounding a campaign which starts with an imperfect organization. Towards the end of the time, the contrary was efficiently demonstrated by the excellent organization which preceded and resulted in the successful evacuation of the Peninsula. The Regiment's casualties at Gallipoli were 10 killed and 25 wounded, but a large number were evacuated with the various diseases with which the place abounded.

"After a month on the Island of Lemnos the Regiment proceeded to Egypt at the beginning of 1916, and there had plenty of time to refit and adapt itself to a campaign in the desert. A few months spent on the Canal inured everyone to heat and sand, but in August the Regiment moved to Matruh about 125 miles west of Alexandria, where it settled down for the autumn, nominally as a protection to Egypt from the attacks of the Senussi, but actually to a life of comparative comfort and enjoyment. The Senussi remained at a respectful distance of over 100 miles.

"During all this time the Regiment drilled and manœuvred as dismounted cavalry, but in the autumn it was decided that all the Yeomanry in Egypt who had come out without their horses would be of much greater value as Infantry; and at the end of the year the West Kent Yeomanry amalgamated with the Royal East Kent Mounted Rifles under the comprehensive title of 'The 10th (East and West Kent Yeomanry) Battalion, The Buffs'. The amalgamated Regiment joined forces at Sollum, and in March, 1917, moved to Alexandria where it was made up with drafts from the Buffs, and became a part of the 230th Infantry Brigade, of the 74th Yeomanry Division.

"The Yeomanry Battalion in April, 1917, took part

in the second Battle of Gaza and spent the rest of the summer digging, fortifying new lines and finally in intensive training in open warfare. This terminated in the Battle of Beersheba on October 31st, 1917. The Yeomanry Battalion was one of those which captured the defences round Beersheba and a few days later took part in the Battle of Sheria where the Turks were finally put to rout and chased by the cavalry for a distance of upwards of 50 miles. The Battalion itself was withdrawn to the sea but a few weeks later commenced the advance towards Jerusalem, and on the 6th December, 1917, again played a leading part in the Battle of Jerusalem which resulted in the capture of that city.

"After a few months of great discomfort, owing to cold and lack of provisions, in the rocky hills round Jerusalem, in March, 1918, the Battalion took part in a further advance towards Nablus (the ancient Shechem). It is believed that an advance on a much larger scale was in contemplation by the authorities when the serious state of affairs in France made it necessary to withdraw the 60th and 74th Divisions intact and large portions of other Divisions from Palestine to the Western Front.

"On the 1st May, 1918, the Battalion arrived in France. The next three months were spent in various places behind the line refitting and training, until at the end of July, 1918, the Regiment went into the line in the Merville section, and in a few weeks advanced the line about 1,000 yards.

"At the beginning of September the Battalion moved to the Somme, and throughout that month took an active part in the advance on the Hindenburg Line. The conditions during the month can be described as anything but pleasant, as the Germans were naturally using every means in their power to resist our advance. General Sir Henry Rawlinson in thanking the Division for its good work wrote as follows: 'The work of this Division during a period of severe and continuous fighting is worthy of the best traditions of the Yeoman stock of Great Britain. Brought to this country from a hot climate where they took part in a very different method of war-

INTRODUCTION

fare, the 74th Division has quickly adapted itself to the altered conditions and has fought with a determination and courage which is beyond praise.'

"The Battalion was immediately afterwards moved again to the north and for the last month of the war actively participated in the pursuit of the enemy, finally being the leading troops of the brigade to enter Tournai. The Armistice was declared on the following day. Subsequently the Battalion settled down in various villages in Belgium and remained there until June, 1919, when it was disbanded. The colours of the Battalion were deposited in Canterbury Cathedral at the memorial service to all the battalions of the Buffs on the 17th of that month.

"The casualties of the 10th Yeomanry Battalion in Palestine and in France were 8 officers and 134 men killed and 24 officers and 486 men wounded. Ten men died of sickness.

"During the 1914–18 war when the 10th Yeomanry Battalion was composed of East Kent Yeomen, West Kent Yeomen and recruits from the Buffs, the members of the various regiments wore their distinctive badges, but all wore a diamond shaped flash on the left arm consisting of the White Horse of Kent on a black background. This has been retained by the Kent Yeomanry as their regimental badge ever since.

"In 1921 the regiment was reformed and converted into artillery, the Royal East Kent Mounted Rifles[1] becoming 385 and 386 Field Batteries with headquarters at Canterbury and Ashford respectively, the Queen's Own West Kent Yeomanry becoming 387 and 388 Field Batteries with headquarters at Maidstone and Bromley. All four batteries formed part of the 97th Field Brigade R.A., Kent Yeomanry, a title that was subsequently changed to the 97th Field Regiment."

The following account of the Regiment from September, 1921, to December, 1939, is by Lt.-Col. H. W. Lucy, O.B.E., T.D.

"The years between the two World Wars were very

[1] For history of R.E.K.M.R. from 1914–18 see Appendix H.

difficult ones for the Territorial Army. This was mainly due to public apathy, lack of training grants and equipment, and to the open opposition of one political party whose main claim to distinction was the number of conscientious objectors among its leaders in the 1914–1918 war. Advocating 'peace at any price', hindering recruiting, and endeavouring to disband Officers' Training Corps and Cadet Corps, its members were largely responsible for the unpreparedness of the fighting forces at the outbreak of the war in 1939.

"In 1938 the passing of the Conscription Act caused a very large influx of personnel into the T.A., and by early 1939 the strength of the regiment was double the War Establishment. There was no reserve of trained Officers and N.C.Os to keep pace with this rapid expansion, and only a small quantity of extra equipment was available. This shortage of Officers, N.C.Os, and equipment seriously hampered training. To overcome the personnel difficulty extra classes were started to train Officers and N.C.Os, and the regiment owes much to the work of Lieut.-Col. G. W. Mansell, who was Captain and Adjutant at the time, and did much to achieve the end in view. Thanks to these classes the regiment was able, on the outbreak of war, to make up a shortage of seven junior officers from its own resources, and to provide a very useful cadre of Officers and N.C.Os on the formation of the second line regiment, 143 Field Regt. R.A. whose first C.O. was Lieut-Col. F. N. Richardson, then serving as a B.C. in the 97th.

"Despite the difficulties experienced, the old Yeomanry spirit of comradeship and service flourished, sustaining the regiment then and throughout the war, and still living on in the 'Old Comrades Association' of to-day.

"On the outbreak of war the regiment mobilised at Mote Park, Maidstone. During the early stages it was without an adjutant, Captain G. Mansell having unluckily had a serious accident. His place was taken on the 10th September by Captain A. B. Blaxland.

"Other and more serious difficulties were encountered

INTRODUCTION

in the work of mobilising a T.A. regiment for war. For unlike the regular army the T.A. had no mobilisation stores at its depots. These had to be collected from all over the country and for a short time life was very hectic, although not without its amusing side. It was only a hasty application of paint that prevented us from advertising 'Kent's Best' and the merits of two rival laundries in northern France, while the day before the regiment entrained it was found that the Ordnance had issued us with over seven hundred sets of webbing equipment without any belts. An officer had to be flown in a bomber, kindly loaned by the R.A.F., to the nearest Ordnance depot to retrieve the missing articles. Eventually however these and other difficulties were successfully overcome.

"Organised into two batteries, 385 and 387 Field Batteries, of three troops each, the regiment embarked for France on the 25th September, 1939, leaving a small cadre behind to form a second line whose subsequent history is given in a separate account. Although armed with 25 pdrs. belonging to another regiment we at least had the satisfaction of knowing that we were complete in every detail and were one of the first, if not the first, T.A. regiment to go overseas.

"The main body landed at Cherbourg on the 26th and left the same evening by rail for La Hutte, where it detrained the following morning and marched to the billeting area, Piace, some 20 miles north of Le Mans.

"Meanwhile the guns and vehicles, which had travelled by a different route, and disembarked at Nantes on the same day, had started moving up by road. So that by the 29th September the whole regiment had concentrated in the Piace area.

"The next five days were spent in overhauling our equipment for the march up to the Belgian border, and at 0700 hrs. on 5th October, we left Piace to march 97 miles in convoy with two other Fd. Regts., a Coy of R.A.S.C. and a Fd. Amb., to Louviers, 18 miles South of Rouen. The following day the march was continued, and after covering 80 miles the Regiment bivouacked at Behen, 5 miles S.W. of Abbeville. The 7th October was spent in maintenance, and on 8th October the regiment marched 72 miles to a hide in a wood at Moncheaux, some 6 miles North of Douai.

"Next day we moved to the Auchy area, some 15 miles South of Lille, R.H.Q. being billetted in the Ferme La Planque, 385 Bty. at Visterie and 387 Bty. at Ferme Du Chapitre.

"During the whole of this period 'secrecy' was the order of the day. Everything was so secret that nobody knew what was happening, and much confusion resulted. Thanks to 'secrecy', no warning was given to the advance party that the regiment had arrived in France and was on its way to the billetting area. The warning order arrived three days after the regiment had settled in. In another case, despite repeated assurances that the Gun and Vehicle parties were still on the high seas, they surprised everybody by arriving in the billetting area at Piace before it was known that they had disembarked. There were many other such incidents which indicated that super secrecy was defeating itself.

"At Auchy the regiment became part of the Corps Artillery of the 1st Corps. Digging began on 11th October, and apart from the reconnaissance of positions to cover the Bachy switch line, gun pit digging, and individual training, there was little of excitement during the rest of October and November.

"So started what was to become known as the 'phoney' war."

On 1st December Lt.-Col. H. W. Lucy was invalided to a Base Hospital and vacated command of the regiment having completed 17 years service with the 97th, and severing a connection with the Kent Yeomanry which had extended over 29 years. Lt.-Col. F. Lushington assumed command of the regiment on the same day.[1]

[1] For list of commanding officers since the amalgamation of the two Yeomanry regiments as an artillery unit in 1921 see Appendix A.

CHAPTER I

FRANCE

September 1939—June 1940

"Now we have begun. Now we are going on. Now with the help of God, and with the conviction that we are defenders of civilisation and freedom, we are going to persevere to the end."

WINSTON CHURCHILL

I

THE winter of 1939/40 has been described as the period of the "phoney war" when the armies of France and Britain held a line against an enemy for the most part invisible and almost wholly non-belligerent. Along the whole length of the Franco-Belgian frontier where most of the British troops were deployed, defence works were practically non-existent and the winter was largely spent in digging and constructing fortifications which in the event were never occupied. Some distance south of Lille the famous Maginot Line began and later in the year a proportion of British troops, including the 51st Highland Division, were sent down to the Saar to hold a part of this line.

The Kent Yeomanry, being a Territorial unit, had not reached the same standards of training and efficiency as the regular army units of which the bulk of the army in France consisted. To remedy this defect the regiment that winter spent more time in active training and less in purposeless digging than the rest of the B.E.F. This proved to be of the greatest value when the testing time came.

All those who served with the regiment in those early days will remember two things, the cold that froze their bodies and the intense enthusiasm that warmed their hearts and minds. Everyone, whatever his rank or duty, was determined to learn how to do his job better than anyone else, with the result that by the end of that hard winter the cheerful body of amateur soldiers which had left England in September had become transformed into an extremely efficient fighting machine, perhaps superior in some respects to those regular field regiments who had spent many years in attaining their high standard. Hard work and enthusiasm were not however the sole reasons for this, although there was plenty of both. As a Yeomanry regiment and a part of England's Territorial army, the 97th had two great advantages over their brethren in the regular army. First the standard of education among all ranks was generally higher. Superior intelligence makes for quickness in learning new things. Secondly, the fact that everyone came from the same county and very often from the same town or even the same village, was responsible for a family feeling which is the nucleus of that esprit de corps without which no regiment can become an efficient fighting unit. "It is the spirit that quickeneth, the flesh profiteth nothing." This saying of St. Paul loses none of its cogency by being applied to a field regiment or for that matter any other military formation. For without a good regimental spirit the material aids to warfare, guns, shells, and petrol engines are of very little value.

After a period in Practice Camp at Sissons early in December the regiment moved down to the Somme area near Marieux to put in a fortnight's intensive mobile training in bitter cold weather. In spite, however, of the wintry conditions, and the difficulty of keeping lorry engines from freezing, much useful work was done, and it was unfortunate that, owing to a false alarm that the enemy had marched into Belgium, the regiment had to return in great haste to Auchy. Two months later it again went down to the Somme this time to the villages of Toutencourt and Pushevillers.

By the end of this second period of intensive training which lasted from the middle of March till the middle of April the efficiency and spirit of the regiment were extremely high. It only needed forging in the fires of battle.

Before going on to give an account of the battles which led to the evacuation at Dunkirk and the disaster at St.

FRANCE

Valery a few brief incidents of the regiment's stay in France may be recalled. Looking back on that strange winter of 1939/40, the lull before the storm, the scenes that the writer remembers best are Christmas Day at Monchaux; the snow on the ground, the men's dinner in the big barn with everyone down to the last joined gunner drinking champagne; New Year's Eve on the Somme; the visit to the British cemeteries where lay those who had fallen in the 1914/18 war followed by luncheon in the little restaurant at Bapaume, the laughter and talk, the paper caps and crackers, the peroxide blonde who publicly kissed the shy and embarrassed Captain, the snow-ball fight in the garden ; the second visit to the Somme in March; the night operations that took place over the old Somme battlefields, the four rusty German howitzers at Bazentin, their muzzles still pointing at the sky, the battered steel helmets, coils of rusty barbed wire and ancient gun pits, the skeleton arm that someone dug up still wearing a wrist watch, and the 18 pdr. shell that exploded under the cook's fire in the courtyard at Courcelles causing the first casualty; visits to Amiens and Lille, talks over the fireside at La Planque; the regimental band at Pérenchies and the coming of Spring.

II

[1]It was April and spring was well on the way when the regiment returned from the Somme and moved into the III Corps area at Pérenchies near Lille. On the 25th of the month 385 Battery, who were billeted in the neighbouring village of Premesque, were ordered south to report to 1st R.H.A. who were in support of the 51st Highland Division on the Saar. A fortnight later I was given permission to visit them and travelled down by road, with Ernest Berkeley, the doctor. We spent the first night at Rheims, famous for its cathedral and its champagne. Early the next morning we were awakened by the sound of gunfire and falling bombs, and when we came downstairs learned from the hall porter that the

[1] This account of the retreat to Dunkirk is by Lt.-Col. F. Lushington.

German armies had attacked the two neutral countries of Holland and Belgium and would doubtless soon be marching into France. The phoney war was over.

That morning we drove on to Metz, and late in the afternoon found the headquarters of 385 Battery at Beckerholtz. Paying a hurried visit to each of the troop positions and handing over to Derrick Mullens the magnum of champagne we had collected in Rheims we started on our journey back. The towns and villages, which had presented so peaceful and smiling an aspect the day before, were already beginning to show unmistakable signs of the horrors of war. I remember particularly a house in a little square overlooking an open-air café whose marble-topped tables were protected from the sun by some gaily coloured umbrellas. The house had been cut in two by a bomb and its inner rooms most indecently exposed. The marble-topped tables were overturned and the umbrellas torn to shreds. Two women were poking sadly among the ruins whilst a third sat weeping by the roadside.

By the 12th May the 1st and 2nd Corps were in position on the Dyle. The regiment however, being part of G.H.Q. reserve, were still at Pérenchies. As it was now impossible for 385 Battery to come back to us we had been made up to strength by A/E Battery from 1st R.H.A. commanded by Major Matthews. Two days later we joined the 5th Division, which had been hurriedly recalled from the neighbourhood of Amiens where it was on its way to embark for Norway, and early the next morning we marched to Ghoy in Belgium.

On this day, the 15th, the Dutch army laid down its arms and the Germans, breaking through the French line between Sedan and Mezières with ten armoured divisions, began their swift advance towards Amiens and Boulogne. But of these great events we, of course, knew nothing.

On the 16th General Georges, the French commander of the sector, gave orders for the B.E.F. to withdraw to the line of the Escaut stopping one day on the Senne and one on the Dendre. To cover this retreat the 5th Division was ordered to hold the line of the Brussels-Charleroi canal.

Still in happy ignorance early that evening we moved forward, but, owing to the appalling congestion on the roads, one division moving up and the rest of the British army moving down, it was early morning before the guns had covered the few miles to their battery positions.

"Looks as if we was going the wrong way if you asks me," said Holdstock, my batman, as we passed a troop of medium guns trundling westwards; and I began to wonder if this was indeed the case.

Half an hour later we drove into Brages, a small town completely empty except for the headquarters of the 13th Infantry Brigade who were moving into some cottages at the northern end. Leaving Holdstock gloomily unpacking my kit in the largest and cleanest house we could find I walked up the street to report to the brigadier. Brigadier Dempsey, who became better known four years later as the commander of the British 2nd Army, told me the situation as far as he knew it and invited me to dine. By the time I returned my small R.H.Q. staff, including John Warde the second in command, Neil Campbell the adjutant and David Warner, who had miraculously turned up from Boulogne, had settled in, but there was still no news of the guns. Soon after midnight Brigadier Dempsey rang up to say he had reliable information that a large force of enemy tanks was approaching to cut us off and would we take appropriate action. I could only reply that as we still had no guns I regretted we could do nothing about it.

Early the next morning the guns arrived and about the same time the infantry made contact with the enemy. There was desultory firing during the day and in the afternoon an air battle took place over Brages in the course of which an enemy plane dropped a large bomb at our back door missing my driver, Gunner Collard, who was reading a novel on the doorstep, by a foot. Fortunately the bomb failed to explode. At my request a party of sappers came later to blow it up. It took the roof off the house and made a hole in the ground big enough to hold a 3-ton lorry, but failed to disturb some sheep who were tethered close by and who, after the explosion, were found still peaceably grazing.

That evening we received orders to withdraw to Ghoy again.

"I told you we was going the wrong way," said Holdstock as we drove slowly along the road in the darkness. "When I was a kid I was a great one for history and if you reads history you can't help noticing that the British army always starts its wars with a retreat."

"Nonsense, Holdstock," I replied, "that's an unnecessarily gloomy view. We shall be advancing again in a few days you mark my words."

The Very lights were going up in the sky behind, lighting up the dark shapes of the marching infantry beside us while far in front a red glow on the horizon marked the site of a bombed and burning Belgian town.

"All the same," Holdstock went on, "it was a pity about them sheep. I daresay we shall be glad of a bit of roast mutton later on."

At Ghoy the inhabitants who had greeted us so warmly and with such obvious relief on our way forward, were barely civil now that we were going back. One can hardly blame them. They were busy packing up and leaving their homes because the British army on which they had relied for their safety were once more leaving them to their fate. By evening there was no one left in the town except ourselves.

Just before nightfall we were ordered to reconnoitre and occupy a defensive position in the area of St. Sauveur about ten miles south-west of Ghoy. I was acting as guide to 387 Battery who were approaching their new positions across country in the dark when Major Warde met me and thrust a signal into my hand. It was from the C.R.A., received some time back, ordering all artillery units to move back to Seclin as fast as possible. Seclin was many miles behind the fighting area, and the message looked ominous. Major Warde, greatly agitated, was convinced that the British retreat had become a rout. These grim forebodings seemed to be confirmed when we reached the main road, which was packed with vehicles

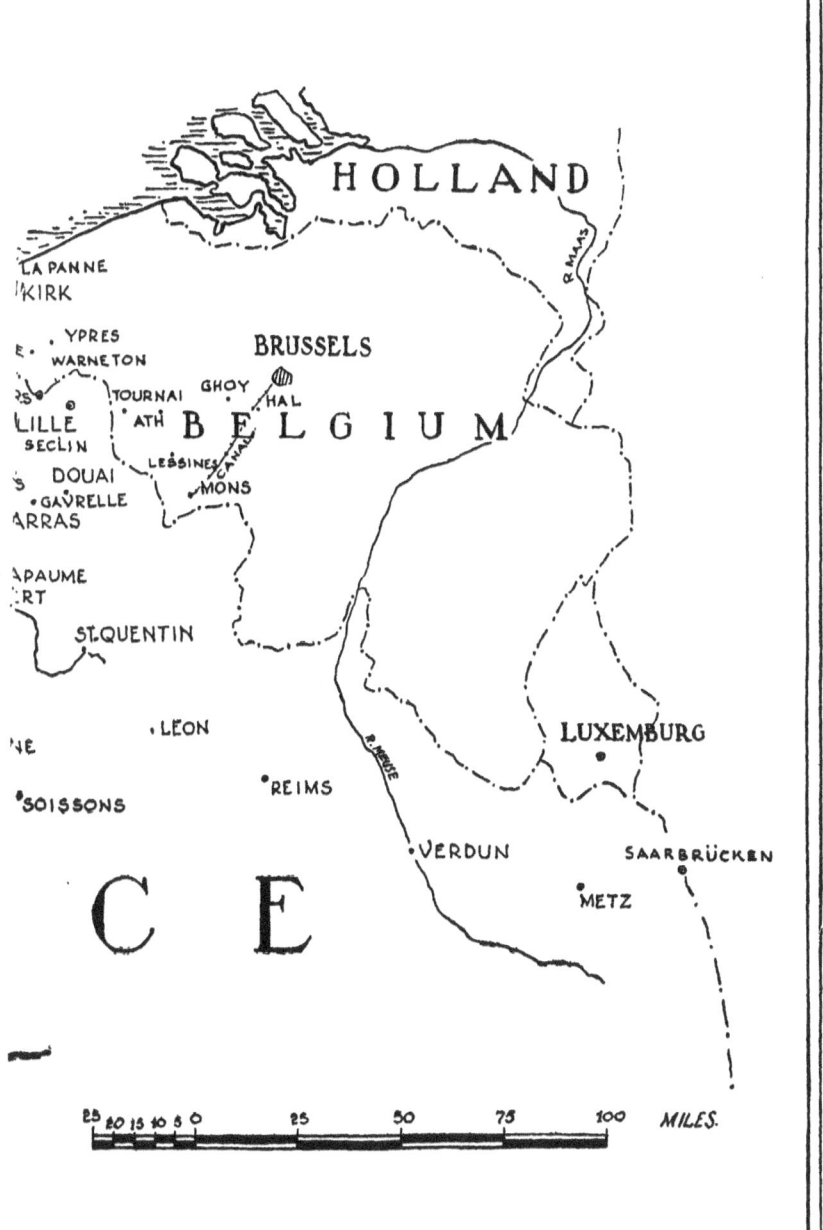

of all kinds and in any order, travelling westwards nose to tail. Joining the throng we tried to keep together as best we could.

This was our first experience of those long night journeys on packed roads which were the worst feature of the long retreat. It was impossible to sleep. No lights were allowed. Like a shunting train the endless succession of cars and lorries moved now slowly, now fast. One moment we were crawling along at walking pace with the bonnet of the car almost touching the lorry in front, the next we seemed to be alone and were frantically putting on speed in order to catch the next vehicle up before it turned off on to another road. Very often for no obvious reason we stopped altogether. When these halts exceeded more than a few minutes the officers got out and walked forward along the road to see what the trouble was. Nearly always it was because some worn out driver had gone to sleep at the wheel. Those behind him, thankful for a moment's respite, had usually dropped off too. So that one had to wake up driver after driver before the long column could get moving again.

Tournai was in flames. We could see the fires lighting up the sky long before we reached the town. On the bridge over the river in the very centre of the town another of those inexplicable halts occurred. I prayed that no enemy bomber would come over. For ten minutes that seemed like hours we made a sitting target, a long line of vehicles, double and treble-banked, brightly lit by the flames of the burning city. At last we moved on.

We reached Seclin at five o'clock in the morning. The guns were parked, the weary men lay down to rest. A small billeting party went in search of the Town Major who was, of course, in bed and asleep. I was standing by the roadside when an old Frenchman came up to me. He explained that he had fought in the last war when the English were his comrades in arms. In this war, although he was too old to fight, the English were his comrades still. He invited me to breakfast and told me to bring my friends. Four or five of us followed him to a tiny two-roomed cottage where he and his old wife lived,

They were obviously very poor. They gave us hot coffee and omelette, bread and cheese and jam. There was not enough bread so the old man went out to buy more. When the time came to go he refused to take any payment, but kept on repeating we were his comrades who were fighting for France. I think we must have eaten everything that he had.

During the day we learned that the British army were holding Tournai and the line of the Escaut and that we had once more been pulled back into reserve. The town was bombed in the morning but little damage was done. I was asleep when they came, but woke to hear the bombs falling. Too tired to worry I turned over and fell asleep again.

A party of fifth columnists marched down the road. Two French soldiers with rifles slung shambled along beside them. Two staff officers from G.H.Q., one of them a Major-General, came to call. They knew nothing about anything and seemed disappointed when I told them that we knew even less.

On the night of the 17th/18th Captain Tony Burrows had been peacefully sleeping in his O.P.[1] on the Brussels-Charleroi canal. He woke the next morning to find the infantry gone and himself alone with his O.P.A.[2] in enemy country. After driving for miles without meeting anyone he came across our front line troops hastily digging in. From there he went from place to place in search of us. Meeting a gun and tractor with its detachment, which were also lost, he eventually brought the whole party back in triumph to Seclin.

Late in the afternoon of the following day we moved to the little mining village of Estevelles. The road was so crowded with refugees and moving troops that it took seven hours to do ten miles.

After a brief night's sleep I drove on to Neuvreuil with a small reconnaissance party leaving orders for the guns to follow. It was a foggy morning and the road was again so crowded with refugees that, although we had started early, it was nine o'clock before we reached our destination.

[1] O.P.—Observation Post.   [2] O.P-A.—Observation Post Assistant.

The little village of Neuvreuil was apparently empty. Some cows were wandering aimlessly down the main street mooing pitifully to be milked, pigs were rooting about in the gardens, and the houses were deserted.

"Looks as if the owners had left in a hurry," Holdstock said, as we walked into a building that had evidently been part shop, part living rooms. Furniture, saucepans, plates, lamps, books, tins, photographs, clothing, flower pots and other articles of intimate domestic use were thrown about in inextricable confusion.

"Still it seems a pity to leave them cows mooing their heads off for want of being milked. I daresay you could do with a cuppa tea and some nice fresh milk in it?" my batman went on.

So while Holdstock milked the cows, and afterwards caught and killed a pig for the men's dinner I went in search of the headquarters of the French batteries we had come to relieve.

The officers were hospitable but casual. They lent us some maps, but were unable to tell us the exact position of the front line. They offered to take us round their gun positions, but couldn't say when they would be moving out.

Slowly the fog lifted. The French guns moved out. Our own moved in. We cleaned out one or two of the houses and began to settle down. In the afternoon 387 Battery moved forward to Fresnes to support an attack by the 5th and 50th Divisions and the 1st Army Tank Brigade. There was another alarm of enemy tanks and the guns were pulled hurriedly out into the open to meet it.

Driving down the road between Neuvreuil and Fresnes I could clearly see the enemy tanks moving in perfect formation along the skyline. I stopped the car and took a look at them through my glasses. They were haystacks.

It was evening. The projected attack had been postponed. I was sitting up in the church tower at Fresnes. Below me lay the silent landscape, the trees and fields, the huddled houses of the little village, and the straight line of the Arras-Douai road empty save for a burnt-out truck. A pillar of smoke rose from beyond Gavrelle and

Douai was burning. Above my head in the darkening sky, like vultures waiting for their prey, the German planes circled and wheeled.

The next day, 22nd May, our attack again failed to materialise and 387 moved back once more to Neuvreuil. During the morning the O.P. was shelled. We at once put it down to the wireless which Lieut. C. Marsham had been using for the first time. From then on we seldom used wireless.

On the 23rd I took over the duties of advanced C.R.A. and set up my headquarters in a house in Gavrelle next door to Brigadier Dempsey. The 91st Field Regiment were in action in the front part of the village which was shelled intermittently throughout the day. Mr. Walker the R.S.M. seemed to regard this as funny. Lying flat on the ground behind our billet with my face in Mr. Walker's boots I failed to see wherein the humour lay. On the other hand the story of a gunner, who had his braces neatly cut by a bomb, as he dived underneath the lorry in the main street at Neuvreuil, struck me as extremely amusing.

In the evening the shelling increased in intensity and the enemy attacked in force. It grew dark but the village was lit by the flames of the burning houses and the flashes of the guns. Brigadier Dempsey was coming out of his front gate. Our infantry had given way and he was about to lead a counter attack in person using his last reserve, his bren carriers. He ordered me to rejoin the regiment in Neuvreuil and withdraw northwards towards Lille. If the infantry could get away he would follow. In Gavrelle the guns of the 91st were being pulled out into the street ready to engage the enemy over open sights should they appear. A blazing ammunition limber lit up the shuttered houses, the men straining at the gun wheels, and the dark shapes of the Bren carriers moving forward to the attack.

At Neuvreuil 387 were already packing up. At Oppy we were joined by A/E. Together we drove on through the night through burning villages and fields littered with the debris of war. In the early hours of the morning,

Gunner Collard, worn out with the strain of driving all night, fell asleep and drove the car over a ditch and into the middle of a field before anyone woke up. I then took the wheel and the adjutant took the map. But we lost our way and it was eight o'clock before we finally reached our destination at Verlinghem, a few miles down the road from where we had started off so hopefully for Belgium ten days before.

At Verlinghem we rested for the day. A battalion of the Buffs were also resting nearby and there were many happy reunions of relations and friends among the men and officers of the two Kent units.

Abbeville had fallen and the enemy had taken the line of the Somme. Calais and Boulogne were invested and Dunkirk heavily bombed. From the point of view of supply all three ports were out of action and rations for the fighting troops had long since ceased to arrive except in very small and irregular quantities. But in the empty villages there was food and wine to spare, cattle and pigs and poultry, well-stocked cellars and gardens filled with vegetables. It was a case of "Help yourself". On a borrowed wireless in our billet we heard the King's speech.

On the 25th we were ordered to reconnoitre the Cantin area near Arras for battery positions. Another attack by us was in the air. It never got any further than that for, soon after dark, having completed our reconnaissance, a despatch rider arrived with fresh orders for the recce parties to rejoin the regiment at Pont-a-Marc and from there move back again into Belgium.

We reached Pont-a-Marc at midnight. It was raining and billets were hard to find. Somewhere in the wet darkness I found Mr. Walker. For an hour or two we lay down on the straw in some barns in a large farm, and then moved off again towards Ploegstreet Wood. In Lille the empty streets were in complete darkness. A few shots were fired as we passed through, possibly by fifth columnists. An hour later the Germans took possession of the town.

In the early hours of the morning, I established my headquarters in a farm just outside Warneton. We were no longer supporting the 13th Infantry Brigade but some Territorials from the 48th Division. They were holding the line of the Ypres-Comines canal with their right flank based on Comines.

One Battery, 387, was in action to our right front on the outskirts of Warneton, the other A/E was to our left rear.

The farmhouse was crowded with refugees most of whom had walked many miles through Belgium. It was a pitiable sight to see the old women and children gathered round their pathetic bundles and to see the look in their eyes when they realised that once more they were in the forefront of the battle.

As we moved in a plane came over flying very low. The whole area was alive with troops including a number of light A.A. In a few seconds every bofors gun and rifle within miles was firing at it. Amidst a roar of cheering the plane was hit and came hurtling down into the wood. An hour later Lt. Mike Savill, who was in charge of the regimental wagon line in Ploegstreet Wood, rang up to say that the plane was ours and had fallen in his lines. It contained two British airman, both dead. This was the first British plane we had seen since the battle began.

The next day at lunch time the Staff Captain, R.A. came to see me, and told me in private of the decision to evacuate the British army at Dunkirk. I was stunned. I knew that things were serious, that the British army had been steadily retreating for days, but that did not worry me. The British army always began a war with a retreat and then, as at Mons, came back again and finished up with a smashing victory. Evacuation was another matter altogether. It would be hard to come back after that. I might have been still more worried had I known that Calais and Boulogne had fallen, that the Belgian army had surrendered, and that at an official press conference, the Germans had already informed all foreign correspondents that the B.E.F. was definitely surrounded and had no hope of escape.

However I soon had other things to think about for in the afternoon the enemy attacked. Our territorial infantry, who were neither well-trained nor well-led, gave way and by four o'clock small parties of Germans were seen advancing on the far side of Warneton. David Warner rang up to say that there was no one between the on-coming Germans and his guns except a small but gallant party of sappers who could be seen digging in in front of Warneton. I rang up the Division and told them the situation. The C.R.A., Brigadier Barry, replied they had no reserves and that the line must be held at all costs even if it was by the guns alone. A few minutes later a despatch rider from Mike brought a message to say that a battalion of the Guards had arrived in the wagon line and were taking over some of his billets, what was he to do? I sent the despatch rider back with a written note to the O.C. the Guards explaining the situation and asking for help. By this time the line to Division had been cut as well as the one to the Wagon Line and the sound of mortar fire and light automatics was drawing ominously nearer.

A quarter of an hour passed with no further news except from David who said that most of his O.P. parties had been driven back to positions close alongside the guns which were now firing at ranges of 900 yards and under. The despatch rider returned with an apologetic note from the Guards' commander, saying he had strict orders to withdraw to Dunkirk and not to get involved in any further action. Soon after, however, the line to Division having been repaired, Brigadier Barry rang through to say that the Guards had been ordered to counter-attack and that their commanding officer would be reporting to me in a few minutes.

At 6 o'clock he and his adjutant arrived in a car. He was a little man, very neat and well-dressed, and his manner suggested that he had just dropped in for a cup of tea and a friendly chat. In the course of conversation I discovered that he and his battalion[1] had just marched twenty-five miles on foot, that they had been fighting continuously all the previous day, and that they had had no food for twenty-four hours. We filled up his car with biscuits and chocolate and bottles of wine and he drove off.

[1] 3rd Grenadier Guards.

Twenty minutes later the whole battalion in line of battle moved past my headquarters. The setting sun was shining on their bayonets, their bren carriers were on either flank; in all my life I have never seen a finer and more inspiring sight. They walked through the guns and the men on them cheered them and made jokes as they passed. The Germans saw them coming, halted and turned back. In less than an hour they had driven the enemy back over two miles to the other side of the canal from where they had started.

The next morning, 28th May, we received orders for a further withdrawal.[1] By 2 p.m. both batteries were in action near Rossignol some two or three miles further back. But the Grenadiers, although suffering heavy casualties from mortar fire, were still holding the line of the canal. All that afternoon we were busy getting rid of ammunition which we were told must not be left behind, and in the evening the retreat began again. We drove through Neuve Eglise, which was on fire from end to end, and joined the vast throng of lorries and men and guns that was slowly moving down the poplar-lined roads towards the sea.

For us this was the last and worst night of the retreat. All semblance of order and discipline seemed to have disappeared. There was no panic, but the men were just too tired to care and lorries and cars double-banked and triple-banked and crawled and halted and moved on again, then halted once more whilst their tired drivers fell asleep over their wheels. Units were mixed up in inextricable confusion and to make matters worse large numbers of French soldiers on horseback and on foot kept crowding in among us and pushing their way past, making anything like continuous movement impossible. At one point a lorry had fallen sideways into a large bomb crater in the middle of the road thereby completely blocking it. David Warner had collected a party of men and was trying to lift it back on to its wheels. The panic-stricken French soldiers however refused to stop and in their eagerness to get on kept pushing the working

[1] See copy of 5th Div. Arty. Orders Appendix B.

party to one side. At last, exasperated, Warner drew his revolver and in his best French threatened to shoot the next man who failed to stop when ordered. His French however was evidently not good enough, or perhaps they were too frightened to listen, for it was not until he had shot one that the lorry was eventually lifted, the crater filled up and the road cleared.

At another place the long procession had halted for nearly an hour. Walking up the line of stationary vehicles I came to a forked road with a sign-post. One arm read "to Poperinghe", a road that was hopelessly blocked, the other pointing up an empty road was marked "to Reninghelst". During the 1914–18 war I had fought over this country and remembered dimly that the road to Reninghelst also led to Poperinghe. So, knowing the others would follow like sheep, I ordered the leading lorry to take it and prayed that I was right.

Poperinghe was being shelled. As we approached it, crawling along at walking pace, we could hear the whine of the shell through the air, and see the flash as it burst in the town. About five minutes elapsed between the burst of one shell and the arrival of the next. As luck would have it one landed in the main square about fifty yards ahead of my car. A despatch rider was hit, and the drivers of the three lorries in front, which were all French, immediately disappeared. Since no one could move while these three lorries were blocking the road we were obliged to search all the cellars in the street, find them, and pull them out, which we eventually did, none too gently.

Daylight came and found the motley army still on the road. Some were on foot, others were riding on horses that the French had abandoned, and the remainder were lying in every attitude of sleep on the heavily laden still crawling lorries. Although we must have made a perfect target from the air no German planes came over to bomb us.[1]

---

[1] Nearly every day till far into the morning the roads of France and Belgium were crowded with marching men and vehicles nose to tail yet not once did the Luftwaffe bomb them. If they had the story might have been very different.

About ten o'clock in the morning the regiment halted at Eikhoek on the Yser canal, found some billets, and immediately went to sleep. Late that afternoon I was ordered to attend a conference in the inn where Brigadier Barry had set up his H.Q.

I found the Brigadier sitting behind a table in the main room with his staff captain and the three Colonels commanding the other three Artillery regiments under his command, the 9th, the 18th, and the 91st.

"Before we begin," he said, "will you, Tony, make sure that we are alone?"

Tony looked behind the bar. There was a frightened squeak, a scuffle, and the proprietor jumped up and was ignominiously hustled out of the door.

"I've brought you here to tell you," went on the Brigadier, "that the 5th Division are embarking for England to-morrow or next day. Two of you will go with it and two of you will remain behind. As I cannot make up my mind which is to go and which to stand and fight I have decided the best thing to do is to toss for it."

Outside the room there was a continuous rumble of iron-shod wheels on cobble pavements, but inside there was dead silence. The Brigadier drew a coin from his pocket. We tossed.

The result of the toss was that the 9th Field Regiment and ourselves were ordered to hand over guns and equipment, including officers and specialists, required by the other two to make them up to strength, and to scrap the rest outside the Dunkirk perimeter before marching to the beaches on foot.

The next morning, 30th May, we reached Moeurs on the outskirts of the perimeter. Driving all our vehicles with their equipment and guns off the road into the fields we smashed up what we could with pick axes and hammers and marched away with sad hearts. Again I established my H.Q. in a farmhouse, and with the rest of the regiment camped in two smaller farms nearby, we sat down to wait for orders.

After breakfast and a short sleep I held an officers' conference in the dining room. An enemy plane flew over very low just as it started and dropped a bomb in the road outside. Most of the officers disappeared under the table. At the conference Major Matthews commanding A/E battery R.H.A., volunteered to go down to the beach about twelve miles away and try to arrange for our embarkation.

The day passed slowly, and it was nearly seven o'clock before Matthews returned to say he had arranged everything. We were to march to La Panne where rowing boats would be waiting to take us off to the ships. The good news soon spread and amid cheers we set off. Matthews had produced a truck for me so that I might go on ahead and meet the embarkation staff officer myself.

It was dark when I reached the little village of Adinkerk, which adjoins La Panne, but I had no difficulty in finding the E.S.O.'s office. Some two or three hundred men, stragglers from every unit in the British Army, were gathered in the street outside silently and wearily waiting for orders. The E.S.O. was weary too. He hadn't slept at all for three nights. I asked where our boats were. Very briefly he told me I must be mistaken. There were no boats. Nothing had been arranged for us. We could sleep on the dunes outside if we liked and he would see what he could do in the morning.

I went out into the street. The tired men were still standing there. A car approached from the direction of the beach with its side lights on. Everyone began shouting "Put out those bloody lights". A cross voice inside said "Is there an officer there?"

I replied "Yes", and put my head in at the window.

"Who the hell are you?" said the voice, still more crossly.

"I am Colonel Lushington of the 97th Field Regiment, Kent Yeomanry." I said "Who the hell are you?"

"I am Sir Alan Brooke, the Corps Commander," replied the voice.

We spent a cold miserable night on the dunes. The enemy was shelling the area. We could hear them coming over but none fell near us. At the same time I doubt if anyone slept much.

As soon as it was light I called again on the E.S.O. He was still sitting at his desk. Near him a junior officer was answering the telephone. On the mantelpiece two candles were guttering in their sockets. There were the remains of food and some cold tea on a table.

"You are to take your lot to Bray," he said. "You will find boats waiting for you there."

I went back and woke up the others, and we set off down the road to Bray. We had marched for about one and a half hours and were on the outskirts of Bray when a squadron of German planes flew over and everyone scattered and took cover. When I came back I found the E.S.O. in a small car looking even more tired and harassed than before.

"I've been looking for you everywhere," he said. "Those orders were a mistake. You are to march back again."

I borrowed a truck and went in search of Corps H.Q. The E.S.O. had told me that they would give me some fresh orders. I was relating our troubles to a staff officer when a Brigadier came in and asked me who I was and what I wanted. I told him I was commanding what was left of two field regiments, the 9th and the 97th, and all I wanted was some orders. He turned on me his blue eyes blazing:

"You're damned lucky to be here at all," he said. "What do you want orders for? Get out."

I got out. I was not to meet Brigadier Ritchie again till just before another retreat, the retreat to Alamein when he commanded the Eighth Army.

I went on to the H.Q. of the 5th Division. Brigadier Barry had already sailed for England, but I found Colonel Bassett the A.Q.M.G. He too cursed me for existing, but softened a little when I told him that none of us had had any food since mid-day the day before.

"You will find some tins of bully and some biscuits in a field just up the road. Go and help yourself and for God's sake don't worry me."

It was nearly ten o'clock when I got back to the regiment, and handed over the tins of bully and biscuits.

The officers were gathered together in a café in Adinkerk. Next door to the café was a small house belonging to two old maids, who offered me the use of their spare bedroom. It was beautifully clean and there were fresh white linen sheets on the large four poster bed. Without bothering to take even my boots off I lay down on the outside of the bed and fell asleep. A heavy A.A. gun just outside my window was firing almost continuously but I never heard it.

I had been asleep about an hour when I was awakened by Matthews.

"We are to march to Bray," he said. "Boats are waiting for us there."

I went downstairs. Lined up in the street were the most wonderful collection of old French vehicles I had ever seen, including an enormous bus into which nearly a hundred men of the regiment had been crammed. I took the seat next the driver and we set off. Everyone was riding on something. If they could not get a seat in a lorry they found bicycles and even horses.

At Bray the same thing happened as before. There were no boats and we were ordered to turn back. I decided to go on to Dunkirk. We were all sick and tired of Adinkerk, and in any case the big French bus was too large to turn in the narrow road. I gave the adjutant a rendezvous at the St. Malo cross-roads on the outskirts of Dunkirk and jumped into a passing two-seater. There were already three people in it, but they willingly drove me on to St. Malo.

The little town was packed with French soldiers. At the Casino on the sea front where I had been told I might find a British E.S.O. there were literally hundreds of them all milling about doing nothing, but no sign of any English.

Back at the cross-roads I met the regiment again, and after a short discussion decided to go on to Dunkirk. As there was not enough room for everyone in the old French vehicles, some of which had already broken down, a party of about forty of us including the adjutant and myself marched in formation down to the sea.

The immensely long sandy beaches were crowded with men, some trudging slowly along towards the quays at Dunkirk, about two miles to our left, others standing in little groups gazing hopefully at the sea, which was crowded with ships great and small, most of them lying a long way out from the shore. Great columns of black smoke were rising from Dunkirk itself and far away to our right a big ship was being bombed. We could see the fountains of water rising round it and the white puffs in the sky where the shells from her anti-aircraft guns were bursting. Two sailors in a rowing boat drew near and we hailed them, but they went further up the beach to pick up someone else. Another sailor who was wading about in the sea close by promised to send us the next boat.

For a long time we waited, but no boat came. At last just when we had almost decided to march on to Dunkirk two boats arrived. We waded out to sea up to our waists and were hauled on board. In a few minutes I was in the wardroom of the destroyer *Winchelsea*, had taken off my wet clothes and was thankfully warming myself at the electric stove. Suddenly there was a terrific explosion, all the lights went out and the ship rocked from side to side. A bomb had fallen within a few feet of the stern. After that the skipper decided to go on to Dunkirk and take the rest of our passengers off the quay. By this means we could embark 1,200 men in half an hour instead of only twenty or thirty every twenty minutes as we had been doing.

While we with two other destroyers were moved to the quay a squadron of Heinkels came over. Every gun on every ship in the harbour and outside at once opened fire and the din was terrific. It was too much for the Heinkels who gave it up, dropped their bombs harmlessly in the sea, and fled.

It was nearly seven when we left. From the crowded deck we could see the white wake of our destroyer twisting and turning as we drove at full speed through the fleet of little ships. Beyond the ships lay the land, the shadowy outlines of the beaches, the quays and the

FRANCE

buildings, and above the land in the slowly darkening sky a great pall of black smoke.

Down below in the No. One's cabin six officers of the Kent Yeomanry and three of the Royal Navy were throwing a party. There were beef sandwiches and beer, laughter and talk and much tobacco smoke. I had thanked the No. One, a large jovial man in a blue jersey, for the loan of his grey flannel trousers and was in the middle of telling him the story of the retreat when I stopped short. There seemed no point in going on as he, like everyone else in the cabin, was fast asleep.

At the beginning of May the B.E.F. consisted of three Corps comprising five regular divisions and five T.A. divisions. There were also three pioneer divisions equipped on a much reduced scale and less artillery, signals and administrative units. The armoured units consisted of seven cavalry regiments equipped with light tanks and two battalions of Infantry tanks, only twenty-three of which were armed with anything heavier than a machine gun. The total strength of the B.E.F. was approximately 350,000 men. The total casualties in killed, wounded, missing and prisoners were 30,000.

During the nine days of the evacuation the enemy air force could drop a bomb anywhere inside the Dunkirk perimeter, ten miles long by five to six miles deep, and be sure of hitting something. Yet, thanks to the R.A.F., to whom they were greatly superior in numbers, they did surprisingly little damage. Our fighters, based in England, could not stay over the beaches for more than twenty minutes at a time. Yet although they were so few they shot down 377 Germans with a loss to themselves of only eighty-seven. On the 30th May, the day the regiment arrived inside the perimeter, the R.A.F. shot down seventy-six German planes for the loss of five.

Over 800 ships and countless numbers of small boats were used in the evacuation. The Port of London alone sent thirty-four motor life boats and 881 ships' boats. All these ships and boats reported to the Royal Navy after the evacuation order had been given and the work had already begun. They had to be maintained, fuelled, provisioned, watered, supplied with life-buoys, instruments, compasses and charts before they could set out. At one time there were as many as 150 ships anchored outside Dover while another fifty waited in the Downs for orders and supplies.

There were thirty Naval officers and 320 naval ratings on duty on the beaches. Neither these nor the officers and men of the destroyers had more than an hour's consecutive sleep for eight or nine days. Thirteen destroyers were sunk, six English and seven French, 171 ships were repaired, 316,663 troops were saved.

CHAPTER II

FRANCE (CONTINUED)

"We shall fight on the beaches, we shall fight on the landing grounds, we shall fight in the fields and in the streets, we shall fight in the hills, we shall never surrender."

WINSTON CHURCHILL

4th June, 1940

I

IT is now necessary to go back a little in our story to follow the fortunes of 385 Battery who left the regiment on the 22nd April in order to join the 1st R.H.A. on the Saar.

The following account is by Major (afterwards Lt.-Colonel) W. J. de W. Mullens, D.S.O.:

"On the night of the 23rd we arrived at Mafrecourt where we were told that we should have to lie up the following day in the Forest of Argonne as the last stage of our journey was to be made during the hours of darkness. Having spent a very uncomfortable day in the pouring rain, we started off at dusk on what was to prove the most unpleasant march. We had to move in groups of five vehicles at close intervals with 250 yards between groups (quite impossible at night) with no lights. The French had arranged 'Ballissage lighting'—little fairy lights on the sides of the roads.

"We eventually arrived at Hagondange, near Metz, in the early hours of the morning tired, cold and very hungry, where we found the advance party. We had driven about 100 miles, in some cases without relief drivers and with the loss of only one vehicle which had gone over a twenty-five foot ravine. Fortunately no one was hurt and the vehicle arrived under its own steam the following day, having been extricated by the French.

"Before arriving at our destination we saw what we thought was a huge fire but which proved on further investigation to be an iron foundry with the lights blazing. We took a poor view of this after our long march with no lights. A French policeman, however, explained that both this foundry and a similar one in Germany belonged to the same firm and an agreement had been reached that neither should be bombed.

"The next few days were spent in reconnaissance of the French battery positions which we were to occupy on the 29th. Battery H.Q. went about seven miles in front of the Maginot Line to stake their claim on a small village. Two or three Officers and several N.C.O's. spent a few days with the French battery from whom we were to take over and it is interesting to note their views and outlook on the war in general in the light of future events.

"At mid-day a six course lunch was served in their mess and at seven-thirty a seven course dinner, this was their usual custom and definitely not done for our benefit. At the O.P. there was always a table with a tablecloth set for the N.C.O's. and this in full view of the enemy who was doing much the same thing. The French B.C. explained this by saying that the only thing either side could do was to gain a few miles of ground as there was the Siegfried Line on the one side and the Maginot Line behind, both of which were impregnable, so why not sit down and make the best of it?

"Two troops were to come into action behind this 'Ligne de contacte' and the third was to remain at Ferange about seven miles back just behind the Maginot Line.

"The Battery's task was to support the 152nd Infantry Brigade consisting of the 2nd Seaforth and 4th Seaforth Highlanders and the 4th Battalion (Queen's Own) Cameron Highlanders.

"On the night of 4/5th May 'B' Troop under the Command of Captain P. B. Wacher, came into action near Bibiche and the following day fired what was probably the first round to be let off in anger by any British battery in France. On the following night 'A' Troop commanded by Captain Mills, came into action at St. Oswalds Château, an indifferent position, in view of the enemy, and visited by their patrols, but with a certain amount of protection and no alternative in the area which we were given.

"A certain amount of registration was done from these positions as well as from alternative 'nomad' positions but the gentleman's agreement that no houses, roads or working parties of less than five men were to be engaged rather hampered things. This agreement was a legacy from the French which we did not keep for very long.

"After 10th May when Holland and Belgium were invaded, the enemy became much more aggressive. On the 15th our infantry were forced to withdraw and we moved back to join 'C' Troop commanded by Captain H. M. Wix in a previously reconnoitred position in Ferange. Here the Battery was engaged in firing harrassing fire tasks at odd intervals throughout the night every night for a week.

"During our 'stay' in the Maginot Line we fired altogether about 4,000 rounds.

"On 22nd May it was decided to send the division to Sedan to fill a gap left by a French Division that had apparently been mislaid, so the next night we moved off and spent a day at Marcheville and the following night moved to a concentration area at Varenne. At Varenne the 'Lost' French Division turned up and it was decided to send us N.W. of Paris to prepare a defensive position behind the River Seine. There was then a further change of plan and we were told that the war was progressing favourably and that we were to go to the neighbourhood of Abbeville to hold the line of the River Somme.

"Having been given our route and final destinations for the march up North (our guns were sent by rail despite a strong protest from me) we sent an advance party forward to reconnoitre hiding places for the daylight hours. We had been told we would be met by guides just before dawn each day, but on no occasion did we find them. So we hid every morning just before daylight at Vitry, Sezanne and Henonville on the 25th, 26th and 27th, finally arriving at our concentration area in the Haut Foret d'Eu at dawn on the 28th.

"We halted there one day and then went into action at Marquenville. The next day we came into action at Ercourt in support of the 154th Infantry Brigade. Here all troops were shelled though a great number of shells were fortunately duds. Out of 36 rounds landing on one troop position only twelve exploded.

"On 30th May we learnt that an attack on the Abbeville Bridgehead was to be staged and that we must move out of our positions to make way for the 31st French Divisional Artillery. We were given an area near Huppy to reconnoitre. On arriving there every hedge and other bit of cover contained a troop of French '75's' and at last we were forced to put our twelve guns in line in the open on top of a bank. This position we occupied on the night of June 2nd, the command post and battery headquarters being half a mile in front of the guns. The attack was due to start at 03.30 hours on June 4th and the battery was allotted the task of putting down a smoke screen east of Abbeville. This was successfully done and the screen lasted till mid-day, 1,600 rounds having been expended. The initial order of 100 rounds gun fire to 12 guns was a proud moment for me even though it was only smoke.

"About 2 per cent. of these rounds were prematures and landed on a French battery about 1,000 yards in front of us, which annoyed them considerably. The attack was a failure and we withdrew to a more covered position at Doudelainville a few miles behind. We were in action here all day on the 5th but found the shooting very difficult owing to enemy aircraft who appeared to be paying particular attention to Huppy.

"We had intended to remain till the following day but late that night, having received orders to withdraw, we went into action near Rambures. A few hours later, at two o'clock in the morning of the 6th, we were again ordered to withdraw and lie up in the Forest of Eu there to await further orders.

"This was a very unlucky day for the battery, first we lost L/Bdr. Payne, Gnr. Hogben and Gnr. Hammond, who were on their way to R.H.Q. with some documents. Knowing nothing of the withdrawal they went straight into a village occupied by the enemy. In the afternoon we had to move the battery in daylight and were severely bombed, having three killed and seventeen wounded, including Captain Wix. After great difficulty we evacuated the wounded, mostly with the help of the French medical staff.

"That night we went on to Fresnoy to lay up once again and wait for orders.

"We were ordered to support the Royal Scots Fusiliers who were holding a line from Le Tréport to Eu, and came into action at Floques, one time site of the No. 6 Genera Hospital, and could undoubtedly have held this position for a considerable time, but the enemy had pushed through on our right and once more we were forced to withdraw to conform to the line. It was here that we heard it had been decided to evacuate the Division from Le Havre. The 154th Brigade with the 17th and 75th Field Regiments were sent back there to hold the town for the withdrawal of the rest of the Division.

"We came into action at Brequemont on the night of the 9th but did not contact the enemy. Here Lt. Bowring with Burbridge, Howland and McGlushon left to act on Arty. Liaison duties with the Border Regiment. I never saw them again until I arrived at Southampton Water. They found the Border Regiment just as they were ordered to withdraw and after numerous unsuccessful attempts to find us again managed to get through to Le Havre and after 'calling' at Cherbourg returned to Southampton.

"After a short but very unpleasant march on the night of the 10th we again withdrew S.W. of Dieppe. Here the enemy attacked in considerable force and the regiment was largely instrumental in repelling the attack.

"The next evening we were ordered to abandon all our kit and to hand over as many vehicles as possible to transport the infantry on the next withdrawal.

"It was now apparent that the enemy had cut us off from Le Havre, and plans were made to evacuate British and French troops from St. Valery en Caux.

"We were in action at Blosseville sur Mer soon after dawn on the 11th June and on the same day a bridgehead was formed round St. Valery, the 152nd Brigade holding the east side, 153rd Brigade part of the south side and the French the rest of the south side, with the line of the Durdent River west of the town.

"At mid-day it was decided to make an attempt to start to evacuate the Division that night, and the battery were ordered to come into action in the immediate outskirts of the town of St. Valery to cover the withdrawal of the infantry. As we approached the town, we were met by the French pouring out, saying that the enemy held the town. This we found to be untrue and after a certain amount of difficulty and obstruction by the French and their vehicles, we went into action and dug a perimeter camp, nearly every man being armed with a weapon ranging from a Service rifle to a French cutlass. Behind us St. Valery was being heavily shelled. There was also considerable rifle fire taking place between the British and French troops in the town.

"While we were here we learnt that they were going to attempt to evacuate everyone in one night instead of two, starting at 22.00 hours and that we were to be one of the last units to go at 03.40 hours on the 12th. This was rather gloomy news especially as there were no enemy to engage. At about 12.30 hours our C.O., Lt.-Col. W. H. T. Peppé, M.C., R.A., arrived at our camp and told us that he had seen the other battery (B/O) out of action and that he was going to stay with us till we were due to go down to the quay. This was indeed a brave act as it was fairly obvious that the chances of the battery getting off were very slight.

"Having destroyed the guns and vehicles that had served us so well, we marched down to the town, only to be told that there were no boats. It was raining and, as they were still shelling the town which was full of troops, we marched back and hid in a small wood on the high ground on the east side. On the way the C.O. told me that the Division would surrender at 09.30 hours and that it was now a case of each man for himself.

"Shortly after this Lt. Allfrey went down into the

town, by this time on fire, and on reaching the harbour saw in the distance some miles to the east some boats. Picking up an abandoned motor cycle which lay by the side of the road he came back with the glad news. I at once decided to try and make a getaway and gave orders for every one to follow me.

"Leaving the wood to the north-east of St. Valery we crossed a few fields and eventually arrived at the cliff edge. From here we could plainly see, lying off the next village, a large number of boats of all descriptions including some French destroyers. Much cheered by this wonderful sight we began to run along the cliff pursued by tracer bullets from German machine guns.

"Near Veules les Roses we found a number of French soldiers, who under the mistaken impression that the village was held by the Germans, were trying to make good their escape by letting themselves down the cliff on ropes. The ropes were too short and most of them fell the remaining fifty feet severely damaging themselves. One party had made a rope with rifle slings which broke under their weight with disastrous results.

"As we approached the village, which was being shelled by French destroyers, Allfrey, who was riding a horse some way ahead of the rest of us, suddenly fell off as if shot. In fact he had only rolled off. Finding himself in a field surrounded by barbed wire he had chosen this method of dismounting. But it was a great relief to me to see him get up and go on running.

"We eventually reached the beach by a narrow track winding down through a wood where we found several other officers from the battery waiting for us.

"There were four groynes leading out to the sea, and three of these were occupied by the French, of whom there were several hundred, and the other by a few British troops mostly from the Duke of Wellington's Own Regiment who had presumably been holding the north-east side of St. Valery.

"Small rowing boats from the bigger ships came alongside the groynes at intervals and took off a few men and rowed them out to the ships about a mile away. But the tide was unfortunately going out very fast, and the boats had to move continuously farther out to sea, where they were being shelled both from the cliffs south west of St. Valery and north east of Veules. When the tide finally receded the groynes were left high and dry and the men had to wade or swim out to the boats.

"To begin with the evacuation, so far as the British troops were concerned, was a very orderly affair with very little interference from the French, with the exception of a few wounded whom we allowed to enter our boats and a few who pretended to be wounded and were not. But later when the boats had nowhere definite to come to, the groyne being high and dry, we were joined by hundreds of panic-stricken Frenchmen who could only be stopped from swamping the boats at the point of a revolver. Finally the naval officer in command of the boats decided that it was no longer safe to come within wading distance of the shore and that those who wanted to be saved must swim for it. The officers, naturally, were among the last to leave and this was how Lt. Connell, while trying to swim out to the boats, was drowned. In one case a boat crowded with men was without oars. Sgt. Terry, who was in charge, made the men use their tin hats as oars, and in this way, after a long row, they eventually reached the waiting ships.

"Our journey to Southampton which we reached 27 hours later, was not a very comfortable one. The ship was crammed full, and our only sustenance was a small plateful of stew and a quarter of a pint of water. At one time during the night we found ourselves heading back to France on the instructions of one of our destroyers, but this was altered shortly afterwards and at last, much to our relief we were safely back in England and enjoying meat pies, tea, chocolate and Woodbines, the first real meal for more than two days.

"During our five weeks of actual fighting we came into action twelve different times, ten of which were during the last twelve days. We were in all probability the first in and the last out of action during the Battle of France.

From first to last the battery fired between 20,000 and 25,000 rounds."[1]

II

There are many stories of individual adventures and escapes by the officers and men of the Regiment during these two retreats. Unfortunately there is not sufficient space to relate them all. The following have been selected and are put down as far as possible in the narrator's own words.

L/Bdr. Steers' story (387 Battery):

On the afternoon of Tuesday the 28th May at Denoutre in Belgium I was ordered by Lt. Savill, the officer in charge of the Wagon Line to report with my truck to a nearby hospital and collect a number of wounded. I left the hospital with three sitting and four stretcher cases in the back and a badly wounded infantryman sitting in front with me. My orders were to report to Dunkirk Hospital. Unfortunately I had no map, food or water, and was told to find my way there as best I could.

After driving down a few lanes, I came to the main road with convoys streaming along it. For the remainder of the evening, and all that night I was driving mainly in first gear. Whenever the stream of traffic was held up, I managed to scrounge water, chocolate or cigarettes for the fellows on the back. Fires were burning on either side of the road where troops were burning surplus stores and equipment. Progress was painfully slow.

On Wednesday morning we were machine gunned from the air; the roads were subjected to dive bombing but were seldom hit; vehicles and guns lay abandoned in the road; and the French Artillery had cut their horses loose. The bridge across the canal was blocked to traffic

---

[1] 385 Battery was probably the only combatant unit to escape from St. Valery, where approximately 10,000 British and 14,000 French were taken prisoners. In the battery itself the casualties were as follows:

Killed	1 Officer	Wounded	19 O.Rs.	Missing	2 O.Rs.
	3 O.Rs.	P.O.W.	3 Officers		
			39 O.Rs.		

and about to be blown up. But I managed to get all the wounded across with the aid of Lt. Savill's white raincoat and a revolver given to me by a wounded officer whom I had in the back of the truck. He instructed me to let the men think I was an officer, and to order them to carry the stretchers across the bridge.

On the other side of the canal I fell in with a corporal from the Ambulance Corps. He had an ambulance and I managed to get the wounded on board. By now the effect of the morphia had worn off, and they were in a sorry state. All the troops available were being formed into one unit, each having to carry as much ammunition as possible and whatever arms they could find. I was then detailed to drive into Dunkirk with the ambulance, as it was the only place they knew of, although the French were coming back saying that the Germans were already there.

I had to throw my grenades away and also my rifle and was told to say that I belonged to the Ambulance Corps if I was captured. The ambulance was sent on ahead and the main party followed on foot. The officer in charge said that he did not think that the enemy would fire at the ambulance, but I did not feel too easy about this. Actually the journey was uneventful and I arrived at Dunkirk early in the afternoon. I could not find the hospital but I met a Scotch medical officer and he stayed with me. The French hospital refused to take the wounded as they needed all their space for civilians.

The town was bombed all the afternoon. We put the wounded in the cellars and then went round the streets with stretchers picking up men who had been wounded in the bombing. I was knocked about quite a bit but never had any bruises or felt any pain.

We stayed in the cellars with the men until Thursday. Some died and many were in great pain. There was no water in the town but we managed to scrounge some light beer. By Thursday the party had grown and there were now three officers, including the Medical officer, six fit men and thirty-five wounded.

The Medical officer decided it was hopeless stopping

there. He called all the fit men together and told us we would have to leave the wounded and go to the harbour to see if we could find a radio station to get into touch with the Navy. Otherwise we should have to try and get a boat and, after collecting the wounded in the night, try and make our way down the coast.

We set off for the beach and, on arriving there, we were amazed to find thousands of men, and many ships burning. But what concerned us most was the sight of a Hospital ship. The Medical officer got hold of some ambulances to collect the wounded from the cellars and at the same time dismissed us to the beaches, wishing us good luck and a safe journey home.

I went to the beach near the Mole and fell asleep. The last time I had slept was on the Monday. After waking I wandered up and down the beach and eventually found Dvr. Ducret, Gnr. Elphick and L/Bdr. Dorien. Later we met Sgt. Vyse and his gun team. Finally we crawled along the Mole, which was then under heavy fire and boarded the destroyer H.M.S. *Winchelsea*.

B.S.M. Moon's story (385 Battery):

On the night of the 5th June the battery was in action at Doudelainville and, as ammunition was running short I was told by Captain Johnson to collect another 200 rounds per gun. I went back to the ammunition dump about nine miles in rear of our position, collected these rounds and loaded them into eight five-tonners lent me by the R.A.S.C. officer in charge.

The journey back with these big lorries was a nightmare. The main Abbeville road was choked with French and British troops and with transport of all descriptions as well as with hundreds of refugees with a varied assortment of strange vehicles. It was 8.30 in the morning before I got to St. Maxent and every one of my eight five-tonners was missing. I was also told by various passers-by that I was going the wrong way as everyone had pulled out. Eventually my drivers turned up one by one. Each of them said he had been ordered back to the R.A.S.C. depot and all showed an evident reluctance to proceed any further. After a little thought I decided to leave them at St. Maxent and go on by myself on my motor cycle to Doudelainville to find out the position. On my way I called in at R.H.Q. and found it empty.

The road into the village of Doudelainville is in the form of a narrow cutting. Turning off this into a small by-road I ran bang into five or six German A.F.V's. with two Jerries standing in front enjoying a smoke. As I flashed past them I had visions of being marched back into Germany and in less time than it takes to tell I pictured all the unpleasant things that happen to prisoners of war. However they appeared not to notice me and I drove on into the deserted village still looking everywhere for any sign of the battery. I visited the farmhouse where the command post had been and then the gun positions and, much to my relief, found they were all deserted.

The only way out for me now was the way I had come and I made my way back to the village street where I took off my steel helmet and did several little things that might help as some sort of disguise. Then making sure that my cycle was in order, I started off. By the time I reached the A.F.Vs. again I was absolutely all out, or rather the cycle was. By now the crews had collected together and, as I went by, one hefty looking fellow made a grab at me, which almost caused me to be unseated. The next hot-and-bothered moment was overshooting the little turning that I had previously come out of and trying to turn round in the road in 'top' (definitely due to wind-up). Eventually I got back to St. Maxent and wasted no time in starting my convoy back to their depot, feeling more than pleased that I had still got 1,600 rounds of ammunition and eight five-ton lorries, and that I had satisfied myself that the battery was safely out.

I was greeted several hours later by Captain Johnson, with "Am I glad to see you?" to which I replied "Not so b——y glad as I am to see you sir."

Captain Wix's story (385 Battery):

After leaving the Battery in the Forest of Eu on 6th June I was sent in a French ambulance with two other wounded men, Ward and Epps, to a French Main Dressing Station at Beauvais. Here we were operated on, and for the next day or so I am a bit vague as to what happened. I do remember, however, that there was no water or anything else to drink, that a woman in my room had continual hysterics, that there was an air raid, and that I lost all my clothes and belongings except a rather dirty shirt which I still had on. I was eventually removed by ambulance to the hospital Foch at Suresnes, near Paris.

The hospital at Suresnes was a beautiful building, but the whole place was crowded out with French wounded and completely understaffed and lacking in organisation. I spent three or four rather miserable days there in a ward with four French Poilus. I only had my wound looked at once and as it was still bleeding I became rather weak. I did, however, make friends with a very nice nurse who spoke a little English and had some English friends in Kent.

At four o'clock on the morning of 12th June she came into my ward and said the Germans were on the outskirts of Paris and if I was fit enough she would help me get out. She produced some boots for me, a poilus trousers, and a great coat, got me downstairs in a bathchair and then went back for another Englishman, Sgt. McLeod of the 4th Batt. Seaforths, whom I had met during the attack at Abbeville. We unfortunately had to leave another chap from the Seaforths behind as he was too bad to be moved. Apart from him I don't think there were any other Englishmen in the hospital. My friend the nurse got hold of a truck, with hard tyres and only two gears and put us in it, in company with eight wounded Moroccans and six Senegalese, and a French Lieutenant who had just arrived. Before we left she gave me 100 fcs. and as neither McLeod or myself had any money at all this proved more than useful.

The driver of the truck found he had only half a gallon

of petrol so we went to Paris and scrounged some more off a French Major. Paris was a pathetic sight, nearly everyone who had intended to leave had already gone, and the rest, knowing it was not going to be defended looked completely baffled and miserable. Since we did not intend to be part of the reception committee for the Boche we told the driver to head for any hospital "vers le sud".

He took us about twelve miles, which was as far as he could go, and put us down at a sort of cottage hospital already filled with civilians. It wasn't of course much good, but both McLeod and myself felt pretty done up, so we decided to stay the night there; in any case we reckoned it would take the Boche a little time to digest Paris before he advanced again.

We got a bed and some food and slept till next morning.

We woke up early and had a talk with the French Lieutenant about what we were going to do. We still had the wounded black troops with us. The Senegalese were very patient and pathetic, never moaned or made a fuss at all; they reminded me very much of a dog with a lame foot. The Moroccans, although the worst of their wounds were only slight, made far more fuss and were a bit of a nuisance altogether.

The owner of the place told us that he and his staff were clearing out as soon as possible, but he thought he could lay on some Paris taxis to take us to another Hospital. This he did after about four hours and we left with a fleet of seven. Apart from our party, there was the owner of the hospital, a crippled girl who was a sort of Red Cross nurse, one proper nurse, one maid, one baby aged about four months (no one seemed to know where that came from) and an old man of seventy-five with a broken leg, who would insist on periodically removing the splints, and readjusting them according to his own fancy.

It was a pretty hectic day, the road south was crammed full of refugees of all sorts, Belgians who had been in the road since the fighting started, Parisians in farm carts which they had hired when they ran out of petrol, not knowing how to harness or drive the horse and often arguing about it while they held everyone else up, and a whole crowd of Reservists complete with rifles who were just ambling along with the rest without any organisation or order. I really don't know how we moved at all. We tied a red flag with a red cross marked in lipstick on the leading taxi, and kept on shouting through the sunshine roof "laissez passés les blessés". This worked for a bit, but far more successful was a man on a motor bike who joined us and shot on ahead blowing a whistle and clearing some sort of a way for us.

We passed through Étampes and Fontainebleau, but all the hospitals we found were evacuated. At last we finished up in the dark somewhere near Pithiviers with nowhere to sleep, so we parked in an avenue of trees and prepared to lie down there. The French Lieutenant went for a walk and returned with a slice of bread and a bottle of champagne all round, and an excellent Corona for McLeod and myself and very soon we were all asleep on the grass beside our taxi.

The next day was the same sort of day, crowded roads and empty hospitals (though we did get some fresh dressings at one of them applied by the Red Cross cripple). All the time we were scrounging petrol off the police and military authorities and what food we could, mainly off refugees. It was quite impossible to buy food anywhere.

That night we slept in a small château near Blois all bedded down in one room. The owner could provide nothing in the way of food except a small quantity of bread and some sort of a garlic paste. To supplement this, however, we had a glass of red wine, a glass of cream and a glass of white wine each. By this time, by the way, we had lost the old man, the baby, the owner of the hospital and the nurse. They were all in one taxi and I don't know what happened to them.

The following day, 15th June, we again headed "vers le sud", and again encountered the same troubles, but in the evening, we at last discovered a hospital near Argenton which was not evacuated. They took us all in and

McLeod and I had our wounds re-dressed, a good meal, and went straight to bed.

Next day, the 16th, I was having lunch in the Officers' Room, when we suddenly heard the men next door singing the Marseillaise. The doctor came in and announced that France was asking for an armistice, and the war was over. The French Officers didn't appear to mind much, but four pilots were greatly affected, and started rating the remainder for the poor show they put up.

McLeod and I were just wondering what the devil to do now, when four Anglo-French ambulances, driven by English girls, arrived at the hospital full of French wounded. We told them our bit of news and said they had better make for Bordeaux as quickly as possible with us. However, they said there were several more ambulances to come, so we waited for them. They turned up fairly soon, and with them were the French doctor in charge, and a young English girl who was his second in command. These two proved a bit of a nuisance as they maintained that they were still under French Command, and could not go till they had orders from the French. I told them I intended to take one of the ambulances for what British wounded there were, whether they liked it or not. Two of the girls had already agreed to come along, and the rest, after a lot of arguing, said they would follow later.

We started off with three British wounded (one ambulance had brought a Sgt. Pilot from the R.A.F.), the four French Pilots and an excellent French Sergeant Major, all of whom insisted that they would take their lives if we didn't take them. The two English women drove in turns all through the night with headlights blazing, and we reached Bordeaux in the early hours of the morning. At Bordeaux we went to the French relations of one of the drivers, who gave us a shake-down and food, and after a bit of sleep I went down to the harbour with the Sergeant Major to see about a lift home. The place was in a turmoil, but eventually we found a stolid looking sailor on guard at the gangway of a British destroyer. The Officer of the Watch very soon told us what to do, so we collected up our party and took a train for a place, whose name I I forget, about eighty miles down the river where there was a boat waiting.

Before I left Bordeaux a Colonel of Marines stood me champagne and rolls for breakfast. He was an excellent chap and appeared to be running everything in the town, including a very nice Belgian Countess.

When we got near the boat we found an almighty crush. I should imagine everyone left in France who could scrounge a British passport, no matter what nationality he was, was trying to get on board. We didn't fancy much scrambling in the middle of that mob, so we lay down in the sun on the quay, hoping someone would eventually make room for us. This happened and in due course, we found ourselves in an improvised hospital in the ship, very ably looked after by members of the A.T.S.

We sailed the same night, 18th June, and in three days landed at Falmouth.

Lt. Keith Rae's story (385 Battery):

On the night of 11th June I was with my battery at St. Valery. We were acting as part of an inner circle of defence with orders to keep the enemy off while the 51st Division embarked. Very early the next morning, having destroyed our guns and equipment in accordance with pre-arranged orders, we marched down into the town only to find there were no ships to take us off. Major Mullens therefore led us back into the woods above the town, and as it was pitch dark and raining hard, I wandered into an empty house, sat down and went to sleep.

When I awoke it was just daybreak, so I went back into St. Valery to try to find the rest of the battery and to see if there were any orders. I had not gone far when I met John Goschen of the R.H.A. and Harry Freeman-Jackson. They told me that the whole division was to surrender at 9 o'clock and that those who wished to try to escape might do so. They had decided to try to get away and asked me to go with them. To this I readily assented, and after a hurried consultation we decided that the only possible way was by sea. Accordingly we walked down to the river, where we found a small canoe. Having removed our heavy equipment and boots we paddled down the river and out to sea. We had only gone a few hundred yards when German machine gunners on the cliffs spotted us and opened fire with several heavy machine guns. The first burst was all round us, and it was a miracle that no one was hit, so we upturned the canoe and started to swim out to sea, dragging the canoe with us, hoping to get out of range, and then right the canoe and paddle up the coast to the fleet which we could see in the distance. This proved quite impossible and eventually we were forced to swim ashore. It was quite a long swim and we were all very exhausted when we got there, and sat for several minutes under the cliffs, where we were out of sight of the Germans. There I luckily found a pack with a dry shirt and a corporal's overcoat. While I was changing the Germans started dropping hand grenades down the cliffs, and shouted to us to come up and surrender. As they had not fired at us swimming ashore, Goschen and I felt that it was only fair to scale the cliffs and surrender, which we accordingly did.

When we got to the top of the cliffs we were searched and then left to wander round the German positions. I watched a 3.7 anti-aircraft gun firing at the fleet who promptly retaliated and gave us the worst shelling I had experienced since the war started. I lay in a large bomb crater with the crew of a 3-inch mortar, and we were all covered with soil thrown up by the shells which repeatedly fell on the edge of the crater.

The shelling eased off after half an hour, and we were marched off by a particularly objectionable little German who kept prodding me in the back with his bayonet.

After walking for about two miles, we reached a sort of enclosure or compound where there were about 1,000 English soldiers who had been mopped up the previous night.

We were kept there for an hour when all the officers were taken by lorry to a château which, I imagined, was a

Divisional H.Q., where we were searched and questioned. From there we were taken by stages to Rouen where we were put into an empty camp surrounded by barbed wire, with machine guns at each corner, and guards armed with tommy guns, wandering round. We were given plenty of very stale bread and jam and cold tea to drink. We stayed at this camp for two days, during which time fresh batches of men and officers arrived continually, including most of the officers of the 1st R.H.A. and Pat Mills from our battery. I also met the Embarkation Officer who told me that most of my battery had been taken off by the fleet.

From Rouen we set out for Germany. The first two days we were taken by lorry, being placed in similar camps each night. They then told us that we should have to march the rest of the way to Germany. The food became steadily worse and our normal ration became three or four hard biscuits and a cup of weak coffee early in the morning and a bowl of bean soup in the evening on which we were expected to march twenty to twenty-five miles a day. Needless to say the French were much sharper than we were and always got the best of everything that was going.

After several days of this Pat Mills, Hopkins (known as "Hoppy") and I decided to escape. As I have already said, these camps were fairly well guarded, but on the march we had several times seen good opportunities of escaping and felt that this would be the best way of getting away. Escaping on the march was made easier by the French who each carried a couple of large suitcases or a heavy pack. Naturally after a few miles they began to tire, and gradually the column began to straggle, which materially diminished the efficiency of our guards. It was towards the end of one of these marches, that our opportunity came somewhere between St. Pol and Béthune.

The column was nicely straggled out and when we halted for ten minutes rest, the nearest guard was 200 yards away, so Pat, Hoppy, and I slipped under some blackberry bushes unseen, and a few minutes later the column moved on without us. We had no fear of our absence being noticed as our names had never been taken and we had only been counted once.

We waited in our very uncomfortable hideout till night as a considerable amount of German transport was passing up and down the road. As soon as it was dark we set off across country making due west in the hope of reaching the coast somewhere south of Le Touquet. We had no compass only the stars, but luckily it was fine. It took us a fortnight to reach the sea, doing about seven miles a night.

How we hated our march to the coast! Walking by night across unknown country occupied by the enemy is one of the most nerve-racking experiences.

During the day we hid in the woods and begged food off the farmers. The farming community in occupied France were magnificent and never refused us food or advice.

We were nearly caught on two occasions. Once we were hiding in a wooded ravine when I was awakened by the sound of a lorry. I crawled up to the top of the ravine, and there, just above us, were several Germans dismounting from a lorry. I rushed down the bank, woke up the others, and we just had time to gather our belongings together and crawl under a bush, when a German soldier came crashing down through the undergrowth, laying a telephone line just where we had been sleeping. The second occasion was when we were trying to cross a river valley by night. We had just scrambled through a very difficult hedge when I saw a very small light. I pointed it out to the others who merely laughed and said it was a glow-worm. We had only gone a few steps further when we were challenged by a sentry. Luckily it was very dark and he could only hear us, not see us, so we walked steadily on between rows of tents full of snoring Germans and out the other side. In the darkness we had walked slap into the middle of a German camp, but luckily the sentry had been half asleep and must have thought we were some of the cows moving about the field.

A few days later we reached the coast, arriving at a

small village called Groffliers near Bercle Plage, where we hid in the grounds of an empty château with a lot of scrubby bushes running down to the sandhills. From the top of these sandhills we could see quite a number of fishing boats moored in the estuary of the River Authie.

That night we crawled down to these boats and, although the village people had assured us there were German patrols on the beach, we never saw or even heard any. After a thorough reconnaissance, we came to the conclusion that the only hope of taking one of these fishing boats out to sea with any chance of success was when there was a fairly strong offshore wind, which would allow us to drift out to sea, and when we were some way out to raise sail and get well out of sight of land by daybreak. We stayed a long time on the coast, waiting for the wind to change to the right quarter, but it blew with remarkable steadiness from the west, and never looked like changing. The old concierge of the château used to bring us food every day.

After we had been there five weeks Hitler began to concentrate his army round the northern ports preparing for an invasion of England, and a regiment of "horsed" artillery arrived in our château. We then decided to make for unoccupied France. So, changing our uniforms for peasant clothes, we set off.

Until we reached the Somme we marched by night, as the country was very heavily occupied. This took seven days. We crossed the Somme with some difficulty, near the village of Long. From here onwards we marched by day, doing about eighteen-twenty miles a day, Mills and Hoppy in front while I followed about half a mile behind, so as not to appear too much of a crowd. We kept to the third-class roads the whole time and, where possible, to the footpaths. We always skirted the occupied villages and at night, if possible, tried to find an isolated farm. In most cases we would be invited in to feed with the family and then be allowed to sleep in the barns. We frequently met Germans, but they never stopped us as they took us for labourers going to work in the fields. We were nearly caught once again when one night's march

FRANCE

from the frontier between occupied and unoccupied France.

We were walking through a large wood when we saw a German on a bicycle approaching. As we always avoided the Boche wherever possible, we all dived into the ditch, but unfortunately he had spotted us, and came over to see what we were doing. We must have looked very suspicious sitting in the bramble bushes, and he asked us in very bad French what we were doing there. Hoppy, who speaks excellent French, replied that we were resting as we had walked some way. He then remarked that it was a peculiarly uncomfortable place to rest. We replied that it was a lovely place and that we always rested in similar places. He then asked if we were soldiers, whereupon we roared with laughter and said "Good lord, no." I said that I was much too young to be mobilized, Mills added that he was too old, while Hopkins said that he had six children and that he had never been mobilized. This answer seemed to satisfy him, and he began to ask us if there were any deer about. He had a shot gun with him and was obviously out shooting. We told him that there were quite a lot of deer on the other side of the wood, and if he hurried he might get a shot at them. This news seemed to please him, and he got on his bicycle and made off while we walked for a couple of hours in the opposite direction just in case he decided to ask any more questions.

Two nights later we crossed the Cher which is the frontier, without as much difficulty as we had expected. We separated to cross the river, and crossed about two miles apart. I swam across just as it was getting dark, about 500 yards from the nearest German post. We had arranged a rendezvous the other side and the next day I met Pat at the arranged place. While we were waiting for Hoppy who was held up by an unexpected patrol, I went off to see an Englishman who lived nearby.

He was not very encouraging, and assured us that by far the best thing would be for us to give ourselves up and be interned. He said that the Germans had complete control of the French Police, and also the Army, who had orders to arrest all Englishmen and intern them. He told us that there were no ships coming or leaving Marseilles, and that we had no chance of getting there either by train or by walking. I told him that our minds were made up to try and get to Marseilles by train as we did not feel like walking another five hundred miles and persuaded him to cash me a cheque for 1,000 francs.

When Hoppy at last arrived we walked into Loche where we bought some new clothes, leaving ourselves just enough money to pay for our tickets to Marseilles. When we originally escaped we had between us about 4,000 francs, the remainder of which paid for the new clothes. The owner of the clothes shop put us up for the night, and the next day we walked into the station and bought tickets for Toulouse without any difficulty, and there bought tickets for Marseilles. Nobody asked us for papers, either on the train or at the station, which was undoubtedly very lucky, as I found out later that nearly all the trains were being searched.

We arrived at Marseilles at about 10 o'clock at night, and started to look for somewhere to live. We asked at a number of small hotels, but always with the same answer, that we must show our papers first. Luckily the last place we tried was owned by an English woman who said that we could sleep in her drawing room for the night, but that we must leave early in the morning, as a French detective came round every morning checking up on new arrivals.

The next morning we went along to the American Consul hoping that he might be able to help us. He sent us along to the British Consul who was working under the Americans. The British Consul was most disappointing, and said he could do nothing to help us until we got ourselves interned, and then he would let us have an allowance of £5 per month. At last after a considerable amount of arguing he agreed to let us have £5 each if we were really trying to escape, and told us to come back in a few days to collect it. He advised us, if we did not want to be interned, to live at the "Home for Distressed Seamen" on the Rue Forbin. We accordingly went along to this place, where we met a very charming padre called Caskie, who told us that we most certainly might stay the night, but advised us not to stay long as a detective came round every two or three days, and took all British soldiers along to Fort St. Jean where they were interned. This fort apparently was run by the Foreign Legion, who collected there before being sent back to North Africa. Officers and men were well treated and were allowed out on parole, and received the monthly grant from the Consul. This cheered us up quite a lot and we felt that at the worst, we should only be interned, instead of being prisoners of war.

That evening a Captain B. turned up, who had come down to see us, as he had heard that some other British officers had arrived. He told us that he had been interned but had escaped, and was living in a Polish hospital where he was working on a plan to escape. He said that he could fix us up to stay at the hospital too, and he told us of his plan to escape. The next day we went up to the hospital where a Polish Colonel received us very kindly, and told us that all the Poles were trying to get back to England to fight again. There were about 300 Poles at this hospital all magnificently fit and sunburned and all pretending to be ill. Each had a temperature chart above his bed; some wore bandages; and a permanent squad was detailed to stay in their pyjamas so that they could jump back into bed if any French officials came round. We were given a room with the door leading out into a shrubbery, where we could hide if anyone came round inspecting the hospital.

The Poles had discovered that Poles of non-military age could get across Spain on a Polish passport. Accordingly they were issuing passports with false ages to all Polish soldiers. They also gave us passports of non-military age. I was called Yez Yosef and was aged seventeen, Hopkins was forty-eight, but Pat by this time had gone off on his own and we never saw him again.

Having got our passports the next step was to go to the Chinese consul and buy a Chinese visa for 120 francs. With these visas we went to the American State Express

Company and bought a ticket for Shanghai, paying an advance of 200 francs, the rest to be paid at Lisbon. Armed with these we went to the Portugese Consul and bought Portugese visas, paying 150 francs in the morning and 400 francs in the afternoon. Taking all these papers with us, we then went to the Spanish Consul and bought a transit visa across Spain for 11 francs. We were now eligible for an exit visa out of Marseilles and with this would have been able to get to Perpignan on the Spanish frontier, where we were told we could get exit visas out of France. The Poles were sending one Englishman with each batch of Poles, but unfortunately, shortly before we were due to go, the frontier was closed by the Germans and we were forced to abandon this scheme.

Our next plan was to try to stow away on one of the occasional neutral ships that visited Marseilles. We met a doctor who had already tried this twice. On both occasions he had been caught, after spending several days in intense discomfort, as nobody except the German Control knew when these ships would be allowed to leave. He told us that all ships were very carefully searched by their own crews, and it was almost impossible to escape detection.

The only other shipping leaving Marseilles were the troop transports taking the Legion back to North Africa. So we decided by hook or by crook to get on board one of these.

A few days later, when we were in the British Consulate collecting the £5 we had been promised, a strange individual came up and asked us if we were British officers trying to escape. Thinking he was a French detective we refused to tell him anything until he told us who he was and what he wanted. He then said that he was an Austrian Quaker called Natzler, whose parents lived in London, and that he was trying to get back to England to join the army. He said that he had got papers that would take him to Casablanca, and that if we would like to go with him he thought he could fix us up with the necessary papers. We were only too glad to find a way out of Marseilles, and gladly accepted this offer. We arranged to meet him next day, by which time he said that he would be able to procure the papers for us.

The next day we met him as arranged. With him was a Hungarian who assured us that within twenty-four hours he would forge some demobilization papers for us, Twenty-four hours later we met at the same little café, and were given demobilization papers for two Rumanians. These papers stated that I was a Rumanian, who had been born at Timisoara, and lived in Paris for six months before the outbreak of war, when I had joined the 2me Pioneer Battalion of the Engagés Volontaires Étrangers, which is part of the Foreign Legion. The papers also said that I had only joined for the duration of the War, and would be demobilized at Casablanca. Hoppy's papers were identical. We put our fingerprints on them and signed them, and the Hungarian stamped them. We paid him 800 francs for these papers. On arrival at the Treasury we placed our papers on the counter, and were paid the 1,000 francs, which is a bounty paid to all demobilized soldiers. This was accomplished without the least difficulty, and we then went and bought the medal to which we were entitled.

In the afternoon, we went up to the Camp St. Marthe, the demobilization camp, and demanded to be sent to Casablanca. Our papers were stamped, and we were told to report for Roll Call at 7.30 hours a.m. and to catch the boat leaving at mid-day. The next morning we answered our names at Roll Call, and proceeded down to the harbour where we hung about beside the ship for a couple of hours, with about twenty-five other Isolé's as we were called waiting to go aboard. At first we imagined that all the others were genuine cases, but on becoming friendly with them, we found that the whole lot had false papers of some sort.

Eventually after a brief examination of our papers, we were allowed by the German Control to go on board. We were then packed down into the hold with a large number of Arabs. As we couldn't face this we got back on deck, hired three deck chairs, and stayed there for the duration of the voyage. Luckily it was quite calm and fine, and we were well fed by the ship's cook. We kept very much to ourselves, and rarely spoke to anybody.

After three days steaming through Spanish territorial waters, we reach Oran. At Oran we fell in on the quay and were marched by an N.C.O. up to the Demobilization Camp. Here, after a long wait, our papers were stamped, and we were told to go to the station and catch the next train to Casablanca. On enquiry at the station we were told that we could either buy tickets and go on the civilian express or travel free on a slow military train. Eventually we were forced to take the military train, which left at midnight. We spent three very cold nights and three very hot days in the train, having taken sufficient food for the journey with us. At first we travelled third class, but there was such an influx of Arabs, that we could stand it no longer, and for the price of a few francs, we bribed the guard to allow us to travel first class.

We had no trouble at Oujda on the frontier between Algeria and French Morocco, where our papers were once again stamped. On arrival at Casablanca our papers, by this time very imposing looking documents, were again stamped by the military officials. The first thing to do was to fix ourselves up at an hotel, and we soon found a room for three in a small hotel in the Arab quarter. This was much easier than at Marseilles. Our demobilization papers were as good as any identity cards, and we had no trouble whatever.

Once settled in we set about making enquiries about escaping. First we went to the British Consul working under the Americans, who was more pleasant than his counterpart at Marseilles, but not really very helpful. He advised us to go to the British Club where we introduced ourselves and created quite a stir. Nearly all the British population at Casablanca as well as some residents from Algeria, who had been thrown out after the Oran incident, were there and had been trying to get back to England for five or six weeks. They, of course, could only resort to official means, as they were well known to the police.

FRANCE

We were told that the British blockade allowed no ships into Casablanca and the Italian Control allowed no ships out, so there was no chance of stowing away. We next made enquiries about crossing the desert to Nigeria, but found that this was completely out of the question except with a well-equipped expedition. The only alternative left seemed to be to try to sail a fishing boat to Gibraltar, a distance of about 250 miles, with a good chance of meeting a British warship on the way. On making further enquiries with a variety of shady characters we found a Spanish fisherman who was taking a party of twelve to Gibraltar in a few days time. There seemed to be no snags to the scheme, but Hoppy and I were slightly suspicious of it and, in addition, there was only room for one of us, as there was already a crew of eleven comprising four Belgians, two Moroccans, one Czech, one Austrian and three Frenchmen. Eventually this scheme fell through and, as the authorities were on the watch, we began to feel desperate.

Then, once again, we had a stroke of luck. We had by this time become very friendly with an Englishman working for one of the American Oil Companies, and he introduced us to a friend, another Englishman, who, to us, seemed a modern "Scarlet Pimpernel". We never knew his name and, when referring to him, we always called him Mr. "X". We showed him our papers and, on seeing they were Rumanian demobilization papers, he told us that he could easily get us out of Morocco with them. He explained that the first step was to go to the French Police and apply to be repatriated. He also said that he was a friend of the Chief of Police and would come with us to the latter's office and help us through. By this time three other Englishmen had arrived, a Swiss called "Dubois", a Yugoslav under the name of "Stevanovitch", and a Bulgarian named "Poppoff". The five of us, and Mr. "X", accordingly went along to the police station and were shown into the Chief of Police's office. There we solemnly sat down and were given large forms to fill in. These forms required the usual details of place of birth, date of birth, etc. We knew most of the answers, as we had been previously coached by the Hungarian at Marseilles. The only question that we had not thought of, was the names of our fathers and mothers. Hoppy and I sat for several minutes thinking hard, and finally in desperation, I wrote down Carol Benon, and Helene Benon (née Frederica). I then glanced at Hoppy's form and saw that he had written down Frederic Nagy and Marie Nagy (née Lupescu). I then made a very grave blunder, and signed mine with my own name "J. E. K. Rae". Luckily Hoppy noticed this, and jogged my elbow So when no one was looking, I crumpled it up, slipped it into my pocket and hastily filled in a second form.

Our papers filled in we handed them to the Chief of Police, who promised to get the necessary exit permits as soon as possible. Three days later the papers were returned with the necessary exit permits. Our friend Mr. "X" then told us that those papers would be useless at Lisbon and that we had better get temporary British passports. These, our only genuine papers, we got from the British Section of the American Consulate. Hoppy then took them along to the Portuguese Consul, who for the sum of 150 francs attached the necessary Portuguese visa. In this way we now had papers both to get out of Casablanca and into Lisbon.

The next job was to find a ship going to Lisbon. Mr. "X" advised us to go to a small Portuguese shipping agent who might be able to help us. We told him our story, and he said that he had a 200 ton coastal steamer leaving for Lisbon shortly, and that for the sum of 4,000 francs we might travel on deck without food to Lisbon. As we then had very little money left, we arranged with the British Consul to pay him the necessary £125 when we reached Lisbon. Handing our British passports to the captain of the ship we proceeded down to the harbour where we were given yet more papers to fill in and where our small amount of baggage was thoroughly searched by the customs. We then passed through the Italian Control and showed our papers to a fat Italian N.C.O. who stamped them and allowed us to go on board.

Already on board were about eighty other passengers

of all nationalities, including a large number of French Jews who seeing what had happened to their fellow countrymen in Germany and other occupied countries, were getting to the United States while the going was good.

After a long delay we were allowed to sail. I think it was one of the best moments of my life as we slipped under the hull of the *Jean Bart*, the newest of the French battleships, past a number of destroyers of the Toulon Squadron, which later put a spoke in the wheel of General De Gaulle, and out to sea. Despite the relief of having finally escaped from the clutches of our enemies, the next three days were not enjoyable, and I hope I shall never have to face the Atlantic in a 200-ton steamer again. Personally I managed to survive the journey. But nearly all the other passengers seemed to be ill the whole trip. We passed one British convoy, but as we had no wish to spend the rest of the war at Gibraltar, we let it go by.

We arrived at Lisbon early in the morning, and it was not till late in the evening that passengers with British passports were allowed ashore. The other passengers were still on board when we left. We fixed ourselves up very comfortably at one of the best hotels and the next day went to see the British Military Attaché. He was very pleasant, told us not to shout about who we were, and promised to get us passages in the flying boat leaving for England the next morning. He said that the Consul would pay the £28 each for our passage. On hearing this, we hadn't the courage to tell him that he already owed our little shipping agent £125, so we persuaded someone else to tell him when we were safely on our way to England. The flying boat left early the next morning and after a very pleasant and uneventful trip, we landed safely at Poole on 19th September, exactly three months after we had escaped.

CHAPTER III

INTERLUDE BETWEEN BATTLES

June 1940–June 1942

"Let us therefore brace ourselves to our duties and so bear ourselves that if the British Empire and Commonwealth last for a thousand years, men will still say 'This was their finest hour'."
WINSTON CHURCHILL

I

BY the 17th June the whole regiment were once more re-united at Abergele in North Wales. The chorus of mutual congratulation had however barely subsided when the two Batteries were again separated, 385 moving to Liverpool to take over the anti-tank defence of the Wirral peninsula and 387 marching south to undertake similar duties in Swansea and district.

Before giving an account of the part played by the Kent Yeomany in the critical months that followed a brief sketch of the war situation at that time as a whole will not perhaps be out of place.

The campaign in France was over. On 21st June at Compiégne, in the railway carriage used by Foch for the 1918 armistice, the armistice of 1940 was signed by the French delegates. Three days later they signed one with Italy. Holland, Belgium, Denmark and Norway had already fallen and most people outside England were of opinion that the war was as good as over and that the capitulation of the British Empire was only a matter of time. The British people themselves, however, held a different view. Their determination to carry on alone was much strengthened and their courage heartened by the speeches of their great leader, Winston Churchill.

But for the moment the island, which for centuries had successfully resisted all attempts at invasion, was weaponless and almost defenceless. The number of armed and equipped soldiers barely amounted to a brigade. The R.A.F. was perilously weak. The Navy was still intact, but it was doubtful if the Navy alone could save the

INTERLUDE BETWEEN BATTLES

country from invasion. With the whole of the European coastline at his command Hitler was free to use it to attack Great Britain by sea, by air, or by submarine blockade. He prepared all three, and on 8th August began the necessary preliminary—a series of daylight air attacks. These attacks, and their repulse, which was aptly named the Battle of Britain, lasted till the end of October. On them the whole issue of the war turned; for had they been successful there is no doubt Britain must have shared the fate of France.

But the R.A.F. though constantly outnumbered, had the better of almost every engagement. In the whole period the number of German aircraft brought down in daylight was 2,375. On one day alone, 15th September, 185 were destroyed. The R.A.F. lost in all 375 pilots killed and 358 wounded. But in the end they were victorious, invasion was baulked, the daylight attacks were abandoned and the enemy turned to night bombing. In the immortal words of Mr. Churchill "Never in the field of human conflict was so much owed by so many to so few."

Meanwhile on the continent of Europe a Free French movement was formed under General de Gaulle, while in October, Italy, using Albania as her advanced base, had launched an unprovoked attack against Greece. The Greeks resisted with courage and success and in the following month the great victory at Taranto, in which three out of six capital ships of the Italian battle fleet were crippled by torpedoes from naval aircraft, restored British naval supremacy in the Mediterranean.

In Africa the Italian armies in Libya and Abyssinia had invaded Egypt and Kenya. Early in September a great force under Marshal Graziani crossed the Egyptian frontier and harassed by British patrols, had finally halted at Sidi Barrani. Three months later, on 11th December, a mixed British force under General Wavell began an offensive which in sixty-two days drove the Italians not merely out of Egypt, but out of Cyrenaica, capturing 133,000 prisoners, 1,300 guns and an immense quantity of stores. This brilliant victory was accomplished by a striking force only about 30,000 strong and greatly inferior to the Italians in equipment.

In America the sale of war supplies to Britain was first permitted on a basis known as "cash and carry" and later greatly facilitated by the introduction of Lease-Lend. An agreement was also concluded between the two countries whereby in exchange for fifty American destroyers Britain leased certain naval and air bases to the United States.

Early in the new year Great Britain, at the request of the hard-pressed Greeks, sent a small expeditionary force to that country from Africa thereby seriously depleting General Wavell's strength. In March Germany attacked Yugo-Slavia, bombed Belgrade ruthlessly and fell upon the rear of the Greek army in Albania. Both Greece and Yugo-Slavia were over-run and the British were compelled to retire. Once again a British Expeditionary Force was rescued by the Navy after leaving behind its guns, its equipment and its transport.

Ejected from the mainland the British attempted to hold Crete, an island of great strategical importance in the Mediterranean. But the Germans stormed it from the air and, lacking fighter protection, the garrison was over-run. About half were evacuated, again at serious cost to the British Fleet.

The British forces in Libya, threatened by the presence of a large enemy army in their rear in Italian East Africa, were further depleted by the losses in Greece. At the same time, early in the new year the Italian colonies of Eritrea and Somaliland had been invaded by two forces which eventually met like pincers in the heart of Abyssinia. Although these operations were eventually successful and the bulk of the Italian armies were cut off and destroyed, they occupied a number of troops who were badly needed elsewhere.

In April the Germans, having moved a large air force into Sicily and an equally large tank force into Libya, had attacked our lightly held line in the west of Cyrenaica, and in a very short time driven the British army back to the Egyptian frontier. They were unable, however, to take Tobruk which was still held by a British garrison.

INTERLUDE BETWEEN BATTLES 63

At the beginning of May the Iraq army under the leadership of a man named Raschid Ali rebelled and seized Baghdad where the British Legation was besieged. The bulk of the women and children had been evacuated to the R.A.F. cantonment at Habbaniya, which was also surrounded and besieged by a strong force of rebels with artillery. To meet these threats a battalion of the Essex regiment was flown up from Basra and a small relieving force despatched across the desert from Haifa. By the end of the month the rebellion collapsed.

In June the British were forced to send an army into Syria to put down the Vichy régime who were collaborating with the enemy. Enemy objectives in the Middle East, the Iraq oilfields, the Persian Gulf and the Suez Canal, were threatened by a pincer movement, one force coming down through Turkey, Syria and Palestine and the other attacking along the North African coast.

In the event the first arm of the pincer never materialized. By 11th July the Syrian campaign came to an end and Syria was handed over to a French administration under General de Gaulle, supported by British and French troops. Hitler then turned his attention in another direction, and on 22nd June attacked Russia.

For nearly nine months, from 7th September, 1940, to 16th May, 1941, the British people had endured an intensity of bombing hitherto unprecedented. London, the greatest sufferer, was raided in the beginning on eighty-two out of eighty-five consecutive nights. Over a million houses were damaged and twice as many made uninhabitable. In the provinces nearly all the big towns were also heavily bombed, including among others Liverpool and Swansea.

The regiment, whose duties did not include active air defence, was forced to suffer with the rest of the population this new form of warfare, and with them to maintain that most important of all measures of passive defence, the upkeep of morale. Although neither failed, in many ways it was easier for the soldier than for the civilian. First, although aware that those nearest and dearest to him were in equal danger, the soldier was at least spared the sight of their agony. Secondly, he was so fully occupied with preparations against invasion that he had little or no time for imaginary fears either for the present or the future.

At Swansea the regiment, in addition to manning the anti-tank defences in the area, was made responsible for all the anti-invasion measures in the town and docks, a responsibility which was later extended to include the Gower Peninsula. In this they were assisted by a Holding Battalion of the Welch Regiment, two Field Bakeries R.A.S.C., who had fought as infantrymen at Dunkirk, and about 2,000 men of the local Home Guard. At first the number of weapons available was pitiably small and sandbags were the only means of protecting defensive positions. Later a number of 4.7 in. and 4 in. guns belonging to the Navy were found in the docks. These were mounted on the sea wall and manned by men from the regiment. Rifles from America were issued to the Home Guard and the men in the Field Bakeries. Lewis guns began to appear in small numbers and men were trained in their use. Gradually, as more and more stores and equipment began to arrive, the beaches were covered with barbed wire entanglements and concrete pill boxes, while tank traps and gun emplacements sprang up in the docks and at vital points on the surrounding hills.

The Imperial Chemical Works produced two armoured cars armed with Vickers machine guns, the gift of Sir Roger Keys. These, together with two 13 pdrs. pulled by light lorries and manned by the regiment, with a platoon from a newly-formed battalion of the Welch Regiment that had lately joined the garrison, formed an impressive mobile striking force.

Exercises were held on Sundays with the Home Guard in which the importance of guarding against fifth columnists was emphasized. Captain Allfrey disguised as a dock labourer was captured and thrown into the guardroom. Major Warner with a band of Kentish pirates boarded a small sailing boat and attacked the harbour from the sea.

Meanwhile the enemy bombing continued. At the

INTERLUDE BETWEEN BATTLES 65

Llandarcy Oil Refinery two oil tanks were set on fire and burned like vast flaming torches throwing out columns of black smoke for two days. But with this solitary exception the actual military damage was trifling. For some reason the enemy aircraft, who came over in small numbers, seldom more than three at a time, confined their attentions almost exclusively to the residential part of the town.

Early in August 385 Battery left the Wirral Peninsula and moved to Carmarthen. Battery H.Q. was established at Llangain, mid-way between Carmarthen and Llanstephan, and guns were taken over from 387 Battery and from the 77th Field Regiment at Carew Cheriton Aerodrome.

As well as being responsible for the defences of Swansea and the Gower static anti-tank guns, 6 pdrs. and 4 inch, were now being manned by the regiment from Tenby to a few miles west of Cardiff. On the 16th September the moment came to test these defensive preparations. About ten o'clock at night the secret code word Cromwell, indicating that the long awaited invasion was actually taking place, was received from Area H.Q. at Abergavenny. The necessary orders were issued by telephone and all defensive positions were manned.

There was one difficulty however which, although it had been foreseen, seemed insurmountable. It had been discussed many times between myself, who as officer commanding the regiment, was also responsible for the defences, and my friend Mr. Jones, a local solicitor, who was also the commander of the Home Guard. How were we to turn the Home Guard out at night when they were all in their beds asleep and nothing short of the crack of doom would be likely to awake them? Telephones were no good. Most of them were not on the telephone. A house-to-house visitation would take too long. There were over two thousand of them. There seemed only one thing to do in the event of a really serious emergency, and that was to ring the church bells. There were strict orders against ringing the church bells except in the case of an actual enemy landing. We were not clear whether the magic word Cromwell indicated that the enemy had landed on the east coast or on the west, or whether he had not landed at all but was merely on his way. But now that the moment had come both Mr. Jones and myself decided that on no account could we run the risk of the Home Guard not being there to meet them. So we rang the bells.

Cromwell turned out to be a false alarm. There was no invasion. But the sound of the bells ringing in Swansea was taken up by the towns on our right and left and spread and spread till eventually the church bells over half England were pealing. In many a sleepy hamlet the sexton, wakened by his wife by the direful words: "John! John! the invasion. Can't you hear the bells?" rushed out half-dressed into the night to climb the belfry tower and pull and pull till the clanging peal was answered by another from a neighbouring village. And so on and on through the night the tocsin sounded while the innocent authors of all this returned peacefully to their beds and slept.

Next morning the Area Commander rang up in person demanding an explanation. I rather gathered from the agitated way he spoke that someone of importance at the War Office had been asking him to explain.

In December the regiment was re-formed as a Field Regiment and moved to Builth Wells to mobilize and train. R.H.Q. and 385 Battery, less one troop at Newbridge, were billetted at Builth and 387 about seven miles away at Llangammach.

Before leaving Swansea a large number of recruits straight from civil life had been enlisted. These had been taught marching and saluting and other elementary military movements on the barrack square by a party of specially selected N.C.O.'s under Mr. Walker, the R.S.M. They had reached such a high standard that some of the veterans appeared a little slipshod and slovenly beside them. It was decided therefore to devote the first month at Builth, while waiting for our new guns and equipment, to smartening up the whole regiment. A period of intense activity followed in which marching,

INTERLUDE BETWEEN BATTLES 67

saluting, guard mounting, and arms drill competitions were the order of the day. During December the ground shook to the stamping of feet and the slapping of rifles, while the winter air was rent by the deep baying of the R.S.M. and an ex-guardsman sergeant-major lent by the A.A. Training School at Llandrindod Wells. Particular attention was also paid to turn-out and a fresh supply of regimental flashes was purchased and issued to all ranks. By the New Year the regiment, by now fit to stand comparison with a battalion of the Guards, turned with relief to the training with guns and transport, which constituted the reason for its existence.

In February the regiment left Wales by road for Essex and took over the defence of the beaches in the Harwich peninsular in support of the Essex Division. R.H.Q. was established at Great Bentley, 385 Battery at Harwich, Great Oakley and Thorpe le Soken, 387 at St. Osyth and Clacton. A month later orders were received to mobilize for overseas and the regiment proceeded to Great Baddow to re-organize on a three battery basis. A new battery, 470 Field Battery, was formed by transferring a troop from each of the old ones, and Major K. Miller who had taken the place of Major Warde while the regiment was at Swansea, took command. The new formation, which remained more or less constant until the end of the war, now consisted of 385 Battery, B and C troops, 387 Battery D and F troops, and 470 Battery A and E troops.

The following month the order to mobilize for overseas was cancelled and the regiment returned to the peninsula.

The next three months were devoted to intensive training punctuated by inspections by a variety of general officers. In May the regiment went to Practice Camp at West Down. On 1st June the anniversary of the return from Dunkirk was celebrated by a parade on Great Bentley green followed by a thanksgiving service in the church. At the end of July the regiment moved into camp at Skreens Park, near Chelmsford, for final training and mobilization before proceeding overseas. On 14th August the Honorary

Colonel, Colonel C. E. Ponsonby, O.B.E., T.D., M.P., and other old members of the regiment visited the camp and were entertained at an all-in wrestling match and to a guest night, run on traditional lines, in the officers' mess. A week later the Inspector General of Artillery, inspected the regiment and confessed he was much impressed by the turn-out of all ranks as well as by the march past of the regiment to the strains of its own band. On the 28th the regiment embarked on the SS. *Orontes* at Glasgow and two days later sailed for the Middle East.

Before concluding this account some further mention must be made of the band which was formed at Llangammach under the leadership of Major Warner, ably supported by a number of talented and enthusiastic O.R.s. The band consisted of two parts, a dance band which played regularly throughout the following months at dances organized for all ranks as well as on special occasions for the officers and their friends, and a marching band, probably the only one in existence belonging to a field regiment, which played at church parades, inspections and on other ceremonial occasions. Great credit is due to all concerned for the work done by both these sections of the band, which was undoubtedly partly responsible for maintaining the high morale of the regiment and fostering esprit de corps, as well as giving a great deal of pleasure to a large number of people outside the regiment. The band took their instruments with them when they went abroad and only ceased from functioning as a band after the retreat to Alamein had caused heavy casualties to their members.[1]

II

The following account of the voyage to the East is by Major (later Colonel) D. B. H. Warner, T.D.:

"On the 30th August, 1941, about eleven o'clock in the

[1] This band should not be confused with the drum and trumpet band manned by 385 Battery in France, a short account of which appears at the end of the book.

morning our ship the *Orontes* took up her position as flagship of the convoy and we got under way. H.M.S. *Repulse* and a number of destroyers acted as escort. The aircraft-carrier *Furious* also started, but soon turned back with engine trouble.

"Our course lay to the west and gradually the size of the convoy grew to twenty-eight ships as others joined us, some from Liverpool, others from Swansea, including among the latter one very old coal-burning ship, the smallest and slowest in the convoy, carrying all our guns and vehicles.

"In the evening we learnt that another convoy, sixty miles ahead of us, was being heavily attacked by submarines and from the air so we altered course to the south and doubled our look-out. The *Furious* had already left and visibility was poor. Later that night we again altered course to the west and continued steaming west until the 2nd September when we received wireless orders from home to proceed due south to avoid a pack of hostile submarines ahead. About the same time the *Furious* reappeared. Our new change of course had taken us far too close to the coast of France to be comfortable and the sight of the great aircraft carrier's vast bulk ploughing along behind us was very reassuring.

"By now most of us had found our sea-legs and were even becoming resigned to the numerous, to the landlubber, irritating rules and regulations peculiar to troopships. Among these was an order that all ranks must remain on deck from nine till twelve in the morning. There was nothing to sit on but the deck itself since to use your life-belt for the purpose was strictly forbidden. Those who were not sufficiently padded by nature were therefore compelled by this harsh rule either to walk up and down for three hours or to lean disconsolately over the rail. Frequent calls to boat stations were another source of annoyance involving as they did standing for hours in a tin hat in a draughty part of the ship waiting to be inspected by the O.C. Ship. Since there were not in any case sufficient lifeboats to accommodate more than half of us most people would have preferred to resign themselves to a watery grave from the beginning rather than stand in a queue dismally reviewing in their wind-chilled minds the remoteness of their chance of safety.

"But by far the worst of the sufferings imposed by these regulations was the one that compelled all ranks to sleep below decks at night. As the weather grew warmer the heat and stench below decks after dark became more and more unendurable so that by comparison the Black Hole of Calcutta would have seemed an air-conditioned paradise. The only ventilation was by means of blowers. Those who were fortunate enough to sling their hammocks in the direct path of one of these contrivances usually contracted a severe chill in the minute area exposed to its blast while the rest of their bodies sweated and sweltered.

"These little trials and troubles made up the debit-side of life at sea. But there were many credits and compensations. The food was excellent. Concerts, cinema shows, boxing competitions, lectures by experts on a variety of subjects, and games of all kinds all helped to overcome the monotony of our days. The regimental band played regularly and an excellent revue by the officers and men of the regiment was staged and produced by Lieut. David Clarke.

"Early in September all ranks put on tropical kit for the first time. While the sun shone benignly down on 3,500 pairs of lily white knees and their somewhat self-conscious owners, a small drama of the sea was being prepared beyond the horizon.

"Sunday, the 7th September, was a particularly lovely day and the colours of the sea were more than usually brilliant. The convoy, less nearly all its escort, including the *Repulse* who had gone off to a secret destination to refuel, slid over the glassy water like a group of toy steamers pulled by invisible strings. In the *Orontes* the usual church parade had been held on the boat deck, accompanied by the band, and the entire ship's company had settled down to a typical Sunday afternoon of sunbathing and sleep when from the bridge a small smudge of smoke was seen dead ahead. All eyes and glasses were turned on the horizon and there was much speculation as

INTERLUDE BETWEEN BATTLES 71

to the identity of the stranger. The position of the sun made identification difficult but gradually the superstructure of a capital ship began to emerge and more smoke and masts indicated that she was not sailing alone. The general opinion was that we had run into the *Scharnhorst* who, having learnt of the absence of the *Repulse* and our escort, was now bent on our destruction.

"The alarm was sounded and the 'danger' signal hoisted. All hands went to action stations and guns were loaded and smoke canisters prepared. The 'dispersal' signal, already made out, was beginning to go up when a light was seen to flash from the now fast approaching ship and she was identified as the *Repulse* who, as we afterwards learned, had refuelled quicker than she expected. The feeling of relief on the bridge was so great that a general move was made to the Commodore's cabin for the purpose of calming the nerves. It was quite a long time later that someone remembered that the 'All Clear' had not been sounded and that the rest of the ship's company were still standing at 'action stations'.

"Five days later we entered Freetown where we stayed for a further five days to take on a fresh supply of water. The weather was extremely hot and sticky; there were continuous tropical rainstorms; and no one was allowed ashore. The troops amused themselves watching the local boys diving for pennies and, when that became monotonous, turning the hosepipes on them. Everyone was relieved when on the afternoon of the 18th we at last weighed anchor and once more felt the welcoming breeze on our faces and heard the swish of the water against the ship's sides.

"On the evening of the 20th we crossed the line but, owing to our numbers the customary ritual was not observed.

"For the next week life went on as usual. By day we watched the flying fish. At night, the rule about sleeping below decks having been mercifully relaxed, we lay on the deck and identified the Southern Cross in a sky bright with stars. On the 30th, as day broke, we saw for the first time the imposing bulk of Table Mountain outlined against the brightening sky and soon after breakfast secured alongside the quay of Cape Town. A few hours later the regiment, which had spent the whole of the last two days polishing boots and badges, and whitening their flashes and lanyards, paraded through the town behind its band.

"The hospitality of the South African people to the convoys who touched at their shores was unbounded, and their kindness and generosity will never be forgotten. There were dances every night; drives were organized into the interior and to places of interest in Cape Town itself; and every man was adopted by a family and made to feel that he was indeed an honoured guest. Many lifelong friendships were made and correspondence between the men of the regiment and their kind hosts, I believe, still continue.

"This extremely happy interlude soon came to an end. In the afternoon of the 3rd October the *Orontes* once more set sail. On the following day we were rejoined at sea by the *Repulse* and the other half of the convoy who had been equally royally entertained at Durban.

"For the next three weeks little of importance occurred to disturb the even tenour of the voyage. Once more we crossed the line. The *Repulse* was relieved by the *Chatham* which in turn was replaced by the cruiser *Glasgow*. On the 17th all doubts as to our destination, at one time believed to be Singapore, were set at rest when the convoy split, one half steaming due north and the remainder, including the *Orontes*, setting course westward for Bombay.

"For a few days there was a hectic rush of farewell parties, including a fancy dress cocktail party in the officers' lounge. Early on the morning of the 23rd we reached Bombay, unloaded our kit, and re-embarked on H.M.T. *Devonshire* which was lying alongside waiting for us. The weather was sultry and sticky in the extreme and it was evening before all our baggage was stowed away and everyone had found their place in the new ship. As, however, we were sailing again the next morning all those who could get leave at once set off to explore the town.

INTERLUDE BETWEEN BATTLES

"At ten o'clock in the 24th October we once more steamed out to sea this time on our last lap and alone. Our final destination was now known to be Basra. Many of our vehicles had left the docks at Swansea with the word 'BASRA' chalked in large letters on their sides. But in the atmosphere of intense secrecy prevailing at the time no one believed that this was anything but another security measure.

"The next six days, in a ship built for the comfort of the troops it was designed to carry, were like a peace time pleasure cruise and it was with mixed feelings that we finally sailed up the Shatt-el-Arab river and watched the date palms on its banks sliding by on either side. Our long voyage was over. Since the day we embarked at Glasgow we had covered approximately 12,000 miles and spent sixty-four days at sea. A new land and a new life awaited us. What we wondered had the future in store?"

III

The regiment having disembarked at Basra entrained the same night for Zubair. It was 2 o'clock in the morning when the train stopped in what appeared to be the middle of nowhere and the Arab guard informed us in broken English that we had arrived. It was pitch dark and cold, and the men were still in their shorts and shirt sleeves without blankets, tents or food. There was no one to meet us: and, when daylight appeared, there was nothing in sight but a group of tamarisk trees, the railway line and the bare desert. Once again the powers of masterly organization, for which the staff who control base ports are so well known, had excelled even the most sanguine expectations. Eventually a neighbouring Indian battalion, the 1/19 Hyderabads, came to our aid, produced transport and tents and helped collect our stores and equipment, most of which was still lying fifteen miles away on the quayside.

A fortnight later, once more fully equipped with guns and lorries, the regiment proceeded in convoy to Baghdad staging on the way at Sulaiba (eighty-two miles), Ur of the Chaldees (forty-one miles), Samawa (sixty miles), Khamjadal (sixty-nine miles) and Lancer Camp, Baghdad (fifty miles).

It is difficult to convey to those who have not been there the strangeness of this strange new world in which we now found ourselves. A mere description of things seen is not enough—the camels and the palm trees and the sand. Everyone who has read any book about the East, or who has been to the pictures, or paid a visit to the Zoo, knows what camels and palm trees are like. The heat, the smells and the flies—all these are available in some measure and at certain times and places at home. It is only a question of multiplying them tenfold. But the atmosphere of the East, the sensation of being strangers in a strange land, these are as hard to convey as that other feeling, the feeling of being unconsidered midgets in space and time, of no more and no less importance than the flies that settled on the children's faces or the insects that bit us when we went to bed at night.

Driving up the desert track from Basra to Baghdad this sense of the infinity of time and space increased. Time almost ceased to exist. For in this ancient land where Abraham had grazed his flocks and Belshazzar had hunted the wild lion it was hard to conceive time in terms of minutes and hours. Space too seemed limitless. In the desert where the horizon never changes there are no landmarks to mark your progress. An endless sea of sand broken up by wide valleys and gentle rises, too low to be dignified by the name of hills, and covered with patches of low scrub and camel thorn, stretched interminably before us. From time to time we passed an Arab village consisting of tumbledown mud huts which looked as if they had been recently bombed. A crowd of children, ragged and dirty, ran towards us with hands outstretched screaming the one word common to all the people of the east "Bucksheesh! Bucksheesh!" Mangey looking pi-dogs skulked at their heels or scampered snarling up the narrow, filthy streets. We crossed the Euphrates, and long after the river was out of sight could see the white sails of the feluccas gliding as it were over the desert itself.

INTERLUDE BETWEEN BATTLES

From now on we were to travel many thousands of miles across the desert, and as the procedure was always the same a short description may not be out of place here. David Warner, with Mr. Walker, the Quartermaster, was the first to leave the camp, followed shortly afterwards by the advance party consisting of the cooks' lorries from each battery. The whole regiment would then move off in column of route, the guns and tractors being grouped under a selected officer in rear.

Having chosen the site for the new camp the Quartermaster would mark out the area with empty petrol tins. In a short time the advance party would arrive and take up their allotted positions; and, while the cooks prepared the evening meal, the battery captains' party would carry on the process of marking the exact position of each gun and lorry in the battery. By the time the leading vehicle appeared all was ready.

The setting sun glinted on the petrol tins, and shone on the naked torso of the second in command, already as bronzed and polished as the top of his bald head. In thin blue columns the smoke from the cooks' fires rose in the still evening air. From a distance of at least a mile the Quartermaster's cheerful bellow could be heard welcoming the newcomers. One by one the lorries and guns swung into position and the men jumped out of them laughing and shouting. As if by magic a mushroom growth of tents and bivvies, trestle tables, benches and latrines covered the ground.

The sun went down and the moon came up. Men's voices and the sound of singing slowly died away. In the still desert night there was no sound but the tramp of the sentries' feet and the mournful note of a jackal baying at the moon. The regiment was asleep.

We stayed three days in Baghdad and were visited by a Russian mission. Since this is the only occasion during the whole of the war when either regiment of the Kent Yeomanry encountered our Russian allies the writer has felt it his duty to record it.

On the 21st November the regiment moved into a tented camp by the lakeside at Habbaniya and became part of the divisional artillery of the 10th Indian Division under Major-General W. T. Slim.

The next two months were spent in training for desert warfare and in making ourselves comfortable. To say both seemed to us almost equally important may outrage the feelings of those who believe that a soldier's first and last duty is to fight, but the risk must be taken. The winter in Iraq can be very cold. The camp at Habbaniya consisted of tents only and was fully exposed to the frequent sand-storms that swept across the desert. On these occasions it was impossible to see more than a few yards in front of one's face, tents were often blown down, and everything, clothes, blankets, food and books were smothered in sand. Even the ink bottles became filled. There were no amenities in the camp, no recreation or reading rooms, no hot baths and no means of keeping warm. But in the R.A.F. cantonment one and a half miles away everything had been provided that the ingenuity of peace-time service backed by an apparently bottomless purse could devise: brick buildings, hot baths, centrally heated messes, recreation rooms, clubs. swimming pools, a cinema and a well-equipped hospital. It was even said that the aircraftsmen, all of whom belonged to the ground staff, slept in beds with sheets and were called in the mornings by Arab orderlies with cups of tea.

Unfortunately the Group Captain commanding the station was unable to see his way to allow the army to participate in these luxuries, even to the extent of an occasional hot bath, and the cantonment was out of bounds to troops. The only concession made was to allow the soldiers to come to the cinema in the evenings. Their numbers materially swelled the box office receipts and, provided they left the cantonment area the moment the performance was over, they could do little harm.

Faced with the discomforts of camp life in the desert in winter the regiment set to work to overcome them. Iraq is the home of the brick-making industry. Somewhere about 4000 B.C. the earliest inhabitants of Iraq, the Sumerians, invented the art of baking mud bricks in the sun and binding them together with a little chopped straw, and bricks in Iraq have been made in this way ever since. It was not long before someone discovered an old deserted brickfield guarded by a solitary Arab caretaker. Men who in private life were bricklayers and builders took the lead and in a few weeks the camp was transformed. Brick dining halls and recreation rooms sprang up like mushrooms; beautiful brick kitchens, fitted with the latest oil and water burning devices were the pride of each battery; and fireplaces of ornate design, many of them stamped with the emblem of the White Horse of Kent, decorated the tile-floored messes of the officers and sergeants. General Slim, who came to inspect the regiment on a day when a particularly unpleasant sandstorm was blowing, was greatly impressed and ordered that parties from other units should visit the camp and take note. This was how things should be done, he said. A unit that knew how to look after itself must ipso facto be a good fighting unit.

He was less pleased, however, when some months later his A.Q.M.G. brought him a bill for £300 which had been presented to most of the military and civil departments in Iraq. It was for bricks and was supported by a number of chits which read as follows:

"To the Desert Brickfield,
    Thanks very much for bricks. Will call again for more to-morrow.
                        Yours faithfully,
                            CLARKE GABLE."

or:

   "Your bricks are excellent. We never use any others.
            Signed   MUSSOLINI
                     CHARLEY CHAPLIN
                     POPEYE THE SAILOR."

Training in desert warfare and in learning to find one's way about the desert presented no difficulties since the desert itself lay at our doorstep. North, east and west it stretched and one had only to drive for ten minutes in any direction to find oneself as completely out of touch with the landmarks of civilization as in the middle of the Sahara. Unfortunately, after a Christmas which many will remember as one of the happiest the regiment ever spent—it was the last time that so large a number of the old originals were to spend Christmas together—the all important training was brought to an end and orders were issued from above that the regiment should take its part in digging the defences on which the whole of the rest of the army in Iraq as well as thousands of hired labourers were engaged.

During the winter of 1941/42 the Powers-that-Be were obsessed with the fear that the enemy might attack the Iraq oilfields through Turkey marching southwards towards their ultimate objective, the Persian Gulf. The lesson of the winter of 1939/40 that static defences dug in the ground are of no avail against modern weapons and modern methods of offense and that a fully-trained mobile army, however small, is worth hundreds of miles of concrete dug-outs, had not yet been assimilated. All over the country from the Mosul area in the north where the 8th Indian Division were stationed to the Hindiya Barrage in the south, occupied by the 21st Indian Infantry Brigade and working parties from the regiment, men were feverishly digging. Regimental training was resumed again in February, but it was not until the second week in March that the regiment joined the 20th Indian Infantry Brigade at Baiji and serious training of all arms together began. It was then found that the standard of training of the infantry who had been digging the whole winter was far below that of the artillery and that combined operations were consequently of much less value. This error in military policy was to have serious repercussions in battle in the near future.

In April the C.O. with other senior officers from the army in Iraq went on a month's tour of the Western Desert. Officers and men of the regiment were granted leave and shooting parties were arranged in Kurdistan and elsewhere. Captains Wix and Wacher with Lieut.

INTERLUDE BETWEEN BATTLES 79

Bryant and nine O.Rs. from 385 Battery succeeded in shooting three wild pig and a quantity of duck and partridge while Bdr. Law with another party from the same battery, shot an ibex near Rowanduz Gorge. A number of officers and men acted as escort to Mr. Adrian Holman, the newly-appointed Counsellor at Teheran, and spent an enjoyable leave in Persia.

Meanwhile the war as a whole was not progressing favourably for the Allies. On 7th December, without warning, Japan attacked every American and British base within reach and her aircraft sank two American battleships and disabled three at Pearl Harbour. Three days later the new British battleship *Prince of Wales* and the battle cruiser *Repulse*, which had escorted the regiment out from England, were likewise sunk by Japanese bombers in the Gulf of Siam. Hong-Kong fell on Christmas Day and Singapore early in February. In swift succession the Japanese conquered the Dutch East Indies, Borneo, the Philippines, the Andamans and Burma. Her armies threatened India and Ceylon and her fleet was only prevented from dominating the Indian Ocean by the British occupation of Madagascar, till then under Vichy control.

The winter of the Japanese disasters would have been still more gloomy had it not been relieved by the rally of the Russians who took advantage of the severe cold, from which the German armies suffered far more terribly than themselves, to dislodge the enemy from one position after another. Eventually Hitler himself assumed personal command. A Russian offensive against Kharkov in May was defeated; Sevastopol was taken and the Crimea overrun. Two huge German armies then attacked the Russian line between Donetz and the upper Don, one turning south to take Rostov and push on towards the Caucasus, the other moving east to reach the neighbourhood of the Volga at Stalingrad.

In North Africa the story was much the same, an initial success followed by set-backs. General Wavell had been succeeded by General Auchinleck, who on 18th November had opened another offensive. Tobruk was relieved and on Christmas Eve Benghazi was once more in British hands. Early in the year, however, a strong counter-attack by the German and Italian forces under General Rommel at El Agheila drove the Eighth Army back to Gazala where, for a time, the line remained stabilized.

These reverses were not without their effect on the regiment. Although they had taken no part in active operations since Dunkirk many officers and men were of opinion that there had been far too much retreating since then and that the time had come to make a stand even if this meant fighting to the last round and last man. During the whole of the late winter and early spring the argument which became known as the "Last Round Last Man argument", whose chief supporter was Major Mullens, raged intermittently. Little did we know how soon we were to be given an opportunity to put it to the test!

CHAPTER IV

THE WESTERN DESERT

June 1942—December 1942

"Do not let us lose the conviction that it is only by supreme and superb exertions, unwearying and indomitable that we shall save our souls alive.... Long dark months of trials and tribulations lie before us. Not only great dangers but many more misfortunes, many shortcomings, many mistakes, many disappointments will surely be our lot. Death and sorrow will be our companions, hardship our garment and valour our only shield."

WINSTON CHURCHILL

I

ON the 18th May, 1942, the 20th Indian Infantry Brigade Group, of which the regiment now formed a part, were ordered to Egypt. On the 19th the regiment moved from Baiji to Taji on the outskirts of Baghdad, where they remained four days. Here some alarm was caused by the news that the regiment was to be reduced to two batteries and that 470 Battery were to become part of the newly-formed 164 Field Regiment. The B.R.A. Tenth Army (Army in Iraq), Brigadier John Hallifax, M.C., however, promised that he would do everything in his power to prevent it and the regiment, complete with 470 Battery, left Baghdad for Cairo on the 23rd.

The following account of the march through Iraq, Transjordan, Palestine and Egypt to Tobruk and of the subsequent retreat to El Alamein is taken from a number of sources.

From Baghdad we took the road that leads south of the lake at Habbaniya. For three days we drove west across the desert, halting each night at the oil stations, those little collections of tin bungalows surrounded by barbed wire and known only by letters and numbers, G5, H3, H4, which mark the course of the pipe line from Mosul to the sea.

It was very hot. Out of a burnished sky the sun blazed down on a brazen earth. Dust devils, like whirling djinns summoned from some Arabian hades, chased one another across the burning sands. On the horizon lakes shimmered and in the lakes fantastic palaces grew. Camels walked on stilts twenty feet high, and strange-looking vehicles, with wheels four times as big as their bodies, appeared and disappeared. The sweat ran in little trickles into our eyes and made a salty taste on our cracked lips. Small rivulets of sweat made patterns in the sand-filled hollows between the nose and cheek bones and streams poured down our bodies so that we sat in damp pools of sweat.

DESERT FORMATION

Driving along hour after hour with nothing to look at but the wheel tracks in the sand and the dust cloud from the vehicle in front my thoughts went round in an endless circle composed part of thankfulness and relief at leaving Iraq, part of speculation as to where we were going. No one seemed to know exactly, though a bombardier had confided to the mess cook, who had told the padre's driver, who had told Holdstock, who had told me, that we were going to the Western Desert. The bombardier had had it in strictest confidence from a native woman in the bazaar at Mosul. So it must be true. Besides there was a rumour that Rommel had attacked again and that the Eighth Army were fighting hard. Obviously they could not get along without us.

THE WESTERN DESERT 83

Another less well substantiated report had it that we were on our way back to England, where we were going to take part in the invasion of France that was coming off in the near future.

Holdstock did not believe this. "It stands to reason that they wouldn't have sent us out all this way just for a picnic. No, I reckon we got to do a bit of fighting here first before we start going back to France."

I was inclined to agree with him.

We passed Rutba where the track forks, one fork going northwards to Damascus and the other still in a westerly direction to Mafraq and Palestine. Here the track became a tarmac road and the sand of the desert slowly changed to a black lava-like formation, scarred with deep fissures and cracks, and lying in great blocks across the plain as far as the eye could see. No man, nor beast, nor engine invented by man could live or move in such a country. It was the very picture of desolation, the end of the world.

Beyond Mafraq the country changed again. Green grass began to appear and little stunted trees.

Crossing the Jordan by the bridge of Jisr el Majamie there was another change and the spirits of the men rose at the sight of the green hills and the green trees, the fields of waving corn and the rich orchards filled with oranges and apricots, figs and pomegranates. On the oldest road in the world, the road once used by the caravans from the Euphrates to the Nile, we drove through Semakh, the southernmost Arab town on the Sea of Galilee, to Tiberias, where Salome danced before Herod for the head of John the Baptist, and then upwards over the range of the Nazareth hills past the Horns of Hattin, where on a hot July day six and a half centuries earlier the Crusaders had been finally defeated by Saladin. From a point near by it is possible to see to the east the Sea of Galilee, like a sheet of blue glass far below with the barren hills of Gilead beyond; to the west the Mediterranean and the range of Carmel; to the south Mount Tabor and the Plain of Esdraelon; and far away to the north the snow-capped top of Hermon shimmering in the haze. The road then descends gently to the plain, winds round Tabor, and travels across Esdraelon, scene of twenty battles, to the pass of Lejjun near Megiddo.

Megiddo, now a heap of grass-grown mounds, stands at the entrance to the most famous of the passes in the Carmel range through which have marched back and forth the invading armies of the Hittites, Egyptians, Assyrians, Greeks, Romans, French and English, through which Thotmes and Sennacherib, Alexander and Vespasian, the Crusaders and Napoleon and Allenby have come and gone, have fought and conquered and vanished into history. Here, fifteen centuries before the birth of Christ, Thotmes III, the greatest of the Pharoahs, defeated the Hittites. Here Barak defeated the Canaanites and "the stars in their courses fought against Sisera". Here Gideon, with three hundred picked men, utterly routed the hosts of Midian and chased them across Jordan to Succoth, "faint yet pursuing". And here Pharoah Necho, King of Egypt, slew Josiah, King of Judah, when he opposed him on his way up against the Assyrians.

Along this mountain road, which has echoed and re-echoed to the thunder of Assyrian chariot wheels, the trumpeting of the elephants of the Antiochi, the tramp of the Roman legions, and the clank and clatter of the armed knights of Richard Cœur de Lion, rolled the lorries and guns of the regiment the men in them unaware that only a few short years before Allenby's victorious cavalry with jingle of bit and spur, had trotted up this same pass to miss capturing by a hairsbreadth the German general, Liman von Sanders.

Through Tulkarm and Lydda rumbled the guns and ever southwards along the maritime plain, past Ashdod and Ascalon, cities of the Philistines, to Gaza. At Gaza we turned east to Beersheba, and from there south once more till, thirty miles on, at Asluz the desert again swallowed us up.

For two whole days the long column wound its way over the narrow tarmac road across Sinai until at Ismailia we crossed the canal by the military bridge and drove, without halt or pause, along the road to Cairo.

From the backs of the lorries the men stared curiously at this their first sight of Egypt. To the left the sweet water canal ran close beside the road. Feluccas, loaded to the brim with bales of cotton and logs of wood, moved

slowly over its surface, their tall masts bent in a tapering arc, their patched white sails bellying gently to the breeze. On the banks patient Egyptian buffaloes walked in circles, harnessed to the sakiah, the creaking wooden water wheel which plays such an important part in the irrigation of this ancient and fertile land. Veiled women dressed in flowing black, carrying pitchers on their heads, moved up and down from the water. Their feet were bare, gold and silver bangles jingled on their arms and ankles while their half-naked children played and splashed in the mud beside them. On the other side of the road in a narrow strip of fertile land, their menfolk laboured from dawn till dark. Donkeys plodded to and fro, white birds flew over the green fields or followed in flocks the plough as it turned up the rich dark earth, while crows picked the ticks from the backs of the buffaloes as they wallowed in the ooze.

On all this rich and varied life the sun beat down, covering the fields with light, sending vivid splashes of light through the palm and eucalyptus trees beside the canal, lighting with a shimmering haze the illimitable desert that stretched beyond. One felt enriched as well as enervated by the heat as if one had already become a part of this age-long and abundant fertility which, emerging from the primeval slime centuries ago, still continued to give birth to an endless succession of buffaloes and birds, donkeys and naked children, to produce crops, and to pour out such a flowing tide of life that wars and invasions, battles, pestilence and death, had no effect on it.

"So this is Egypt," Holdstock said. "Don't think much of it myself. Sooner 'ave a nice tram ride down the Old Kent Road."

"You'll like it better when we get to Cairo," I replied. "There are plenty of trams there as well as picture palaces and pubs and everything else you can think of."

"Them women in their veils and black clothes! They don't look decent to me."

"You'll find the women in Cairo are all right," I said soothingly. "They all wear silk stockings and proper European clothes."

But we didn't stop in Cairo. We drove straight through —over the Kasr-el-Nil bridge and down the Mena road, past the Pyramids and Mena House, and along the desert road towards Wady Natrun. At Wady Natrun we halted for the night and next day drove on to Amriya, a vast camp of tin huts and tents and low brick buildings which seemed to sprawl for miles across the desert. Stopping

THE WESTERN DESERT

here for an hour to get rid of our heavy baggage we drove straight on along the coast road past Fuka and Daba, where we halted again for an evening meal, and then on through the night to Matruh.

It was dawn when we reached Matruh and the weary

men flung themselves on the ground to sleep. But within an hour they were up again, and were eating the breakfast the tired cooks had made ready, and within less than another hour we were once more on the road making for Sidi Barrani and Sollum. At Sollum we spent the night and the next morning climbed the steep cliff road that leads to Fort Capuzzo, completing the last hundred miles past Gambut by mid-day on 4th June, and finally coming to rest on a stretch of bare cliff between the sea and the road about twelve miles short of Tobruk.

In ten days we had travelled over 1,600 miles across three deserts and through four countries, Iraq, Transjordan, Palestine and Egypt.

It was late afternoon before all the guns and vehicles were in. The men were tired but cheerful. They were busy unpacking their gear, putting up tents, mounting guards, and on all the hundred and one tasks that confront the soldier on arriving at a new place. Outside the camp on the road there was continuous activity, convoys going up to Tobruk and convoys coming down, despatch riders on motor-cycles hurtling to and fro and, every now and then, some important personage in a staff car hooting to get past. But above the din of the traffic and the noise of men hammering in tent pegs there was another sound, a continuous distant rumble, ominous, menacing like the roll of drums or of far-away thunder presaging a storm.

"That's gunfire that is," said Holdstock, stopping what he was doing for a moment to listen.

"Yes," I answered.

"Sounds like a battle to me," he went on. "Getting closer too. Shouldn't be surprised if we weren't in the thick of it before long."

Again I was inclined to agree.

* * *

From Alexandria the coastal belt of North Africa slopes gently upwards in strips of undulating country gradually diminishing in width from east to west till it reaches the foot of the great Libyan plateau at Sollum. At its widest this belt of land stretches inland for nearly forty miles before it merges into the desert. It is most fertile nearest the sea, but on the high desert plateau beyond the cliffs, in the flat scrub-covered country, the vegetation begins to grow less and very soon the real desert begins, stretching away to the Siwa oasis and beyond Siwa over unexplored country to the distant Sudan. From Sidi Barrani to Sollum the coast road winds among the sandhills, covered

THE WESTERN DESERT

here and there with a kind of feathery undergrowth that looks like withered bracken, with the great buttress of the Scarp running parallel frowning down on the blue waters of the sea. In the spring the harsh slopes are gay with flowers, with salt-wort and sea lavender, samphire and yellow nettle, with iris and ranunculus, campanula and bushes of Spanish broom. Between the ridges of the hills and the sea scarlet poppies mingle with fields of swaying asphodel, while in the evening the whole land is scented with masses of sweet-scented stock. But during the rest of the year no vegetation grows there save patches of scrub and camel thorn and a plant which when crushed by the wheels of a truck gives out a faint smell of thyme, while beyond the stark line of the hills the desert stretches, mile after mile of hard limestone covered with dark shining pebbles with, in places, stretches of dried mud cracked by the sun into thousands of little fissures so that the ground looks as if it had been paved by some capricious but meticulously exact road maker.

Where the Scarpe joins the sea swinging round to form a little horseshoe-shaped bay, two roads climb the hill into Cyrenaica, one the continuation of the main coast road winding up the cliff-side in the centre of the horseshoe and the other leading up the famous Halfaya Pass further south. At the top of the first road stands Fort Capuzzo. Beyond the fort, among the battered buildings and flamboyant monuments, the two roads join and travel first north to Bardia, and then eastwards again along the coast to Gambut and Tobruk. A few miles short of Tobruk the road forks again, the left arm leading up a gentle slope known as Belhamed to El Adem. Opposite Belhamed and about three miles south of it, at the end of a long ridge of high ground, which stretches like a camel's hump eastwards and westwards lies the little eminence of Sidi Resegh. It was on these two small hills, Belhamed and Sidi Resegh, which command the southern approaches to Tobruk, that the Brigade finally dug themselves in.

The news from the front was not good. The winter campaign had led to the relief of Tobruk and the establishment of a line from Ain Gazala in the north to Bir Hakim in the south. Beyond Bir Hakim in the open country to the south and west armoured cars and mobile columns patrolled daily while both sides prepared for a new offensive in the spring. In April the battle for Malta reached its peak figure of one thousand sorties a week, and under cover of this tremendous bombardment from the air great numbers of Axis convoys slipped across the Mediterranean with reinforcements and supplies for Rommel's army. Meanwhile every effort had been made to build up the Eighth Army by using Tobruk as a supply base and by pushing forward the desert railway across the wire into Cyrennaica, so that by the beginning of May the British had a seven to five superiority in tanks and an eight to five superiority in guns. The R.A.F., though inferior in numbers to the enemy, whose new squadrons had been drawn largely from Russia, were superior in skill and equipment.

On the 26th the Germans attacked. Using the old tactics, that had been employed by every commander since the desert campaign began, Rommel brought his two armoured divisions in a wide sweep round our open flank at Bir Hakim and thrust northwards towards Acroma and El Adem. For three days there was very heavy fighting in this area, the pivotal points being the defensive position at Knightsbridge, west of El Adem, which was held by the Guards and that at Bir Hakim which was held by the French. The enemy, however, eventually succeeded in making a gap in our minefields some five miles north-east of Bir Hakim and through this gap, which became known as the Cauldron, they tried to supply the bulk of their armour battling to the east. After much bitter and inconclusive fighting, with heavy losses on both sides, on 6th June they succeeded in breaking through. Three days later the garrison at Bir Hakim, surrounded, outnumbered and running short of supplies, received orders to withdraw.

The loss of Bir Hakim proved to be the turning point of the battle. With great speed, using the whole weight of his armour and guns, Rommel thrust north and north-east towards El Adem, inflicting heavy casualties on our

THE WESTERN DESERT

tanks without suffering any corresponding loss himself, and on the 13th a general withdrawal to the old frontier line at Sollum began.

The individual who takes part in a modern battle sees very little of what is going on around him and knows even less. To us marooned on our two little hills there was nothing to show that a great battle was taking place near us and that the British army was in full retreat.

It was very hot. The sun shone down on the empty road, on the barbed wire and silent guns, and on the men digging in the hard rocky ground. Their throats were parched and the flies, settling on their hands and faces, were brushed off in clouds when they stopped to mop the sweat from their brows. They were short of water. Two pints of brackish water per day does not allow a man much margin for splashing. They felt dirty, as well as thirsty and those who were lucky enough to get a bathe in the sea near Tobruk were so smothered in dust in the lorry coming back that they felt the experience was hardly worth it.

In default of definite news rumours began to circulate. A sister regiment, the 157 Field Regiment, R.A., with whom we had lived side by side at Habbaniya, had been swallowed up at Knightsbridge. Only the doctor and two others had survived. The French, who had held out so long and so gallantly at Bir Hakim, had been over-run and lost to a man. Another brigade was surrounded and was fighting for its life at El Adem, only a few miles up the road.

On Saturday, 13th June, this last rumour crystallized into the definite news that the enemy had raided a supply depot at El Adem, as a result of which an attack was planned for that night. Under cover of darkness one troop of 387 Battery was moved up to Ed Duda and at 21.30 hours commenced firing. Later in the night the infantry attacked. The result was highly satisfactory so far as it went. A number of lorries were set on fire and the small enemy force, taken completely by surprise by the gunfire, did not wait for the arrival of the infantry, but made off hurriedly into the night.

On the same day the L.O.Bs.[1] under David Warner went back to Sollum where they encamped by the sea at the foot of Halfaya Pass. For the next week this party, when not bathing, was engaged in organizing the defence of the Egyptian frontier and in selecting positions for seventy-two field guns and an equally large number of A/T guns.

It was not until Monday, the 15th, that things began to happen. A General came in an armoured car; came and went. There were conferences and a constant running to and fro. A small column of guns and infantry, under Hubert Allfrey,[2] went out to find the enemy and came back at the end of a long hot day without seeing anybody. Somehow this lack of contact only served to accentuate a feeling that had been growing with the hours, the feeling that we were very much alone. For we knew now—perhaps the General had told us—that there was no one between us and Rommel's army. The rest of the Eighth Army, with the exception of a large force locked up in Tobruk, was behind us, and we stood alone, a very small rearguard, with orders to delay the enemy as long as possible, and then to withdraw if we could. It was those last three words that sounded so ominous.

The next morning I was wakened by Holdstock with the words: "The Germans have arrived, sir. What would you like for breakfast? There's only them tinned sausages left."

"What do you mean the Germans have arrived and where's Cole? Tell him I want him."

"What I say, sir. They're just outside. You can see 'em quite plain from the top of the hill. And Cole's gorn, sir. He's finished all right. Napoo as you might say. One of them Wog lorries drove over him and Bombardier Collard in the night when they was asleep and squashed 'em flat."

"Good God! What an awful thing! Did it kill them?"

[1] L.O.B.—Left out of Battle. By order of Higher Authority a number of key men from each unit were left out of battle and sent back to the rear, the intention being to use them to replace casualties later on.

[2] Major H. M. Allfrey, M.C. commanding 387 Field Battery.

"No they ain't dead—leastwise not yet." Holdstock, like all bearers of bad news, hated to spoil a good story. "But they looked pretty gashly when we picked 'em up."

Slowly the day went by. The enemy seemed to be feeling their way. Large numbers of them were concentrated round Sidi Resegh, two miles away. Through the heat haze that hung over the desert we could see more behind, tanks and armoured cars and hundreds of trucks, a whole division.[1] There was something sinister about this slow approach of a vastly superior force. It was like that of a boa constrictor who hypnotizes his prey before crushing it.

The defensive position at Sidi Resegh manned by the 6th Rajputana Rifles and 385 Battery was being heavily shelled. The main position at Belhamed, which contained the Brigade H.Q., the 1st South Wales Borderers, the 3rd Gharwali Rifles, and the remainder of the regiment, less 470 Battery, who had been lopped off on our way through Cairo, was shelled whenever our guns opened fire. The guns at Sidi Resegh had orders not to fire until the enemy came within anti-tank range—800 yards. The same orders issued by higher authority, whose ignorance of the proper handling of artillery in battle was one of the main causes of the subsequent disasters, prevented more than one troop from firing at Belhamed.

On Sidi Resegh B.S.M. Harris, one of the original members of the battery, and one of the most popular, was killed by a shell splinter. Later in the afternoon the enemy having picked up the mines on the western edge of the position, made a further advance and suddenly appeared among the guns of the forward troop. Two unarmed detachments of C Troop were standing on their guns at "tank alert" when the Germans rushed the pits. Despite being wounded Sgt. Stevens blew up his gun before being taken prisoner. The detachment under Sgt. Burgess also managed to blow up their guns. The remaining two guns were man-handled back to join B Troop some 300 yards further east.

[1] The German 90th Light Division.

The western half of the position was then abandoned and a defensive perimeter formed round the remaining guns. By this time all communication with Belhamed had broken down and with night coming on, and the enemy in unknown strength only a few yards away, the situation began to look desperate. All codes and secret documents were destroyed and a steady rate of fire was kept up from the guns, more to keep up the morale of the infantry than in the hope of doing much harm to the enemy who was by this time invisible.

Meanwhile in Belhamed the desultory shelling that had been going on all day increased in intensity in the evening.

"Pretty poor shots, them Jerries," Holdstock remarked when he brought me my tea. "They've been shelling the cookhouse this last hour and ain't hit nothing yet. Shall I do you a bit of larver bread?"

"No thank you, Holdstock."

"There's a nice bit of bacon fat over. It wouldn't take a minute to fry you up a bit."

"No, thank you, Holdstock. Not to-day."

"Beg pardon, sir—but are we staying here long?"

"I don't know I'm sure. It depends on a lot of things. Why do you ask?"

"Well, sir, I was only thinking . . ."

"What were you thinking?"

"I was only thinking it might be a good idea if I was to pack your things. Them Jerries—there's quite a lot of them out there and they might take it into their heads to come on sudden like."

"I shouldn't let that worry you," I said. "We're quite strong enough to stop them if they do."

"Ah well! Perhaps you're right, sir. Anyways it can't be any worse than Dunkirk." With which comforting reflection Gunner Holdstock took himself off.

Just before dark there was a wireless message from Sidi Resegh.

"We have been attacked and over-run. The enemy are . . ." and then silence.

I took it to the Brigadier who with his staff was sitting,

THE WESTERN DESERT 95

like the prophets in a cave, burning all their secret documents.

"Our turn next," he said, coughing in the smoke of the burning paper.

At midnight Keith Rae arrived with more definite news from Sidi Resegh. He had walked through two mine-fields in his stockinged feet under the impression that the mines were less likely to go off if he trod on them without his boots on. Later that night a message was sent to Sidi Resegh ordering what was left of the garrison to withdraw into the desert.

The next day the enemy, still going slow, reconnoitred all round our wire. In the evening the Brigadier held a conference to decide whether we should stay and fight or try to get away after dark. His cave was so filled with smoke that, preferring death in the open to death by asphyxiation, I left before the end.

At nine o'clock the brigade major rang up. We were moving in half an hour; the artillery to report with all available guns at an R.A.F. aerodrome the other side of Gambut, the infantry to join the rest of the Eighth Army in Sollum one hundred miles further east. 385 Battery were already at Gambut. I had ordered them back on my own responsibility after dark. Leaving Hubert Allfrey in charge and ordering him to keep well out in the desert and avoid the coast road in case it had already been cut by the Germans, I drove off with Neil Campbell[1] to try and catch 385 at Gambut.

It was an eerie drive. The empty road, usually so crowded with traffic going to and from Tobruk, seemed filled with ghosts, the ghosts of the men that had marched and fought along it since the war began. Endlessly the black ribbon of the road wound in and out among the white sandhills on which the moon, coming out from behind a cloud, shone with a glimmering light.

Once we stopped for a puncture and, while Wood, the driver, muttering under his breath changed the wheel, Neil and I stood by with revolvers loaded and cocked.

[1] Capt. N. A. Campbell, Adjutant 97th Field Regiment, Jan. 1940–Oct. 1942.

Once we stopped to pick up a truck belonging to 385 that had lost its way.

At Gambut we halted again. It was past midnight. There was no sign of the battery. The two single-storied huts that marked what had once been an Arab village were empty and silent.

There was trouble over the car. Wood was muttering again. Another puncture and the back axle broken. There was nothing we could do. We piled everything we had into the truck and left the car to its fate.

An hour later we picked up 385 moving slowly behind a long convoy that stretched interminably eastwards, the flotsam and jetsam of a beaten army. Together we drove off the road into the desert and waited for daylight.

On the aerodrome the planes were rising into the sky. One by one they roared across the flat ground, lifted effortlessly into the air, circled and disappeared. In a few minutes there were none left. The guns drew up in a long line, unlimbered and dropped their trails. Behind them the sun was rising. A chill wind blew across the empty airfield and fluttered the papers that the airmen had left behind. The cooks began to make tea.

An hour passed, and then another hour. The wind dropped, the sun burned hot on our backs, and the flies buzzed in swarms over the débris of the camp.

"We had better get on. It's no use waiting any longer. I'm afraid something must have happened to Hubert."

It was my own voice. In the silence and loneliness and emptiness it had sounded like someone else's.

Where were the enemy? Where was 387? What next? Shall we go or stay? If we go shall we take the coast road or drive across the desert? A thousand questions hammered at my tired brain, but no answer came.

"When in doubt do something. Never sit still." Somewhere at some time someone had said this. It seemed as good advice as any.

All day we drove and saw no one. Only the same anxious questions still buzzed in my brain like the flies buzzing on the windscreen of the truck.

THE WESTERN DESERT

It was nearly dark when we reached the wire and drove through a gap in the minefields down the Pass into Sollum.

II

It was on the evening of the next day, Friday, 19th June, that 387 Battery arrived in Sollum with the news that after leaving Belhamed the brigade had been ambushed soon after midnight near Gambut. They had managed to get away with the loss of four guns and a number of officers and men including Lieutenants Savill and Streeton. At dawn a little force, consisting of what was left of the battery and R.H.Q. with some anti-tank guns and a few truck loads of infantry, all under command of Major Allfrey, found itself surrounded. Charging under heavy fire through a gap between two converging columns of tanks they had escaped in a cloud of dust and sand into the desert.

The following account of the action is by Major H. M. Allfrey, M.C.:

"At 21.30 hours on the 17th June, having destroyed as much of our water and stores as we could, the withdrawal from Belhamed began. My orders were to move back 35 miles but not to use the main coast road till we reached Gambut. D Troop were to fire a few harassing rounds during the departure of the Brigade and then join the column in rear. Owing to the darkness the departure was not easy and one tractor driver thought fit to try the effectiveness of our own mines while another drove over the escarpment. Leaving these two wrecks behind we started on our journey of 20 miles over rough desert by compass.

"We managed to make about 3 m.p.h. up till about 03.30 hrs. when we were confronted with a large and magnificent firework display. Tracer of all description were being fired by what we took to be our own withdrawing troops and the R.A.F. defending the aerodrome at Gambut. As the going had become extremely difficult and rugged I decided to halt for half-an-hour to reconnoitre the route ahead and find out if possible the cause of the firing. I was not too happy about the position. All through the night there had been white Very lights going up on our right and the rumble of tanks moving and I could think of no satisfactory explanation of these unusual phenomena except that the enemy were close round us.

"Having reconnoitred a way through a very narrow defile in some rocks we pushed on. The going was so bad that about twelve men were pushing on the side of each of the larger trucks to prevent them from toppling over sideways. Soon we came upon Mike Savill and the R.H.Q. party who had joined up with D Troop. D Troop had been up on the coast road near Gambut and found it blocked by enemy tanks. They had fired a few rounds and were now trying to work their way round them.

"Joining forces the whole party pushed on to the southeast, but not for long, as we ran into a large number of vehicles which in the growing daylight looked suspiciously like Germans. A short reconnaissance in Bren carriers soon left us in no doubt about this. Seeing that the coast road was blocked our obvious plan appeared to be to travel due south and try to make a wide sweep round. Unfortunately this plan was as obvious to the enemy as it was to us and we had no sooner started than a column of about ten enemy tanks and fifteen armoured cars moved off on a line parallel to our own. We tried to appear unaware of this manœuvre.

"As we had several crocks among the vehicles that could not move at a fast speed we decided to abandon them. In order not to give ourselves away completely by burning them we smashed the radiators, raced the engines and filled them up with sand.

"The moment we started off again, after rendering immobile all unwanted trucks, the watching column on our left also moved. Still travelling due south, after about three miles, we came face to face with another column. Again we halted and formed up into a leaguer with the guns trail down on the outside. The column in front of us thereupon despatched some tanks to our right who came into action hull down about 400 yards away from us.

"We were now surrounded except from the rear, and it appeared to be only a question of time before we were completely hemmed in. To sit there and do nothing while this happened seemed foolish to say the least of it. Looking carefully through my glasses I thought I could see a narrow gap between the column in front and our shadowers on the left. So I decided to gallop head on at it and hope for the best. I therefore gave orders to limber up and move slowly forward towards the column in front as though we were going to surrender, and then at a given signal to turn suddenly half left and make a dash for the gap. This we did and a pretty warm reception we had passing between the two columns. However about fifty per cent. of our party got through, and, once through, met with no further opposition though two or three of the slower moving vehicles were chased and caught by armoured cars.

"After about a further three miles we were once again confronted by a single armoured car. I unhitched a gun, laid on it over open sights at a range of about 200 yards, loaded and was about to pull the plug when the inmates started waving flags frantically. On closer inspection it turned out to be a South African armoured car out on patrol. They had produced the recognition signal of the day, but that, of course, was complete Greek to us. They had no idea that there were any Germans within 40 miles.

"On our way back to the frontier wire Gunner Sloman died of wounds received going through the gap and we buried him in the desert. The next day we reported to the regiment at Sollum."

The regiment made up, not without difficulty, to fifteen guns, went into action in the Fort Capuzzo area in support of the 25th Indian Infantry Brigade, and was in action in its new positions a bare twenty-four hours when the news of the loss of Tobruk came through.

The retreat to the frontier had deprived the R.A.F. of

the landing grounds near Gambut, and Tobruk was out of range of fighter air support. The enemy on the other hand were able to use landing grounds as near as Gazala. In addition to these handicaps the newly-arrived garrison had had little time to organize the defences. The whole of the large defensive perimeter was new to them and many of the defence works, held so gallantly and for so long during the previous year, had fallen into dis-repair. Early in the morning of the 20th the enemy attacked. The ground attack was preceded by a violent artillery bombardment, supported by intensive dive bombing by Stukas on a relatively narrow front. By mid-day the German tanks had broken through and were engaging many of our positions from the rear. By evening all organized resistance was at an end.

The loss of this important fortress with its garrison of 28,000 men, eighty tanks and great quantities of material and stores once more changed the plans of the Higher Command. With Tobruk still in British hands Rommel dare not move too far east and leave his communications exposed to an attack from the rear. Now that this threat was removed it was felt he would waste no time in continuing his advance. Since time was essential to enable the battered Eighth Army to reorganize it was decided to abandon the frontier line and to fall back as quickly as possible to Matruh. From Sollum to Matruh was 132 miles, from Matruh to Tobruk nearly 250. It was thought that at least a fortnight's respite would be gained before the enemy could stage a serious attack on the new line, during which time reorganization could be put in hand and reinforcements sent up from Syria and Egypt.

"What's this I hear about another retreat?" Holdstock said that evening as he was cleaning my boots.

"I'm afraid it's true, Holdstock. We're going back to Matruh in a day or two. You might keep the news to yourself though. No point in spreading it about. You never know who may be listening."

"That's all right, sir. Everybody knows anyhow. They was talking about it in the cookhouse this morning. Seems to me the British Army never does anything else but retreat. Any chance of our going the other way one day, d'you think?"

"I expect our turn will come soon. Meanwhile we've just got to . . . well, grin and bear it."

"Oh, well, sir, I can't say it worries me much. One gets kinda used to it somehow. Only I thought it would be a nice change like to go forward and chase Jerry for a bit instead of him always chasing us. As I was saying to poor old Cole the other day when he was talking about his garden at home, 'There will be plenty of time for flowers,' I said, 'when we've chased Jerry back to where he come from'."

He stopped to spit into the tin of brown polish and continued rubbing harder than ever.

"Can't seem to get a shine on my leather like what I used to," he grumbled.

"I shouldn't worry, Holdstock. Those boots look all right to me."

Holdstock shook his head. "No, sir. They ain't as good as they should be and that's a fact, and it's all on account of this 'ere shortage of beer."

"I can't see what that's got to do with it I must say."

"Why everythink, sir! The whole secret of good leather work is polish and spit, and if you ain't got the right kind of spit, with plenty of beer and baccy juice in it, it stands to reason you won't never get a proper shine on them boots. As I said to Cole, 'You ought to drink more beer,' I said, 'instead of always worrying about flowers. You won't never make a good batman until you do,' " I said.

This question of beer was rather a sore one. One of the largest N.A.A.F.I. dumps consisting mainly of tinned beer had been put out of bounds to troops since our arrival and had now fallen into enemy hands. We were continually shelling enemy transport on the road to the dump and, while it was some satisfaction to know we were preventing the Germans from getting it, it was at the same time galling to see so much good beer, as it were, under fire.

On the 21st the B.B.C reported that "the enemy were

battering against the impenetrable defence of Sollum against which they could make no headway", but in point of fact the enemy were doing very little and appeared to be in small numbers. The day before 470 Battery, who had left us in Cairo to become part of the newly-formed 164 Field Regiment, and were now once more working in conjunction with us, had left the perimeter on a reconnaissance in force and had encountered little opposition.

At 02.00 hours on the 23rd we slipped out of Sollum and, travelling all night, eventually dispersed in the open desert for the day about ten miles west of Sidi Barrani. In the evening, shortly before moving off, three German planes, flying very low, machine gunned us from the air and Maurice Allfrey,[1] who engaged them with a Bren gun, got a bullet through his hair.

On the 24th we arrived at Mersa Matruh and camped for the night to the east of the town at Smugglers' Cove, taking over the next morning from the 4th New Zealand Field Regiment and occupying positions in support of the 21st Indian Infantry Brigade which consisted of the 2/8 Ghurkas, the 4/13 Frontier Force and the 1st Btn. of the D.C.L.I. Our outlying patrols had already reported they were in contact with the enemy and on the 26th 385 Battery went out on column with some armoured cars of the 12th Lancers with orders to harass them by fire and delay their advance as long as possible. In the words of the B.C., Major Mullens:

"We went out in the area of Charing Cross and had a good day's sport, B Troop shooting up two Italian 3-ton lorries full of troops over open sights at 300 yards' range and taking twenty-eight prisoners. A Major on the staff of the German Afrika Corps drove into B Troop position and was forced to surrender. C Troop was unfortunately bombed by the R.A.F., but only one man was wounded."

The next day in the same area 385 Battery engaged a large quantity of enemy transport moving east. They appeared to be by-passing Matruh, presumably with the object of getting round behind it. The following day Captain Allfrey had some good shooting from a position

[1] Captain M. C. Allfrey, D.S.O., brother of Major H. M. Allfrey, M.C.

THE WESTERN DESERT

two miles east of Charing Cross, capturing a 3-tonner and two prisoners from the 21st Panzer Division."

Meanwhile 387 had been occupying defensive positions inside the perimeter and had taken no active part except in an operation which has been described as the battle of the N.A.A.F.I., a highly successful action in which hordes of scroungers, including officers of high rank, over-ran a lightly defended position and departed with much loot.

On the 28th the regiment moved to Gawala, east of Matruh. By this time the whole of the Matruh defence area was surrounded by the enemy and German transport and tanks could be plainly seen on the high ground to the east. Two divisions, the 50th British and the 10th Indian, were locked up inside and the chance of their being able to break out without heavy losses seemed remote. An attempt to do so was to be made that night.

At eight o'clock I went to see the Brigadier.

"You know the situation," he said. "We are going to try and break through the enemy lines to-night. The Brigade will move through this gap in our minefields," he went on, pointing at the map, "and travel due south along the telegraph wire for ten miles. Then we will turn north-east and make for Fuka. I want you to distribute your guns along the column in order that if any portion of it gets cut off it will have guns to protect it."

Half an hour later some Indian troops on our immediate front panicked. Some surrendered wholesale, others turned back through our lines chattering and screaming. Those lined up in trucks, ready to move off, caught the contagion and in a few minutes there was a milling mass of men and lorries and cars on the track leading towards the gap in the minefield. Standing in the roadway, trying to control the traffic, I was reminded of Twickenham after a big football match—of Twickenham with a difference. The darkness, the shouts and cries, the maddened drivers, the inextricable jam of vehicles filled with jabbering, terrified humanity, the sudden flash of flame followed by a shattering roar as a truck went up on a mine—this was certainly no football match.

Gradually the crowd began to thin out. When nearly everyone had gone Neil Campbell and I got into my car and drove after them. We drove slowly. The darkness in front was lit by periodic explosions where trucks were still blowing themselves up on our mines. Our way led up a steep incline over which a crescent moon was rising. By the light of the moon I could see that the ground on either side of the track was rocky and impassable to wheeled vehicles. The Germans will be waiting for us at the top, I thought. Slowly we climbed in an unending stream.

At the top a bare plateau stretched away into the darkness. Along it the telegraph poles stood like sentinels. A little wind hummed in the wires. There was something comforting and friendly in the humming of the wind.

For a long time we drove south along the telegraph line. Those in front had disappeared. We had only twenty lorries with us.

Out of the darkness a crash of golden sparks hit the ground, then another and another. The car ran up a gentle slope. At the bottom, on the other side of the hill, was a German tank leaguer. I could see the dark hulls of the tanks outlined against the sky and the flashes from their guns as they fired.

A shower of golden, red and yellow balls were bouncing on the ground beside us. They were like the most beautiful fireworks I had ever seen. They were so pretty one forget they were dangerous. I did not even notice that the car had stopped and that my driver could not get the self-starter to work.

In less time than it takes to tell we were careering back down the slope with a medley of trucks and cars swaying and bumping beside us.

For half an hour we drove on almost alone with only three trucks following.

The Very lights from the German leaguers were going up in the sky, now red, now white, now green. To the right, to the left, in front and behind the lights went up, while behind us the sky was aglow with the fires from the demolitions in Matruh.

I had just put Wood on the right line and the compass was reading roughly south-east, when we ran into some more enemy tanks. Once more the red, yellow and golden balls were bouncing just in front of the nose of the car.

"Swerve, Wood," cried Neil. "For God's sake, swerve." Wood swerved. The golden balls stopped. We were quite alone driving through the desert in the moonlight.

A big German staff car came out of the darkness not ten yards away. Like a ghost car, one second it was there, the next it had gone.

I wanted to go south. Neil wanted to go east. Wood didn't care. Every time we saw a clump of bushes we thought it was another tank leaguer.

On our left a small column of moving trucks was slipping in and out of the shadows. I wanted to join them. Neil didn't. I thought they were British. Neil was sure they were Germans. We argued for a few minutes and then I ordered Wood to join them. Anything was better than driving round and round in circles. They turned out to be a small column from the 50th division, commanded by General Ramsden, with the General himself sitting in an open staff car in front. The General said he was going to drive south all night and turn east in the morning.

We drove on. To keep himself awake Wood was singing softly to himself. Neil sat huddled in the back of the car, his long legs stretched right across its width. It was dark and cold and the car rocked and swayed over the uneven ground.

Little pictures of the past few weeks kept flashing across my mind; the Brigadier in his cave at Belhamed coughing in the smoke of the burning paper; the drive down the empty road to Gambut; Hubert blowing his hunting horn as he led his guns into action; Collard and Cole being carried away by the light of a flickering lantern, the blood running from their ears; the road from Sollum and a German plane flying very low, the lighted cockpit and the figure of a man inside, something falling out of the plane; a scream, a flash and a truck going up in flames, the plane turning and the figure of the pilot bending over his machine gun; pop-pop-pop went the gun and the little coloured balls went hopping and jumping on the road in front.

At last I fell asleep. I was dreaming that the Brigadier was playing hide and seek with a mermaid. She had sea-green eyes and long golden hair and a tail like a fish, and the smoke from the burning paper made her cough. Derrick Mullens, without his hat, drove by on the roof of a tank. It was all right, he said. There was a destroyer waiting at the Mole to take us off. Within an hour we would be in Dover. Kind people would pass cups of tea and paper bags, full of sandwiches and chocolate, through the carriage window, and I could send a telegram to my wife to say that I was safe.

The question was would we get there in time? There was a big battle raging on which the fate of Egypt, and perhaps the world depended, and we still had five hundred miles to go. "Hurry! For God's sake, hurry!" shouted the Brigadier. But the car had stopped. The self-starter wouldn't work. And the golden, red and yellow balls were bouncing all round.

"Wake up, sir! Wake up! We've run into another lot." It was Neil's voice.

It was getting light. The little column had changed direction and was flying across the desert at top speed. A few stray shells came over and little puffs of sand flew up where they hit the ground. A lorry was hit and put out of action and a man stood beside it waving his arms. We slowed down to let him jump on the step. "There's a Jerry armoured car behind you," he said.

"How far off is it?" asked Neil. The car was lurching and bumping like a thing possessed.

"Not far," the man replied, "but it's losing ground."

"We're running out of petrol," Wood said.

The column was slowing down. We had shaken the Germans off. Wood stopped to pour in the last tin of petrol. A big three-ton lorry passed us. It was the Quartermaster's. We hailed it. Bombardier Stocker was sitting beside the driver holding his face in his hands. He had been shot through the eye. In the back of the lorry was a little man who used to cut my hair. He kept a small barber's shop in Wales, and had only joined the regiment just before we sailed. He had a friendly smile and a willing way with him. But now he lay with closed eyes on a pile of blood-soaked blankets. His face was grey and streaked with sweat.

"He has been like that all night," said the R.Q.M.S. "I'm afraid he's dying." The lorry was riddled with holes, but the petrol and beer were intact.

Ten miles outside Fuka we found an ambulance and put the bombardier and the little barber into it. The driver said the Germans were already in Fuka. All columns had been ordered to report to a place called El Alamein.

We drove on. All round us were small mixed columns of trucks, lorries, cars and guns making for El Alamein. The sun came out and it was very hot. General Ramsden had left us. He was going south.

At mid-day we halted to brew up. Over the hot strong tea we argued about the route. Neil thought the Germans might be in Daba. It would be folly to run straight into their arms.

It was evening by the time we reached El Alamein. There was nothing there, but the sand and the sea and what did duty as a railway station. Two harassed officers were sitting in a tent trying to direct the traffic. They said the 10th Indian Division were twenty-three miles away to the south.

We drove on till it was too dark to see; then lay down on the sand and slept.

CHAPTER V

THE WESTERN DESERT (CONTINUED)

> "Let me then assure you, soldiers and airmen, that your fellow countrymen regard your joint work with admiration and gratitude and that, after the war when a man is asked what he did, it will be quite sufficient for him to say 'I marched and fought with the Desert Army.' And when history is written, and all the facts are known, your feats will gleam and glow and will be a source of song and story long after we who are gathered here have passed away."
>
> WINSTON CHURCHILL

I

IN the retreat from Matruh to El Alamein every member of the regiment had similar adventures to those already described, but with varying fortunes, some finding their way across the desert safely to El Alamein, others being captured by the enemy.

A mixed party under David Warner, consisting of R.H.Q., Signals, L.A.D., and four guns of C Troop, under Captain (Tiger) Wix, came under heavy fire during the night. The guns went into action and replied with full charge over open sights in the direction of the enemy's gun flashes, and effectually silenced the enemy fire. Twice more during the hours of darkness the same procedure was adopted with success until at last daylight came and with it a thick mist forcing the party to close up nose to tail. It was decided to take advantage of the mist to halt and brew up. The brew was almost ready when an ominous rumbling sound was heard in the distance. Fog plays funny tricks with sound in the desert as well as at sea, and almost immediately the rumble broke into the well-known clatter of tanks approaching at speed. In the words of David Warner:

"The fires were put out and everyone stood by his vehicle. The tea was forgotten as we waited in breathless silence while the tanks rattled past and then gradually faded away into the distance. When the danger was over we could see by the tracks how close they had been. So abandoning all idea of tea we changed course to the

THE WESTERN DESERT

south and moved off at once in case others might be following.

"It was difficult moving in the mist, but we lost nobody and gradually the sun came through and the mist went. To avoid being surprised we put out two staff cars well

ACTION
RIGHT · LEFT · FRONT · REAR

THE MOVEMENT TO FINISH POINTING
TO DIRECTION OF ACTION

on the horizon. We also picked up two medium guns which were lost and which made a welcome addition to our fire power. By degrees we altered course to the east and north and made for Daba having heard that Fuka was already in the hands of the enemy. Once we were attacked by Stukas, but the party dispersed so quickly that the bombs did no damage. Finally we met Derrick

Mullens and the balance of 385 Battery and handing over Tiger and his four guns continued on towards El Alamein."

By the late afternoon of the 30th most of the scattered parties had once more re-united. But the casualties had been heavy; there were only six guns left and many officers and men, were still missing. Orders were received to withdraw into Corps Reserve at El Imayid and somewhat wearily, but with a thankful heart, the little party moved off. About 21.00 hours, however, while still some way from their destination, counter-orders arrived and the regiment turned back on its tracks to occupy a defensive position at Deir el Shein. In the darkness the tired men drove back towards the line. It was daylight by the time they reached Deir el Shein.

The following account of the events at Deir el Shein on 1st July is by the Adjutant, Captain, afterwards Major, N. A. Campbell:

"Deir el Shein, a large saucer-shaped depression in the middle of the new Alamein line, was defended by the 18th Indian Infantry Brigade. The brigade, which had been hurriedly sent over from Iraq, consisted of three battalions, the Essex, Sikhs and Ghurkas, who were already in position on the lip of the saucer facing northeast, north-west and south respectively. In addition two batteries of the 121st Field Regiment, R.A., one battery of the 124th, one troop of Matilda tanks and an antitank company of the Buffs were in support. The regiment, by this time reduced to six guns, two wireless sets and a minimum of equipment, was forced to occupy positions in the open in the southern half of the saucer. R.H.Q. was established alongside Brigade H.Q. on a little mound in the centre.

"Early in the morning the C.O., seeing that the regiment was in no fit condition to fight, went off to Corps H.Q. to get the Corps Commander's permission to withdraw for a few days in order to re-fit. This permission was granted and a staff officer was sent back with orders for our withdrawal. But by the time the staff officer

THE WESTERN DESERT

arrived the position was surrounded and the order never reached us.

As a defensive position Deir el Shein followed none of the accepted principles. It was isolated, well out of supporting range of any other formation, only partially defended by mines, without wire or trenches and not located on commanding ground. It was understood that the Army Commander's plan was to withdraw from the position the following day and to hold the ground by means of mobile columns, but unfortunately that plan was never able to be carried out.

"Soon after our arrival the enemy, whom we supposed to be still many miles away, started sporadic shelling of the whole area. One of the first of these shells fell near Captain M. C. Allfrey, D.S.O., killing him outright, a grievous and irreparable loss both to the regiment and to all his many friends.

"About nine o'clock an envoy came in from the Germans under a white flag. He informed us that the position was surrounded and demanded our immediate surrender threatening the most dire penalties if we refused to comply. He was promptly taken prisoner and no reply was sent.

"After this the enemy shelling increased in intensity and at ten o'clock the Essex were attacked by tanks and infantry. After heavy fighting the attack was repulsed.

"About mid-day the enemy attacked again. At a critical time in the battle a heavy sand-storm blew up which restricted visibility to a few yards. Under cover of the sandstorm their infantry lifted our mines and their tanks, entering the position, over-ran the Essex and one troop of 121 Field Regiment. By the time the storm had abated there were twelve tanks within 300 yards of Brigade H.Q. To meet this threat the troop of Matildas, the reserve anti-tank guns, and two guns from 385 Battery were brought into action behind the small ridge on which Brigade H.Q. was situated. These guns engaged the enemy tanks while the staff, including clerks, cooks and batmen, of Brigade and Regimental H.Q. took on the German infantry with rifle fire. As a result of this spirited little action the enemy withdrew leaving two tanks knocked out.

"The afternoon was quiet. Only one company of the Essex had suffered seriously, the others were still maintaining their positions. Plans were made for a counter-attack later that evening with the reserve company of the Ghurkas. At the same time an S.O.S. was sent to the 1st South African Division nearby, under whose command the Brigade was. Some time afterwards a message came back to say that tanks were coming to our assistance.

"An increase of shelling and movement during the afternoon indicated that another tank attack was likely to take place in the evening and arrangements were made to meet it. Captain Wix went forward in a Matilda to act as F.O.O., but his tank was hit and he was very seriously wounded.

"About six in the evening after heavy shelling and mortaring the expected attack took place. Both the Essex and Sikhs were over-run and Lieutenant de Cent, who was manning an O.P. in the area was captured. The enemy then advanced across the open towards Brigade H.Q. driving the Sikhs in front of them. To meet this new threat some reserve guns and the only two Matildas still in action were rushed to the area. At the same time a hastily improvised O.P. was manned on the spot by David Warner and myself and between us we succeeded in knocking out an enemy gun. The very heavy concentration of both shells and mortars put down on the area caused many casualties, and made the manning of guns in the open almost an impossibility. Despite this the sergeant in charge of the Signal Section raised a scratch crew of gunners and infantry and continued firing one of the 6-pounders, whose detachment had all been killed, until the gun itself was knocked out. About the same time both the remaining Matildas were knocked out.

"Seeing that the situation was hopeless, Major Warner had sent the bulk of the R.H.Q. men to the rear, and when the barrage lifted and the Germans were only a few yards away the remainder of R.H.Q., consisting of Major Warner, myself, Lieutenant A. A. Hicks and the

THE WESTERN DESERT 113

doctor also left the position. On arriving in the gun area we could see no signs of the men of the battery, only a few burning trucks and knocked out guns. Thinking that Major Mullens had withdrawn with what was left of his men we therefore continued our retreat and eventually, under cover of darkness, made good our escape into the desert.

"While passing through a gap in the minefields we came under heavy machine gun fire from a tank. The truck in which we were travelling was packed with men when an A.P. shell passed through it about a foot above the height of the floor. By a miracle no one was hurt though the shell went between David Warner's legs and grazed the tip of my finger.

"It subsequently turned out that 385 Battery had not withdrawn when we passed through them, but were lying doggo in their slit trenches awaiting the opportunity to slip away. Although it was a disheartening task firing H.E. with cap on, and watching the shells bounce off the sides of the enemy tanks, they had kept their guns in action while any still remained capable of firing. Lieutenant D. H. Biggleston was standing on one gun which received a direct hit and he and all the detachment were killed.

"When night fell and the Germans were in full possession of the position all those who were still alive and unwounded made their way out on foot through the enemy lines and after a weary trek of 25 miles rejoined the rest of the regiment the next day."

Meanwhile in Cairo the fact that Rommel was knocking at the gates of Alexandria, that the fate of Egypt and the Suez Canal, of India and of all our eastern empire was at stake had so far failed to penetrate the minds of the phlegmatic British who, as ever, in the face of danger remained faithful to the Drake tradition. While the battered remnants of the Eighth Army, after a bare thirty-six hours in which to re-organize and occupy, with greatly depleted forces, the practically non-existent defences of the Alamein line, were once more being attacked by Rommel's tanks, in Cairo the usual cricket match was taking place at the Gezira Sporting Club. When, late in the evening of 1st July, the centre of the position, at Deir el Shein, was over-run, twenty-six guns were lost and an Indian brigade, newly arrived from Iraq, completely destroyed, those members of the community who were not too tired from watching cricket, were making plans to dance at Shepheard's, to visit the Pyramids by moonlight or, after dinner at Jimmy's or Maxim's, to drift down the Nile in a felucca. Had Rommel himself been enabled to visit Cairo in June or July of that year he might well have stood aghast at the spirit shown by the indomitable English.

At Corps Headquarters, however, only fifteen miles from the battlefield, the situation was somewhat different. There the day might have been described as one of uncertainty and almost unrelieved gloom. Only General Auchinleck, who had arrived from Cairo to take personal charge of operations, remained calm and unruffled.

I met the General on the outskirts of the camp. I had come to ask permission to withdraw the regiment for a rest and refit. We had only six guns left. Nearly three hundred men and fifteen officers were missing. After granting my request he said:

"Come back as soon as you can. Remember this is a war of movement and manoeuvre. We shall never win battles by adopting a policy of static defence."

At that moment, though we did not know it, the regiment was losing the last of its guns in the static defence of Deir el Shein.

All that afternoon I sat listening to the rumble of the guns and wondering why the messenger I had sent to fetch the regiment did not return. In the hot and oppressive atmosphere of that stifling day the very air seemed heavy with foreboding. But it was not until the evening that the news came through. General Auchinleck had gone and the Corps Commander, Lt.-General Willoughby Norrie, was at supper. The meal was laid out on a trestle table under the stars and most of his staff were seated round it. One of them had just put down the telephone.

THE WESTERN DESERT

It appeared that about four o'clock in the afternoon the brigade commander at Deir el Shein had wirelessed an appeal for help in code. By the time it had reached Corps Headquarters, and had been decoded, it was too late.

So long as I live I shall never forget that supper party. No one spoke. Our minds were too full of what we had just heard. Most of us were thinking of the chances of stopping Rommel from reaching the Delta. In ten days he had harried the retreating Eighth Army across 300 miles of desert, in twenty-four hours he had captured Tobruk, in the course of an afternoon he had attacked and captured the central position in the new Alamein line annihilating the brigade that held it. There seemed to be no reason why in another twenty-four hours he should not be marching through the streets of Alexandria.

My mind racked with anxiety over the fate of the regiment. I could think of nothing else but the fact that my friends had all gone down fighting and that I had not been there to die with them. At that moment it did not seem to matter whether Rommel took Alexandria or not. Without the regiment to go on fighting with there seemed no point in going on.

That night I slept little and rose very early the next morning. I was shaving with a borrowed razor when I saw three familiar figures walking across the desert towards me. They were Neil Campbell, David Warner, and James Watt the doctor, tattered, dirty and unshaven, but undoubtedly alive.

"We've walked back," said David simply. "The others are on the way."

At Amriya, by the salt lakes, fifteen miles from Alexandria and a hundred and twenty from Cairo, the bits and pieces were being sorted out. Men from a hundred different units were coming in, on foot and in trucks, some with arms and some without. In one corner of the vast camp the remnants of the regiment were waiting for transport to take them back to Cairo. The emotions of the previous day, which had seen so many reunions and had borne mute witness to so many which would never take place, were over. They were still very tired.

"I could do with a month or two in Cairo," I heard someone say. "I ain't half going to get drunk when we gets back there. I've heard you can buy as much beer as you want for five piastres a bottle."

"Beer!" replied another scornfully. "That's all some of you blokes thinks about. A fat lot of beer you'd get if them Eyetalians ever reaches Cairo."

"Eyetalians don't drink beer," the first man said. "They drinks a stuff called vino. I know because my wife's brother was a waiter in a restaurant in Soho once. He brought a bottle home as a present. I didn't think much of it meself—sooner have a good bottle of beer any day."

"Did you see all that beer what the Doctor brought in his car yesterday morning and give to the orficers?" the other replied. "I reckon he's the only man in the world what could find beer in a wilderness like what this is. The wonder is 'e didn't bring a whole truck load of women along with him as well."

"Beer! Women!" said Holdstock, exasperated. "Don't any of you blokes know there's a war on? The first thing we got to do is to chase Jerry back to where he come from and then you can start talking about beer and women."

On my way into Alexandria to have a bath I asked Holdstock about the battle.

"Well, sir, they started up on us soon after you'd gone and me and one or two others got into a slit trench on the side of that little hill. The Jerry shells was coming over somethink cruel. We was wedged so tight in the trench we could hardly move. I'd cramp in both my legs. But we didn't half have a feed. We ate pineapple chunks till we nearly busted and even then there was some left over, not to mention what was left in the truck what Lemon couldn't carry."

"Pineapple chunks! What on earth...?"

"Yes, sir. You see the mess lorry was full of tins of fruit, and Lemon said he couldn't bear to die and think of Jerry having all them tins. So he gets out of the trench and runs across to the truck and comes back with his arms full of tins and every one of them was pineapple.

THE WESTERN DESERT

I suppose it's a bit laughable come to think of it, but it didn't seem laughable at the time."

"No, I suppose not."

"And it isn't so very laughable now," went on Holdstock as we swerved to avoid a stray Egyptian donkey. "When I thinks of Collard and Cole and all them lads what we left behind and shall never see again most likely, not to mention those what is dead and buried, and when I thinks of their wives and kiddies at home and of the little businesses they was interested in, and of their hobbies, such as gardening and growing roses like Cole, or smoking their pipes of an evening and causing no trouble to anyone like that poor little 'airdresser bloke, all I can say is— 'What the hell is there to laugh at?'"

Holdstock's summing up of the war situation was endorsed the next day by Mr. Churchill, who in a speech in the House of Commons said:

"The military misfortunes of the last fortnight in Cyrenaica and Egypt have completely transformed the situation, not only in that theatre but throughout the Mediterranean. We have lost upwards of 50,000 men, a great mass of material, and, in spite of carefully organised demolitions, large quantities of stores have fallen into the enemies' hands. Rommel has advanced nearly 400 miles through the desert and is now approaching the fertile Delta of the Nile. The effect of these events cannot yet be measured. We are at this moment in the presence of a recession of our hopes and prospects in the Middle East and in the Mediterranean unequalled since the fall of France."

By the time the regiment arrived in Cairo the critical nature of the situation was fully realized. Steps were being taken to organize the defence of the city and of the surrounding country, W.A.A.Fs, A.T.S., W.A.A.S.Is, and the wives of British nationals were being evacuated to Palestine, Syria and the Sudan, while at G.H.Q. a veritable holocaust of secret documents was taking place in incinerators specially constructed for the purpose.

Unfortunately the draught in the chimneys was unexpectedly strong and a shower of burnt paper descending on the city only served to confirm the worst fears of the apprehensive Egyptians. The English were undoubtedly going. G.H.Q. was packing up, and the troops were marching out. In a few days Cairo would be at the mercy of the marauding Germans, not to mention the unspeakable Italians whose hobbies were well-known to be murder, rape, loot, and rapine.

Such were the rumours that were flying about the city and gaining in intensity every hour. That Cairo remained calm and no major panic ensued may possibly be attributed if not wholly, at any rate in part, to the Englishman's passion for cricket. It was impossible for the more intelligent Egyptian to conceive that there was any real cause for alarm while cricket and other ball games were still being played at Gezira.

Possibly it was with this thought in his mind that the secretary of the Sporting Club had sent me a little note asking for an assurance that we would dig no gun pits on the racecourse. The regiment, while still resting and recuperating at the R.A. Base Depot at Almaza, had been ordered to reconnoitre troop and battery positions in conformity with an all-round defensive plan. It so happened that Gezira, including the famous club grounds, formed part of our area, where Derrick Mullens, with his customary thoroughness, had not only reconnoitred the possible troop positions, but marked the selected site of each gun. In replying to the secretary's note it was with difficulty I refrained from asking if he thought the Germans when they came would pay any respect to the sacred racecourse and whether the cricket pitch and the tennis courts must also be preserved for the benefit of the sports-loving Panzers.

The chances of the very depleted forces available in Cairo at this time, consisting mostly of the battered remnants of units such as ourselves, holding up the whole of Rommel's army should it succeed in defeating or by-passing the Eighth Army at Alamein, were remote in the extreme. One of the American war correspondents living

THE WESTERN DESERT 119

at Shepheard's had received a cable from his paper in New York asking him to cable back a thousand word article on whether the Egyptian army would defend Egypt if the British failed. His reply was:
"No! No!—A thousand times no."

Whilst at Amriya permission had been obtained from the B.R.A. Eighth Army, Brigadier N. Martin, for 470 Battery to rejoin the regiment. This permission was confirmed when we reached Almaza by the M.G.R.A. at G.H.Q., Major-General A. Maxwell, who ordered that the regiment should be re-organized on a two battery basis. Since 470 Battery had suffered less heavily than the other two batteries it was decided to form the remnants of 385 and 387 Batteries into one battery which should keep the title of 385 and that 470 Battery should be re-named 387 Battery. A certain amount of cross-posting, both of officers and men, took place between all three batteries and the eventual result was 385 Battery, commanded by Major H. M. Allfrey, M.C., and 387 Battery by Major P. C. Eliot, with Major W. J. de W. Mullens, D.S.O., second in command. Major D. B. H. Warner was promoted to command 87 Field Regiment R.A. in Paiforce and Captain C. W. Johnson left to take up an appointment with 2nd Echelon.

On 20th July the regiment moved from Almaza to Cowley Camp, Mena, and joined the 50th Divisional Artillery under command of Brigadier C. Eastman, D.S.O., consisting of the 74 and 124 Field Regiments R.A. Training and refitting continued and the regiment was made up to strength both in officers and men.

Early in August it was decided to fall into line with other Yeomanry regiments and to adopt brass K.Y. title badges to be worn on the shoulder, both in battle dress and K.D., by all ranks. This innovation was to prove of value in many ways. It not only encouraged esprit de corps and helped to increase the pride each man felt in the regiment but also enabled the Kent Yeomanry to be known and recognized as such by outsiders. The reputation of the regiment, already high, in this way became widespread. Henceforth wherever they went the word went round "The K.Ys. have arrived" or "The K.Ys. are back again", and the regiment became known by this title all over the Middle East.

III

On 24th August the regiment returned once more to the Western Desert and concentrated south of El Hamam occupying positions a few days later at El Huweija in support of the 8th Armoured Brigade consisting of the Notts Yeomanry, the Stafford Yeomanry and the 3rd Royal Tank Regiment.

The following account is by the Adjutant Captain, afterwards Major N. A. Campbell:

24th August, 1942.

The regiment, under command of Derrick Mullens, as the C.O. was away on a Senior Officers' Course at Gaza, moved out of Mena Camp at 05.30 hours and moved up to the desert. We halted at Amriya in order to draw water and then drove approximately forty miles west into the desert and bivouacked for the night. We arrived just as it was getting dark and had difficulty in collecting the stragglers amongst whom was the R.H.Q. Officers' Mess.

Lieutenant Ant Hicks was sent to the 10th Armoured Division H.Q., under whose orders we now came, to receive instructions and he returned at 02.00 hours with orders that we were to move again at first light and go into action in a long stop position at the southern end of the Alamein Line.

25th August, 1942.

At 06.00 hours the regiment moved off with the recce parties going on ahead to find the battery positions. Good gun positions were chosen from which to support the Eighth Armoured Brigade who were on the extreme left of the line facing south. The guns were up by mid-day and the rest of the day was taken up by digging in. Rommel was expected to attack at any moment so that time was short.

THE WESTERN DESERT

26th August, 1942.

The regiment received orders to come under the command of the 8th Armoured Brigade, while the remainder of the Divisional Artillery was retained under the C.R.A. in support. As the Brigade was not trained for mobile operations the plan was to move forward to better positions by three stages and the next day was spent in reconnoitring positions further forward and closer to 22 Armoured Brigade.

27th August, 1942.

The Armoured Brigade and the Regiment moved forward to the new positions and dug in.

28th August, 1942.

The day was spent in completing the preparations for our defensive positions.

29th August, 1942.

As Rommel had not yet attacked the Brigadier Commanding decided to spend the day in doing a mobile exercise to practise movement and deployment. Accordingly, at first light the Brigade Group moved out. Most of the exercise took place in soft sand so that the tanks had ample practice in towing both quads (gun tractors) and guns.

That night we did not return to our battle positions as it was not desired to disclose these to the enemy air reconnaissance so we moved back and bivouacked in an area some three miles behind our battle positions.

30th August, 1942.

At 02.00 hours a message was received that Rommel had attacked at midnight and had just penetrated the mine fields at the extreme southern end of the Alamein line. The regiment was to move forthwith to its battle positions. Orders were at once sent to the batteries and the O.Ps, which we had great difficulty in finding, as we had not been able to locate them in the dark the evening before. In some miraculous way the batteries eventually received their orders and the regiment got on the move. After a trying night march with the vehicles continually sticking in the soft sand the regiment was in action by dawn that day. The day was quiet and the enemy only pressed on slowly as the light screen of 7th Armoured Division was effectively delaying his advance.

31st August, 1942.

At dawn the next day the acting C.O. and I set off to find the Brigadier and were surprised to see the last tanks just moving out of position. They had received orders to move at once to link up with 22nd Armoured Brigade, who were approximately five miles to our west, but in their hurry to move they had forgotten to tell us. We at once issued orders to the regiment to move and drove on to catch up the Brigadier. On the way we met the second in command of the Armoured Brigade, who shouted out: "Whatever you do, Mullens, keep your batteries together or they will all be written off." At that moment the Batteries were at least three miles apart! On reaching Brigade H.Q. we found that the recce tanks had made contact with the enemy some two miles east of the 22nd Armoured Brigade, and that the Brigadier had made a hasty plan to attack with the 3rd R.T.R. due south of the position held by the 44 Division.

The guns were dropped into action and the battle commenced. About two miles to our south the whole of the Afrika Corps was stretched out across the desert with their tanks in the front and all that day the regiment and the other 200 guns deployed on that front fired round after round into them. The shooting was not all one-sided by any means, and it was a case of "Hard pounding, gentlemen!" on both sides.

The 3rd R.T.R. attacked, but were soon held up, having lost two tanks, and were withdrawn. The Brigadier then made a further plan to attack with the Notts. Yeomanry, and at 12.00 hours they went into the attack under cover of a heavy concentration fired by the regiment. They pressed on heavily and attacked most gallantly, destroying six enemy tanks, but were held up by anti-tank guns, cleverly concealed in a small wadi about a mile east of 22 Armoured Brigade, whose tanks could be seen in the distance. They had to be withdrawn after

THE WESTERN DESERT

losing eight tanks themselves and the battle paused for lunch. In the afternoon the Brigadier decided to attack again with the Staffordshire Yeomanry and the 3rd R.T.R. This attack made better progress, but was again held up by the opposition from the wadi and as dusk came the tanks were withdrawn.

1st September, 1942.

When dawn broke the tanks were back in their positions of the day before. Reconnaissance was sent out to try and locate the enemy. The wadi was found clear and contact was soon made with 22 Armoured Brigade who had advanced east to meet us. The enemy had withdrawn approximately two miles to the south, but was still stretched out across the desert. A thoroughly enjoyable day was then spent by the regiment which fired thousands of rounds. Only one solitary shell, which landed near nobody, was received in return. In addition the R.A.F. bombed the enemy continuously all day and by night.

2nd September, 1942.

We awoke to find the enemy gone. Patrols were at once sent out to make contact. They reported that the enemy was slowly withdrawing back to his original position.

General Montgomery arrived in the morning to visit 8th Armoured Brigade H.Q. He congratulated all ranks on their performance.

3rd September, 1942.

8th Armoured Brigade was ordered to send out a column to harass the withdrawal of the enemy and as Derrick Mullens was ill the command of the column devolved on Peter Eliot. We had various troops under command at different times, but the column ultimately consisted of:

        2 Batteries of the Regiment
        1 Squadron Crusader Tanks
        1 Battery Anti-Tank Guns
        1 Battery L.A.A. Guns
        1 Motor Infantry Company
        1 Squadron Grant Tanks

4th September, 1942.

The column harassed the withdrawal of the enemy. Many good targets were offered and the enemy engaged. No casualties were suffered by us. In the afternoon the regiment was relieved and withdrawn to rest. During the whole engagement the regiment lost one man killed.

On 11th September the regiment moved to the area Deil el Tarfa on the southern flank of the Eighth Army in support of the 22nd Armoured Brigade, consisting of the 4th County of London Yeomanry, and the 1st and 5th Royal Tank Regiments. This brigade formed part of the 7th Armoured Division, the famous Desert Rats. It was a great feather in our caps therefore when a week later, after an inspection by Lieut-General Horrocks, the regiment was officially recognized as part of the artillery of this division. Not only was the division one of the best as well as the most famous division in the Eighth Army, but it was an exceptional honour for a field regiment to be allotted a role normally given to the Royal Horse Artillery only.

The next six weeks were devoted to intensive training. As the regiment had had little experience of working with tanks the first part of the programme was given up to battery training with affiliated tank regiments. Later the regiment as a whole, in conjunction with the 4th Field Regiment R.A., trained as one unit with the Armoured Brigade. Since both regiments consisted of two batteries only it was decided that for operational purposes they should train and fight as one.[1]

Since the method of operating with tanks was peculiar to the desert, and the conditions under which the 22nd Armoured Brigade trained and afterwards fought are never likely to occur again, a brief description here will not be out of place. The easiest way to grasp the principle on which both tanks and their supporting artillery worked is to regard them as a battle fleet on land. When they

---

[1] Lieut.-Colonel F. Lushington commanded the combined regiments, while the C.O. of the 4th Field Regiment, Lieut.-Colonel R. Daniells remained available should he become a casualty.

moved they moved over the open desert like the ships of a fleet at sea and, like a fleet at sea, they deployed, advanced, changed direction, and engaged the enemy, on the orders of one man, the admiral, who, in the case of the armoured brigade, was a brigadier. The little ships, the destroyers, or armoured cars, moved in front ten miles ahead of the rest of the fleet. It was their business to locate the enemy and to wireless back his movements and general position. The three tank regiments with their attendant field batteries and anti-aircraft guns, moved in arrow-head formation behind, one regiment leading, the other two in either flank, the light tanks, Cruisers and Honeys, spread out in a wide arc to the front and flanks the heavies, the General Grants pounding along behind, while the fourth field battery, acting as a reserve of fire power, brought up the rear.

Each tank regiment had its quota of infantry in trucks that went with them, and the whole, when fully deployed, covered an area about three miles wide and three miles deep. The brigadier and his staff were in the centre in four Cruiser tanks. The artillery commander and his staff travelled near him in two armoured cars. The brigadier was connected by wireless direct to the other commanders, the commander of the armoured cars, the artillery commander and the commanders of the three tank regiments. He gave his orders to them personally over the wireless. In the same way they two were connected by another set to their subordinate commanders, and so on down to individual tanks and troops of guns, so that when the brigade was on the march or in action no responsible officer was without a wireless set glued to his head.

It was a fine sight to see this great fleet of some two hundred tanks and guns, sailing over the desert with pennants flying, to see them change direction and formation as one, to see and hear them come into action, the Cruisers dashing forward in a smother of spray and sand, the heavy Grants waddling up into line, the guns dropping their trails and opening fire almost before their box-shaped tractors had had time to turn round and disperse themselves in rear. It was a fine sight, but it needed a great deal of training for efficient working, nor was it the only form of training required.

Before the armour was free to operate in the open desert it was necessary to break through the minefields in the Alamein line. The enemy minefields in the brigade area were two in number and were known as January and February. They were about 1,500 yards apart and were each believed to be about 500 or 600 yards in depth. The method of attack was to make a night approach in three columns nose to tail. At the head of the three columns Scorpion tanks were to beat three pathways through the first minefield. They would be followed by men from the Royal Engineers who were to pick up any mines left out by the Scorpions. The R.E. were to be supported by infantry in Bren carriers. As soon as the three gaps in the first minefield had been cleared, and the pathways marked with tapes and lights, the three columns of tanks and guns were to pass through into the area between the minefields and the whole process would then be repeated in the second minefield.

It can well be understood that to carry out such an operation successfully at night required not only careful planning, but a high state of training in all ranks. In the open desert some miles behind the lines these operations were practised in every detail first in daylight and then during the hours of darkness.

During the weeks of training and preparation for the coming offensive, the exact date of which was still a secret, only two other events of interest, so far as the regiment was concerned, took place. The first was the decision to reform the third battery. On 26th September a small cadre of officers and N.C.Os under Major W. Prideaux left the desert for Almaza to raise and train the new 470 Battery. The second was the loss of Captain N. A. Campbell, who had been adjutant of the regiment since early in 1940, and who, on 5th October, left to take over an appointment as staff captain of the 201st Guards Brigade. This serious loss was much felt by all and by no one more than the C.O. with whom he had worked in close harmony

THE WESTERN DESERT

for more than two and a half years. His place was taken by Captain A. A. Hicks.

On 19th October a conference of commanding officers, presided over by the Army Commander, was held at 13th Corps H.Q. at which General Montgomery explained the plan and disclosed the time and date of the coming battle. Two days later the plan was revealed in detail to all officers by the C.O. and on the following day, the day before the battle, the men were told. On this day, 22nd October, the C.O. visited each troop in turn. General Montgomery's plan for the coming battle was explained, and since the Padre had unfortunately gone sick with diphtheria, a short service was held without him. The 91st Psalm was read and the following verse from Deuteronomy:

"Be strong and of a good courage, fear not, nor be afraid of them; for the Lord thy God He it is that doth go with thee; He will not fail thee nor forsake thee."

In the years to come, when all other names are forgotten, Ypres and Alamein will perhaps be remembered by our children's children as places where their forefathers fought in the two greatest wars of our century. Just as Mons and Dunkirk mark our army's two greatest retreats in those wars so Ypres and Alamein will symbolize its two greatest and most decisive victories. Yet here the comparison seems to end. At Ypres it was always raining. At Alamein the sun blazed down out of a cloudless sky. Ypres was fought in the mud, in an enclosed and civilized country. Alamein was fought in the dust and sand of the open desert. At Ypres the mud was deep enough to drown a mule if he floundered into it. At Alamein the soft sand churned up by the wheels of hundreds of guns, tanks and trucks, was equally deep. It lay thick along the tracks that led towards the line and hung in clouds over the battlefield. Yet in spite of these superficial differences, to those who, like the writer, fought in both actions there was a curious similarity, not to be accounted for solely by the sound of guns firing and the whistle and crash of exploding shells. Perhaps it was that both battles were something more than a mere struggle for victory between the opposing armies. In both history was in the making and those who were there, however dumb and however stupid, however tired and however afraid, could not help being aware of it.

It was six o'clock in the evening on 23rd October, 1942, when the long column of tanks and guns moved slowly forward towards the battle area. The pennants dancing from their masts, dipped and rose as they passed like ships in a choppy sea. So must Nelson's three-deckers have dipped and rolled as they took up their battle stations before Trafalgar. So must the knights of Agincourt have moved, the pennants on their lances fluttering as their heavy horses trotted into line. A cloud of dust hung over them like the spray of a heavy sea hangs over a rock bound coast and out of the cloud came the roar of their engines and the thunderous grinding of tracks on the hard pebbly sand.

Sitting beside Holdstock in an armoured car, a pair of wireless earphones over my head and a message pad on my lap, I had a feeling that I no longer lived in the old normal world of every day life whose inhabitants were flesh and blood and muscle and bone, but had myself become a part of this strange Wellsian world of metal and machinery that was plunging forward in the fading light. Even the friendly and familiar desert seemed to have changed, to have become somehow less friendly and no longer familiar.

The sun went down and the moon came up as, nose to tail, we passed through the gaps in our own minefields.

I wondered what the Germans were thinking on the other side of that empty waste. Surely they must hear us coming? I imagined them crouching in their holes clutching their arms, their gunners standing by their guns, their observers peering forward into the darkness.

A few minutes later there was an ear-splitting crash and the whole sky was lit with stabbing flashes of flame. Sitting clamped in my hard and narrow seat I could see through the slits in front and on either side nothing but a haze of dust and smoke, of light and darkness, out of which a tank, like some strange mastodon in a prehistoric world, appeared and disappeared.

Slowly we moved forward, stopped, moved on again and came to a halt. There were cries and shouts in the darkness. I caught a glimpse of white tapes marking the edges of more minefields and of a man standing with a lantern. The car rocked and tossed as the noise of gunfire changed from a long steady roll, like the beating of drums, to the sound of individual explosions. We were getting nearer. An ambulance passed. Jeeps darted to and fro in the darkness. All along the skyline in a witch's cauldron of flame and fire the lights were dancing.

It was daylight before any definite news came through. We had broken through the first lot of minefields and were held up by the second. There had been heavy casualties.

Driving up into the forward area in the early morning I could see broken tanks and shattered trucks lying everywhere. Beyond the first minefield where the ground rose in a gentle slope towards the second, the scene was reminiscent of the downs on Derby Day, and it was some time before I could find the tank on which, regardless of the fact that he was in full view of the enemy, the General[1] was sitting. Climbing up beside him I waited till he had finished issuing some new orders to his staff and, while waiting, gazed round me. Between the tanks and guns and trucks that lay scattered in apparently inextricable confusion over the slope, jeeps were bustling in and out, men were cooking their breakfast, and an occasional shell burst in a cloud of smoke and dust. When the smoke cleared away men could be seen running hither and thither like ants who have been disturbed by someone prodding their ant-heap with a stick. But in between the shell bursts a brooding silence hung over the crowded battlefield. It was as if both sides, tired out from the long night's struggle, had withdrawn a little apart and in the grey light of early dawn were watching each other, licking their wounds and waiting for the next move.

We had not long to wait. The General pointed out to

[1] Maj.-Gen. Harding, Commanding 7th Armoured Division.

me the area in which some concealed German guns were holding up our advance, gave me a brief outline of what had happened during the night and of his future plans. Then, as I got back into my jeep to drive away, the storm burst. Shells began falling all round me and our own guns replied with an answering roar.

For a week the battle dragged on as, under the twin peaks of Himeimat, which the French made a gallant effort to capture, our men struggled and fought and died. But no further progress was made.

Meanwhile in the north, near Alamein itself, four infantry divisions closely followed by two armoured divisions had been launched in the main attack. On the first night the tanks had entered the salient made by the infantry but, unable to break through, were finally forced to withdraw again. They, too, had been held up with heavy casualties.

Eight days later we drove north to join them and on the 2nd November, at one o'clock in the morning, the final and decisive attack was launched by the 2nd New Zealand Division, supported by the 9th Armoured Brigade.

For the purposes of this attack the regiment had taken over positions from the 1st R.H.A., old friends from France, and had come temporarily under command of the artillery commander of the 10th Armoured Division. The day before there had been considerable hostile shelling of the battery areas particularly of 385 Battery, during which Lieutenant W. Dawes and seven other ranks were wounded. So intense was the concentration of guns and vehicles in the area that it was found impossible to move the battery to a safer place.

R.H.Q. who were situated only a hundred yards behind 385, and a bare fifty yards in front of a troop of Horse Artillery, also came in for some scattered shelling.

Once the attack had begun, however, the noise of approaching shells was drowned by the roar of the barrage. Seventeen field regiments and a large number of mediums supported the attack and dawn was breaking when the thunder of the guns at last died down and a strange calm, broken only by the rattle of empty shell cases being thrown on the salvage lorries, settled on the battlefield.

I was sitting on an upturned petrol tin. Beside me was the little trench where the doctor and I had spent the night, a new shell hole on its very edge and other fresh evil-looking holes all round. A few yards away some cooks were trying to boil water for tea. In the growing light their unshaven faces looked haggard and grey. Beyond them other men stood or sat round the silent guns while the swiftly rising sun shone impartially on more trenches and wire, on a heap of old tins, on a dead man clutching a rifle, on all the flotsam and jetsam of war.

"Your tea, sir."

"Ah, thank you, Holdstock. What time is it?"

"Half-past four, sir, and a dirty morning by the look of it. Hope you slept well."

"Sleep! How could I sleep? Do I look as if I had been sleeping?"

"Well, no, sir. I suppose not in a manner of speaking. Only I thought you might have. I didn't have a bad night myself. Curled up in one of them trenches at the back and slept all night I did. I should have been asleep now if one of the cooks hadn't waked me."

Another hour passed and I began to doze when someone tapped me on the shoulder.

"You're wanted on the blower, Colonel." It was the adjutant.

"Any news?"

"Yes, the armour are on the way up. We are to join them on Sun track at ten o'clock."

"Then it's all over?"

"Yes, it's all over."

"How many rounds have we fired?"

"Four hundred a gun since zero hour."

"Four hundred in just over three hours! That's not bad going."

"No. And that's not counting all the stuff we threw at them yesterday."

"The men must be tired. They've had no rest at all the last two or three days."

Ant shrugged his shoulders. "I could do with a bit of sleep myself," he said.

The infantry attack was completely successful. Most of the enemy had surrendered in their trenches where they lay too dazed by the heavy shelling to resist. But when the 9th Armoured Brigade went through they were met by a strong anti-tank gun screen and lost nearly eighty per cent. of their tanks.

All that day, 3rd November, having once more rejoined the 22nd Armoured Brigade, we waited for the order to advance, but it was not until the evening that we moved up Diamond Track in the gathering darkness and leaguered for the night just behind the forward positions, ready to break through in the morning.

The morning of the 4th was fortunately misty enabling the Brigade to shake itself out from its close formation, tow out the many vehicles bogged in the soft sand, and move across a very difficult piece of country, without being seen. Moving south-west of the feature known as Tel Accaquir soon after ten o'clock the leading tanks came into contact with the rearguard of the Italian Littorio division and a brisk action ensued which resulted in the loss of several enemy tanks and the withdrawl of the remainder.

That evening for the first time we close leaguered for the night in the open desert west of the Alamein line.

At daybreak the next day the advance continued. But the enemy had gone and all day we drove westward over the smooth stony desert, the only signs that we were in hostile country being a small private battle that we passed between our sister brigade, the 4th Light Armoured, and some German tanks. We actually drove through the firing guns of the 4th Light, but as they did not seem in need of our assistance and our orders were to push on at all speed we left them to it.

General Montgomery's plan for the pursuit was a simple one. The main body of the German Afrika Corps, including what was left of the two Panzer divisions, the 15th and 21st, had retreated up the coast road leaving the Italians to their fate. They were being closely pursued

THE WESTERN DESERT 133

by the two Armoured Divisions of the 10th Corps. Meanwhile the 7th Armoured Division had been ordered to turn south and then west across the open desert and to push on at all speed in an attempt to get behind the Germans and cut off their retreat. It may seem strange that this part of the pursuit should have been allotted to the one division whose tanks had been considered so worn out that in the original plan they had been assigned to what amounted to a static role. One can only suppose that the heavy casualties suffered by the armoured brigades of the 10th Corps, who were all armed with new Shermans, had so much reduced their strength that their numbers were insufficient to carry out both roles, the direct pursuit up the coast road and the encircling movement in the desert. So it was left to the obsolescent Stuarts Crusaders and Grants of the Desert Rats to follow the old desert trail and by driving their part-worn vehicles unmercifully to outflank and get behind the fleeing enemy. That we only just failed to do so after a ten day gallop in which we covered over 500 miles was due to no fault of ours.

Tanks cannot travel without petrol, guns cannot fire without shells, and men cannot march and fight indefinitely without water, food or sleep. The nearest supply column to our advance, which moved forward on an average sixty miles a day, was seldom less than ninety miles behind us. This meant that the trucks carrying petrol, ammunition, food and water had to cover anything up to two hundred miles of desert every twenty-four hours. If one includes the time for loading and unloading, for maintaining the vehicles and feeding their drivers this leaves none at all for sleep. Many drivers went without sleep for days on end. No one can keep this up for ever. Added to all this there was the danger of capture by wandering parties of the enemy. On the night of the 5th the regimental refuelling party was captured twenty miles in rear of the main body and before the guns could move the next morning we had to borrow petrol from the tanks.

On the evening of the third day, the 6th, we leaguered late. It was getting dark when I climbed stiffly out of my armoured car. All round me the desert was alive with little points of light where men were boiling dixies of tea on a half petrol tin filled with sand soaked in petrol. Brewing up the men called it. The moment we stopped, even for a few minutes, they started to brew up. The expression had other meanings. A tank or a lorry set on fire by a shell was also said to be brewing up.

"What's for dinner to-night, Holdstock?" I asked.

Holdstock looked up from the little fire which he had already lighted.

"Char and wads and half a tin of bully per man," he said.

"What no fresh rations? Haven't we got any M. and V. or tinned fruit?"

"No, sir, and no roast pork and onions nor paté de foie gras neither, not unless the supply column comes in from the Ritz Hotel to-night. I've only got one loaf of dry bread what I've been keeping for you and Mr. Hicks. The rest of us has biscuits and likes it."

It had been a good day. Starting at first light and changing direction north towards the coast road we had run into a strong enemy column of tanks and guns, including quantities of soft-skinned vehicles.

The leading tanks had opened fire followed by the guns of all three batteries. The enemy, caught by surprise, had made frantic efforts to get away, his guns and tanks remaining behind to cover the retreat of the remainder.

Their shells were bursting round us in vicious little plonks. One splinter came through the floor of the armoured car between my legs. Almost smothered in smoke and dust we edged up behind a tank whose owner popped his head out for a moment and then put it in again closing the lid with a bang.

But in half an hour it was all over. The enemy were out of range.

We followed them up at full speed. Like ships tossing in a rough sea the Crusaders were bucketting along in a long straggly line, the Grants charging majestically behind. Unable to move fast enough the guns were leapfrogging through one another, one troop in action the other on the move.

A troop of guns from 385 came over a low ridge straight into two enemy eighty-eights, which opened fire at point blank range. One gun was hit and its tractor set on fire when the second troop behind put down a smoke screen between them and the enemy. Then while the troop on wheels got away the troop in action knocked out the two eighty-eights one after the other.

The brigadier passed them standing on the roof of his Crusader.

"Good work!" he shouted, as he raced by. "Keep it up, boys."

But we had to stop. We couldn't go on. We had run out of petrol.

It was late in the afternoon when, after refuelling, we caught up with their rear guard near Sidi Haneish. It was raining and the light was bad. Through the mist the flashes of their guns and the dim shapes of their moving tanks were like pictures thrown on a screen that was out of focus.

We moved forward slowly, closing in for the kill. The wireless was crackling with a stream of orders. Every gun we had was firing. The rain came down in buckets.

A tank was hit and blew up in a sheet of flame and the noise of gunfire grew louder and more intense. The water was dripping off the rim of my steel helmet and making a little pool on my lap. Ant. was swearing softly to himself. Holdstock was cleaning his pipe.

The brigadier wanted us to turn every gun we had got on a group of enemy 88 mm. I had ordered a regimental concentration of three rounds gunfire. The rear battery of the 4th Field put on the wrong range and before we could stop them twenty-four rounds fell plonk into our own tanks. No one was hit, but blue sparks were coming out of the top of the Brigadier's wireless mast.

Night was falling. Four German tanks were blazing in the darkness. Eight others had been put out of action and abandoned by their crews. Twelve German 88 mm.

K

had been knocked out. We had lost one Crusader and one Grant.

I sipped my tea gratefully. The rain had stopped and Derrick had arrived with more petrol. It had been a good day—a very good day.

Holdstock and the wireless operator were having one of their usual arguments.

"I don't see what you've got to complain about," I heard Holdstock say, "with your pack stuffed with wrist watches and cameras and Jerry photographs."

"Sooner 'ave somethink to eat," the Corporal replied.

Holdstock nodded and lit his pipe from the fire with a twist of burning paper.

"There you goes again," he said, "always complaining. If it's not one thing it's another. Some folks are never satisfied."

It rained all night and the next morning the desert was a series of disconnected lakes from which the guns, bogged up to their axles, had to be towed on to the dry ground by the tanks. All morning we toiled and pulled, but made little progress. Late in the afternoon we halted again to dry our clothes and blankets in the sun and allow the stragglers to catch up.

The next day, the 9th, having marched thirty miles before breakfast, we waited till after mid-day for the petrol lorries. From the wireless came the news that the British and Americans had made a joint landing in North Africa.

On the 10th, six days after leaving Alamein, having halted all morning for the supply lorries to catch up, we crossed the frontier wire and altered course to the north towards Capuzzo. The 11th Hussars, our armoured cars, had reported an enemy column of eighteen tanks and sixty lorries moving north-west about twelve to fifteen miles ahead. We pushed on therefore till well after dark in the hope of catching them up in the morning.

Since we left Alamein I had seen very little of Derrick who, as officer responsible for supply, had spent his whole time driving up and down between the supply columns and the fighting troops. For days and nights on end he had driven, usually alone, finding his way by compass, by the stars, or just by guess-work. There was no means of telling exactly which way we had gone. We might start off in the morning on a compass bearing due west and change direction by as much as thirty degrees during the day.

Crossing the wire near Fort Maddalena that night he had run into the brigadier's A.C.V. lumbering along attended by its horde of satellite trucks. Hearing we were just ahead he had driven on in the hope of catching us up before dark. But night fell suddenly, as it does in the desert, and he was forced to stop for fear of getting lost or, worse still, running into the Germans with his precious cargo of petrol.

It was late the next morning before he reached us. I was standing up in my armoured car, a plate of cold sausage in one hand, the wireless transmitter in the other.

"Hello! Where have you sprung from? Have you brought any petrol?"

"Yes. The lorries are on the way. They should be here in half an hour." He was unshaven and there were dark rings under his eyes.

"Thank God for that. We've only a few miles left in our tanks. One battery has run out altogether. Have some cold sausage?"

"No thanks. How's the battle going?"

"Oh! All right. We're still winning. The trouble is the blighters run so fast we can't catch them up."

"I heard some firing just now."

"Yes. The Boche are in Bardia and the other side of Capuzzo, but the New Zealanders are coming up the Pass and with any luck we may get behind them."

Together we drove on towards the sound of the guns past some shattered buildings, a burnt-out tank, a rusty howitzer, its muzzle pointing to the sky, its cartridge cylinders still scattered in confusion round it.

Capuzzo itself was full of the broken monuments of past battles, trenches, wire, empty barrels, and piled up heaps of ammunition boxes. How dreary it looked in the morning light!

In the distance trucks were moving, men were brewing up and a troop of guns were in action.

The wireless was crackling exultantly.

"They've blown the bridge out of Bardia. There are hundreds of trucks streaming along the Tobruk road. We've got them now if we can only push on."

On, on, on! At all costs we must get on. No stopping to brew up, no stopping for cold sausage. Keep moving, keep firing. We mustn't let them get away.

But the tanks had to refuel and it was late in the afternoon before we were able to push along westward once more moving south of the Gambut escarpment with a view to cutting them off in Tobruk the next day.

That night we slept little. Everyone knew that tomorrow must see the end of our long journey one way or the other. Our tanks were old and worn. Many of them had already dropped out on the way. If we caught the enemy he might overwhelm us by sheer weight of numbers. If we failed to catch him we could hardly continue the pursuit without a long halt for maintenance and repairs.

Soon after first light we drove on to the airfield at El Adem. It was empty. The 11th Hussars had already signalled Tobruk clear of the enemy.

An hour later a reconnaissance plane reported large enemy columns on the Derna road some twenty miles further west.

We could go no further. We had travelled 560 miles in ten days and fought two major actions on the way. And now the enemy were out of range and out of reach. Six miles beyond the airfield we came to a final halt.

That night we close leaguered for the last time. The sun was setting in a ball of fire on the horizon turning the sandhills pink and golden and casting long shadows on the flat expanse of scrub-covered wilderness. The men were brewing up as usual. Derrick had brought up some fresh rations and Holdstock was singing as he cooked our joint dinner. Wrapt in a blanket, for it was getting chilly at night, I sat on an upturned biscuit box my mind full of past scenes and pictures. Moving up to Alamein, the

THE WESTERN DESERT

tracks two feet deep in soft churned up sand the consistency of face powder, the rows of belching guns, the roar of the barrage, and Holdstock brewing tea, crouching intently over his petrol tin, not caring if the heavens fell and the earth gave up her dead.

The first day of the break through, the mist, the silence, and the charred corpse hanging head downwards from an upturned lorry; and then once more the wide open spaces and the clean desert air, tanks moving forward, guns coming into action, and the Brigadier waving us on. . . .

The long days of the pursuit, the start in the half-darkness of early morning, the stiffness and cold emptiness, the sight of the tanks, guns and lorries spreading out fan-wise in ordered confusion, the sun coming up behind us, the crackle of the wireless and the first order to halt and brew up . . . the weariness of sitting for hours in an armoured car travelling at twelve miles an hour, the stiffness and soreness, the impossibility of reading or resting. . . .

The tired mob of prisoners, a little group of Italians on a queer Heath Robinson vehicle with caterpillar wheels, the search for souvenirs, wrist watches and cameras, birettas and luger pistols. . . .

Leaguering at night—driving into the sunset, the slow closing together, the sudden darkness, and the first stars; the gathering round the Brigadier's tank, studying the map by the light of a hurricane lamp; tea and whiskey and laughter and talk; the sense of confidence and comradeship, the feeling that the tide had turned at last. . . .

The men—Holdstock always cheerful, always singing. The wireless operator, dour and silent, suffering from a gyppy tummy and an attack of jaundice, but refusing to give in. Ant. in his golf jacket and corduroy trousers, Derrick with his coloured scarves, and Peter in a battle dress jacket two sizes too small for him; the survey officer tearing about in a jeep, happy as a pink-faced cherub in a celestial chariot. And Hubert sticking his head out of his Honey tank, his hair all ruffled and his round faced beaming. . . .

To-morrow, I thought, we must get down to some serious maintenance. The vehicles were in a shocking state. To-morrow, too, we must arrange to bring up some creature comforts, tables and tents and camp beds and beer. To-morrow the adjutant must arrange for someone to get pay for the men and see if it was possible to send some of them to the sea for a bathe.

But when to-morrow came there were so many other things to do. Derrick Mullens took a party off to Sidi Resegh to see if they could collect any stores left there since last June. They found everything just as they had left it. A body still lay unburied in a slit trench, an artillery board was still standing and last, but not least, there was the battery commander's hat none the worse for lying out five months in the open desert.

Ten days later the regiment left El Adem for Cairo taking the old familiar route along the Trigh Capuzzo to Capuzzo, Sollum, Sidi Barrani and Matruh and arriving the 30th November at the Base Depot at Almaza.

Although we did not know it our desert fighting was over. In the brief few months since we left Iraq we had taken part in the longest and one of the most disastrous retreats the British army had ever suffered, had fought in countless minor actions as well as in one major battle, a battle that may well lay claim to be the decisive battle of the war, and had taken the lead in the triumphant pursuit of a beaten enemy which had followed that battle. The record of the regiment, during this period of great and historic events, was one of which no man need feel ashamed.

The men had lived hard and fought hard and the majority of them were not sorry to be returning to Egypt, to the safety and comparative comfort of the base areas. At the same time there was a general feeling of sorrow at leaving their friends in the brigade and of knowing that they were no longer a part of the 7th Armoured Division, no longer a part even of the Eighth Army. For if to the outside world the name of the Eighth Army was now one to conjure with and the story of its exploits had become known all over the civilized globe, with-

THE WESTERN DESERT

in the Army itself the name of the 7th Armoured Division, the Desert Rats, was of all names held in the highest honour.[1] Nevertheless this feeling of sadness was not so much due to the loss of those intangibles, honour and glory, as to the more solid advantages that accrue to those who fight side by side. The regiment and the armoured brigade, the men in the tanks and the men behind the guns, had trained together and fought together, had lived together and died together. They had become in the truest sense of the words comrades and friends, and it is always hard to part from one's friends.

But the orders of the Higher Command must be obeyed. In the re-organization of the Eighth Army that ensued after the battle, it was decreed that certain units should continue the pursuit, certain others should remain behind. G.H.Q. had demanded the release of a field regiment, composed of three batteries, to relieve the 31st Field Regiment R.A. in Cyprus and the Kent Yeomanry were selected.

Before leaving the Brigadier sent the following farewell message to the C.O.:

"It is with the very greatest regret that I learn that the 97th Field Regiment, Kent Yeomanry, is to leave this Brigade.

"I should like all your men to know that the keenness they have shown during the short three months you have been with us is very much appreciated. I know that the batteries have not only achieved the closest co-operation with the Armoured Regiments which they were immediately supporting, but from the reports I have received, I understand, that they have also gained their complete confidence. This state of affairs will, I am sure, make you feel that the work you have done has been well worth while, but I fully realise that such a situation could only have been brought about in so short a time by a regiment with a very fine spirit.

"It seems the greatest pity that we cannot remain as at present constituted, but the decision is far beyond my

[1] See Appendix D.

control, and I can only thank you for all you have done, wish you the best of luck, and hope that we may, in some other theatre of war, once again co-operate in as successful a battle as that which we have recently undertaken."

(signed) S. P. B. R<small>OBERTS</small>,
Brigadier.

22 November 1942.   Comd. 22nd Armd. Bde."

CHAPTER VI

SECOND INTERLUDE BETWEEN BATTLES

December 1942—March 1944

I

THE year ended with the usual Christmas celebrations in Cairo. The Kent Yeomanry dance band was reformed and F Troop of the newly-formed 470 Battery won the regimental football competition. Shortly before Christmas the advance party left for Cyprus.

On 15th January, 1943, the regiment, less guns and equipment, left Cairo by train for Beirut and, embarking at that port on the minesweeper H.M.S. *Welshman*, sailed two days later for Famagusta.

In Cyprus the regiment once more rejoined the 10th Indian Division with which it was to remain until the end of the war. The Division at that time consisted of the 10th and 25th Indian Infantry Brigades and an affiliated Armoured Brigade known as the 10th consisting of the 4th and 8th Hussars. All units were in process of reforming and training while at the same time carrying out garrison duties and local defence schemes on the island.

Having taken over the billets and camp sites of the 31st Field Regiment, as well as their guns and equipment, the regiment settled down to the new life, which differed from the old only in the nature of the training, now chiefly devoted to mountain warfare, and the nature of the country over which the training was carried out.

Cyprus is an island shaped somewhat like a saucepan, bounded on the north by a low range of mountains known as the Kyrenia range and on the south and west by a much higher and more extensive range of which Troodos and Mt. Olympus (6,000 feet) are the culminating points. The port of Famagusta lies on the eastern extremity some fifteen miles south of the handle of the saucepan. To the south lie the much smaller harbours of Larnaca and Limassol while due north of Limassol, about seventy miles distant, the tiny fishing harbour of Kyrenia is situated. On the extreme west stands the little town of Paphos, famous for the visit of the apostles Paul and Barnabas and for its association with the age-old worship of Venus, goddess of Love. The central plain, the Messaoria, lies between the two ranges of mountains and is flat and well-cultivated, filled with orange groves and fields of waving corn, save in certain areas where soil erosion and lack of water are responsible for barren wastes reminiscent of the desert. In the centre of this plain, some forty miles west of Famagusta and fifteen south of Kyrenia, lies the capital Nicosia, a low-walled town surrounded by a moat, with narrow streets, a small oriental bazaar, and a general air of having been asleep these thousand years.

To the men of the regiment the sight of the green hills topped with clouds, of ploughed fields and fruit-laden orchards, of well-kept roads and prosperous villages seemed like paradise after their long sojourn in the desert. In Iraq, Egypt and Lybia brown is the predominating colour. The sun shines from a clear sky. The houses are white, the shadows black. There are no half-tones, no soft colours. All is hard and sharp and bright. In Cyprus the colours are soft green and grey, and it does not need the smell of orange blossom and jasmine, the sound of bells on the two-horse carriages, and the sight of green fields and red pillar boxes, to remind you that you are once more in a country more nearly akin to Europe than to "the gorgeous East" of which, for the time being, they felt they had had more than enough.

Added to all this there is the sea. Cyprus is about 150 miles long and nowhere much more than seventy miles broad. It is difficult to drive in any direction for more than an hour without coming in sight of the sea, not the grey, sometimes sultry-looking sea of northern latitudes, but the blue Mediterranean, a sea of many colours from a deep dark unfathomable blue to the pale azure blue of a thrush's egg, full of light and tipped with the white of dancing waves.

Gaiety and laughter and light! Cyprus has been called the island of love and indeed it would be difficult to find a more ideal place to spend a honeymoon, a place where the moon rises over the mountains to make a golden pathway on the sea, where the smell of orange blossom is almost intoxicating in its sweetness, where in the hills a little breeze sighs softly in the pine trees, and in the plains there is music and dancing under the stars. But like all places suitable for honeymoons, a little of them goes a long way. There is always a thorn within the rose. Under the most innocent looking apple tree a snake has been known to lie hidden. Cyprus brandy is cheap and potent. Cyprus husbands are absurdly jealous and extremely quick with a knife. The Hungarian cabaret girls and other ladies of the town are not always what they seem. The weather in winter can be very wet and cold. In the hills the snow falls heavily and the wind howls across the empty vineyards; in the plains one is glad to sit over a fire in the evening. While in summer Nicosia and the towns on the coast are unbearably hot and sticky.

Richard Cœur de Lion, who to avenge a fancied insult to the Lady Berengaria, his future wife, captured the island in a fortnight, must have known about these things for he did not stay long—just long enough to marry Berengaria at Limassol and to spend a short honeymoon. Then having sold his newly-acquired property to the Knights Templar, he sailed away again on his crusade. A few years later, the Knights having failed to pay up, Richard re-sold the island to Guy de Lusignan, a Norman knight and the last Christian King of Jerusalem.

For over three hundred years the Lusignan family reigned as kings in Cyprus, and it is to them we owe the church of St. Sophia at Nicosia and a number of Crusader castles in the Kyrenian mountains of which St. Hilarion is perhaps the most famous and certainly the most beautiful. Cyprus then fell into the hands of the Venetians who held it for eighty years when it was taken from them by the Turks. The Turks, having landed on the island, besieged and took Nicosia without difficulty but Famagusta, which they attacked both from the land and from the sea, held out for four months. At the end of that period the Venetian Governor, Bragodina, offered to surrender provided the lives of the garrison were spared. The Turks agreed to this condition but, when the gates were thrown open, they broke their word. Entering the town they massacred not only the entire garrison, but many thousands of innocent civilians as well, finishing up by flaying the gallant Governor alive in the market-place.

Cyprus then remained in Turkish hands until 1878 when at the Treaty of Berlin Disraeli negotiated its handing over to Great Britain on payment of an annual tribute to the Sultan. In 1914, when Turkey declared war against Britain, the tribute naturally lapsed and Cyprus has been a wholly British colony since that date.

The regiment having arrived in Cyprus in the middle of January spent the rest of the month settling in. R.H.Q. was established at Athalassa near Nicosia, 385 Battery at Akaki, 387 at Angostina, and 470 at Kokkini Trimithia.

The island was at that time commanded by Major-General Ivor Hughes who, assisted by a Corps Staff, took a keen interest in all forms of training. An elaborate defence scheme against possible invasion was constantly revised and discussed, and training in mountain warfare was the subject of many lectures and practical demonstrations.

In the first week of February the regiment took part in a scheme in the mountains with the 10th Indian Infantry Brigade which began at Saittas and Mandria and ended a week later in the Evrykhou area.

On Sunday, 21st February, a combined church parade was held in the Stadium at Nicosia. It was followed by a march-past in which the acting governor, Mr. Shaw, took the salute. The occasion was the 25th anniversary of the birth of the Red Army.

At the end of the month the regiment took part in another large scale mountain warfare scheme with the 25th Indian Infantry Brigade, under command of Brigadier Arderne. Operations began at Zyyi on the 27th and concluded a week later in heavy rain, followed by sleet and snow, near Mt. Stavrovouni. This exercise was the first of many joint exercises with the 25th Brigade with which the regiment was to train and fight until the end of the war.

SECOND INTERLUDE

March was largely spent in shooting practice near Yerolakko during which air burst ranging played a prominent part. Visits to St. Hilarion Castle and other places of interest on the island were arranged.

On 12th April the C.O., Lt.-Colonel F. Lushington left the regiment to go to the Staff College at Haifa, and Lt.-Colonel W. J. de W. Mullens, D.S.O., assumed command.[1] On the same day the regiment moved up into the Troodos mountains to take part in an exceedingly cold and wet mountain warfare exercise organized by Corps H.Q. and appropriately known as "Exercise Tough". On 15th May the regiment moved to a seaside camp at Boghaz, some twelve miles north of Famagusta, and a month later the regiment left Cyprus for Palestine, sailing to Beirut on 14th June in H.M.S. *Manxman*, and concentrating at Arama, near Safad, the following day.

Since all guns and equipment had been left behind in Cyprus, the next few weeks were largely spent in refitting. Sufficient equipment was however made available to enable the regiment to carry out an exercise on 19th June with the 25th Indian Infantry Brigade which was watched by the Staff College.

The following account of the regiment's activities during the next few months is by Major P. C. Eliot, who had taken over the duties of second in command when Lt.-Colonel W. J. Mullens, D.S.O., assumed command. Major Eliot had commanded 387 Battery since August, 1941, when it was known as 470 Battery. He was succeeded by Major P. Mills.

"The period June, 1943, to March, 1944, was spent partly in Palestine and Syria, partly in Egypt. Training in mountain warfare, which had taken the place of the now obsolescent desert warfare, had in turn given away to the more fashionable 'combined operations'. The first half of July was spent at Afula in Palestine for 'dry-shod' training and the second half in 'wet-shod' training at Kabrit on the Suez Canal.

[1] Lt.-Colonel Lushington had commanded the regiment since 1st December, 1939.

"Dry-shod training consisted chiefly of lectures and practice in embarking and disembarking on 'Mock-ups' contraptions of wood and iron built to resemble landing craft and assault boats. At the Combined Training Centre at Kabrit on the shores of the Great Bitter Lake the instruction under both military and naval auspices was more comprehensive and the assaults made by night across the Canal sufficiently realistic to give one an idea what an invasion of a foreign shore from the sea might involve.

"The regiment returned to Palestine at the end of the fortnight keyed up with a feeling of adventure and expectancy which however failed to materialise. August proved a month of anti-climax in which we settled down quietly again at Arama to do nothing more exciting than carry out a few local schemes in the hills of Galilee.

"At the end of the month the Divisional Artillery consisting of the 68th (South Midland) Field Regiment R.A., the 154th (Leicestershire Yeomanry) Field Regiment R.A., the 13th Anti-Tank Regiment R.A., and ourselves moved to Demeir near Damascus for shooting practice. For a week in the desert, in grilling sunshine, firing exercises were carried out. Operations were concluded by a grand inter-regimental Athletic Sports meeting in the stadium at Damascus attended by all the notables in the district and enlivened by the strains of an excellent band provided by the French Colonial army.

"Practice camp over, the regiment moved back to the coast by one of the loveliest roads in the Middle East, the road followed by the first Crusaders on their long march from Constantinople to Jerusalem, by Alexander the Great on his way to conquer Egypt, by Pharoah Necho, Sennacherib and Tiglath-Pileser, and by a constant succession of invading armies of Hittites, Assyrians, Babylonians, Egyptians, Partheians and Persians. Branching off westward from the valley of Orontes towards the sea the road winds through one defile after another along the narrow passage way between the hills and the shore and across the isolated plains that are cut off from one another by the spurs of the Lebanon mountains. Through

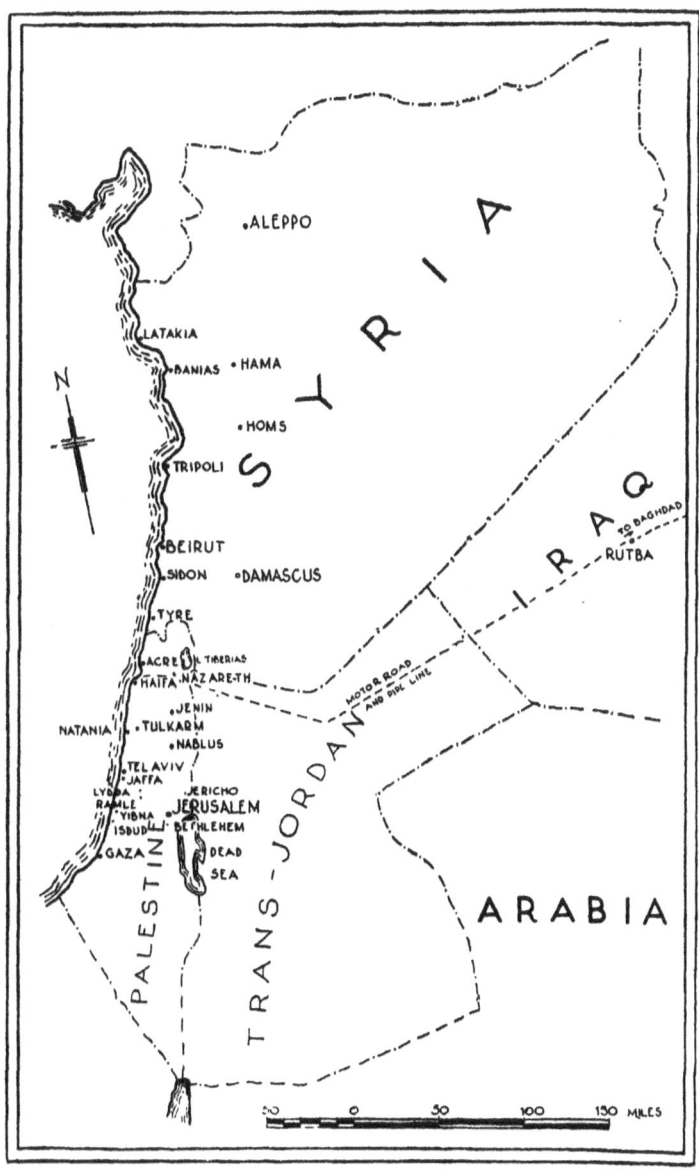

Tripoli and Beirut the road runs until it comes to 'great Zidon' and 'the stronghold of Tyre'. In the days when King Solomon negotiated with Hiram, king of Tyre, for cedar wood and fir trees to build the temple at Jerusalem, Tyre was not only the capital of Phoenicia but the commercial centre of the world, the parent of many colonies and the mistress of the Mediterranean. This great city, one of the oldest in the world, is now reduced to a tiny fishing village signposted for some reason 'Out of Bounds to Troops'.

"At Bayada near Tyre the regiment finally came to rest. After the heat of the desert the joy of sea bathing can well be imagined. But the camp proved ill-fated. A plague of malaria attacked us and within a week more than eighty officers and men had been evacuated to hospital. In the first week of October therefore we moved to Sidon to a well-found camp on the edge of the sea with excellent bathing and attractive mountain country inland. At the same time feverish preparations were put in hand for an attack on the Aegean islands in an operation known as 'Accolade Z'. The C.O. with a small Tactical Headquarters, disappeared to Cairo to form a planning staff. The rest of us packed and labelled, rehearsed and organised. Just before leaving for the port of embarkation however the operation was cancelled.

"By the middle of November the autumn weather made conditions in an entirely tented camp very uncomfortable and the regiment moved into winter quarters at El Bureij in Palestine subsequently moving to Isdud, one of the cities of the Philistines (Ashdod) further north. Here we spent Christmas, made memorable to the many who went to Bethlehem for the midnight service on Christmas Eve.

"The end of the year saw another short move into a hutted camp at Julis where the advent of 1944 was celebrated in the traditional manner.

"Throughout January and February the war seemed very remote and we wondered if we should ever take an active part in it again. The weather was wet but never really cold; training, though continuous, was necessarily restricted. A Practice Camp was established at Asluj in the Sinai Desert beyond Beersheba and troops visited this in rotation. Every advantage was taken to visit Jerusalem and other places of interest. The only pointer towards our

SECOND INTERLUDE

future task was the growing insistence on the practising of river crossings. An inter-troop competition of taking guns across a wide ditch twelve feet deep provided amusement as well as training while on the 'Brigade Level' large forces made imaginary crossings of non-existent rivers through the medium of 'Tewts'.

"March opened with a 9th Army scheme known as 'Crocodile' which lasted a week, and was probably the best and most realistic exercise in which the regiment ever took part. The object was to practice the Division in river crossing. Starting from the Jerusalem area it was directed on Jericho, thence across the Jordan (without using the Allenby Bridge) and up the passes towards Amman. A force to oppose us was collected from far and near and there can seldom have been such a large collection of distinguished umpires. The weather throughout was glorious and the hills on both sides of the Jordan were a mass of wild flowers. Owing to the excessive hospitality of the Northumberland Fusiliers the night before, the exercise went off to a shaky start but gathering momentum it never looked back and provided one of the most sleepless weeks of the war. We poured down from the wilderness of Judea to below sea level; Jericho repeated history by falling; we surged across the Jordan and up into the Mountains of Moab in a breathless rush. By the time that the signal 'Scheme ends' had been received we were ready for two days rest by the shores of the Dead Sea. This was brought to an end by the news that the Division was to proceed immediately to the Italian Front. For the last time we went in convoy down the desert road to Egypt.

"The nine months we had spent in Palestine and Syria had seen the transformation of the 10th Indian Division from a garrison force to a fully mobilized fighting formation again. It was a time of much hard work and no glamour; at times it was discouraging and we became restless with the inaction and the plans that came to nothing. How vital much of our work had been only became apparent later in the Italian campaign. It is doubtful if the Division could have had a pleasanter training ground. Though wet, the winter in the Levant is never really cold. The camps were reasonably comfortable and nearly all had cinemas and good sports grounds. For sportsmen there was plenty of rough shooting, for those who wanted to ride, horses could be had from Remount Depots, for the sightseer there were an inexhaustible number of places of Biblical and historical interest. We left Palestine with regret, enhanced perhaps by the fact that we left it at the time of year when it was at its greenest and pleasantest.

"Our last fortnight in the Middle East was unfortunately spent at Ter Hag which is one of the bleakest camp sites imaginable—a waste of desert, the monotony of which is relieved neither by the so-called 'Sweet Water' canal nor by the proximity of Tel-el-Kebir, the scene of a British victory in 1882. The distance of 60 miles to Cairo made it difficult to pay more than a fleeting visit to our old haunts. Luckily the stay was short and after dispatching the guns and vehicles to Alexandria, the main body of the regiment entrained for Port Said on the 22nd March. The following day the convoy sailed.

"We had passed one more milestone on the road home and were at least approaching the right continent. With this comforting reflection we shook the dust of the desert from our shoes and strained our eyes to catch the first glimpse of Europe."

The situation in Europe had greatly changed since the regiment had sailed for the Middle East. The battle of Alamein, the victory of the Russians at Stalingrad, the capture of Tunis and the clearing of the North African coast line, the invasion of Sicily, and the landing on the Italian mainland, these outstanding victories and successes had completely altered the whole face of the war. Whereas before Alamein the Allies had been everywhere on the defensive against the oncoming and apparently irresistible Axis forces, after that battle it was the Axis who were on the defensive and the Allies who were everywhere advancing with gathering and ever-increasing momentum and power.

SECOND INTERLUDE 153

A brief summary of events from the battle of Alamein onward may help to bring this period of the regiment's history into better perspective with the whole.

Early in November, 1942, while the Eighth Army were still pursuing the retreating Afrika Corps across North Africa the Russian offensive at Stalingrad began and by the end of January a German army of over 300,000 men headed by a field marshal and sixteen generals had laid down their arms. A second Russian offensive in the Caucasus was almost equally successful and by the beginning of March our allies had captured Kursk, Rostov, Rzhev and Kharkov, though the latter was lost again later in the month to a German counter-offensive in the Ukraine.

Meanwhile the Eighth Army had reached Tripoli in January and, joining forces in Tunisia with the First Army and the Americans in April had taken Sfax, Sous, and Enfidaville. The first week in May saw the fall of Bizerta and Tunis and the 13th of the month the surrender of all German and Italian forces in Africa. Over 250,000 men were made prisoners and a vast quantity of warlike stores and material fell into Allied hands.

This great victory, which finally freed the whole of the North African coast, opened up the Mediterranean and enabled Allied ships and planes once more to sail and fly over this great inland sea under fighter protection. Apart from the strategical advantages of quicker communications this was equivalent to adding a large tonnage to our available shipping.

The U-boat campaign, which throughout 1942 had gone badly for the Allies, also showed signs of turning in our favour. Whereas up to now the enemy had been able to build submarines by mass production much faster than the Allies could sink them, in May, 1943, for the first time the enemy losses were greater than their replacements. The use of improved radio-location apparatus fitted both to surface ships and aircraft and the building of large numbers of aircraft carriers were largely responsible for this happy result.

Meanwhile the Allied air attack on Germany's production had greatly increased in strength and accuracy, and by February, 1943, American heavy bombers co-operating with the R.A.F. were engaged in a continuous night and day bombing of Germany's factories and plants. On one German city after another bombs weighing nearly four tons were rained down in such numbers that the defences were smothered. The ever-increasing scale of these attacks brought home to the German people, as nothing else could, the terror and misery of war to which they had so wantonly subjected other nations and at the same time dealt crushing blows to the German war industries.

Throughout this period the whole of the Allied might was concentrated against Germany. But in the Pacific the capture of Guadacanal in the Solomons by American marines in February, 1943, was a pointer as to what might happen when the Allies found themselves strong enough to carry on major war operations on two fronts at once.

On 10th July, 1943, the Allies invaded Sicily and five days later a Russian offensive was launched in the Orel area. The successful landings in Sicily and afterwards on the Italian mainland were the result of many months of planning based on the experience gained by the Americans in the Pacific and by the British in a series of coastal raids of which Dieppe was the most notable. They would never have been possible without large numbers of specially constructed landing craft and the most careful preliminary training of both the Army and the Navy in their use. The establishment of air superiority and the employment of fighter protection based on nearby coastal airfields was another important factor towards ultimate success.

Mussolini resigned on 24th July and six weeks later Italy formally surrendered to the Allies. In the same month, September, Allied troops landed on the beaches at Salerno, the French landed in Corsica and the Russians captured a number of important towns, including Bryansk, Poltava and Smolensk.

For a week the fate of the Fifth Army hung in the balance at Salerno where the Germans, acting with great

SECOND INTERLUDE 155

swiftness, had concentrated the bulk of their forces. Finally it was saved by the arrival of the Eighth Army under General Montgomery, which landing in the toe of Italy on 3rd September, had captured Taranto, Brindisi, and Bari, three important supply ports and then advanced swiftly north to join hands with the Fifth on the 17th. A week later an offensive was launched from Salerno which resulted in the capture of Naples on 1st October.

Throughout the winter the Allies were everywhere on the offensive in Italy without gaining any notable success. The weather was bad, rain fell heavily, and the troops suffered greatly from the cold and wet more especially those who had been accustomed to campaigning in the desert.

On 22nd January, 1944, a new landing was staged sixty miles higher up the western coast on the beaches of Anzio. Taking the enemy by surprise the troops went ashore without loss; but they failed to take advantage of their initial success and four days later the Germans counter-attacked. The beach-head was sealed off and the Allied forces were only saved from being driven into the sea by the accurate and heavy fire of their own warships. Finally they remained, cooped up in a narrow bridge-head, four to eight miles deep, under observed fire from the surrounding hills, for four months, till in May the advance of the main armies relieved them.

At the end of the year 1943 the Russians had made further notable advances capturing Kiev. Berlin was heavily raided by the R.A.F. on five consecutive nights, large numbers of U-boats were announced as having been destroyed in the Atlantic and a conference was held at Mena, near Cairo, between Mr. Churchill, President Roosevelt, and General Chiang Kai Shek.

The Conference, which was held at Mena House in November was followed by another in December at Teheran at which Marshal Stalin was present. President Roosevelt and Mr. Churchill then returned to Cairo for further talks with President Inonu of Turkey. Three members of the regiment played a not insignificant part at Mena. Colonel F. Lushington was responsible for all the administrative arrangements and Lieutenant D. V. Clarke and Bombardier J. Walker were members of the administrative staff.

The year 1944, which saw the landing of the first line of the Kent Yeomanry in Italy, was also to see the landing of the second line on the beaches of Normandy a few days after D day. Henceforth both regiments were to be engaged in almost continuous operations until the conclusion of the war.

CHAPTER VII

ITALY

March 1944—May 1945

I

ON 23rd March, 1944 the regiment sailed from Port Said for Italy, disembarking at Taranto five days later.

The situation on the front at that time might be described as one of stalemate. On the right the Allies held the town of Ortona on the Adriatic coast. The line then stretched southwards and westwards through Lanciano, Isernia and Venafro to Cassino, and thence along the east bank of the river Garigliano to the sea. The key point of the enemy position was undoubtedly Cassino. In spite however of repeated attacks this immensely strong natural fortress held firm and it was not until the middle of May that after a six days offensive along almost the whole front Cassino at last fell and the road to Rome was opened. On the fourteenth day of the offensive the Allied advance along the coast made contact with the forces on the Anzio beachhead, the Germans were outflanked, the Alban hills were forced, and the first European capital to be liberated by the Allies was entered on 4th June.

The following account of the part played by the regiment in these and subsequent events is by Major P. C. Mills, M.C.:

"It was on a sunny morning in early spring that the liner *Franconia*, with the major portion of the Kent Yeomanry on board, lay at anchor in Taranto Bay. She had arrived with the convoy the previous night. Everyone on board was much excited at the prospect of arriving in sunny Italy at last and the bolder spirits who were rash enough to leave the shelter of the weather decks were the first to suffer disillusionment. There was a keen wind of arctic intensity which soon brought in its wake violent showers of snow and sleet. This state of affairs raised the gravest apprehensions in the mind of all the old campaigners who, with blood rendered thin by long sojourn in the mild climate of the Middle East, and further weakened by recent participation in a long and futile tactical exercise in the semi-tropical depths of the Jordan, could only regard their impending departure from the comparative comfort and warmth of an erstwhile luxury liner to the bleakness of a reception area with the deepest forebodings.

"These apprehensions were only too well justified by subsequent events. I have never been able to understand why it is that at the main port serving an expeditionary force, where convoys of roughly the same size arrive with a certain amount of regularity it is impossible to make any arrangements for the reception of the troops. The procedure on this occasion was so typical of many other occasions that I will set it out in a certain amount of detail. At a very early hour all the loud speakers on the ship started issuing long and detailed instructions, followed by various amendments with a result that everyone sat disconsolately surrounded by their hand luggage for some hours waiting to go ashore. (Incidentally if every soldier were given a pound note for every hour during which he has sat patiently surrounded by his kit waiting for something to happen, the country would be too bankrupt to consider ever taking part in another war.) After a time a somewhat garish looking Italian ferry boat came alongside and with masterly Italian seamanship carried away a portion of the gang plank at the expense of the entire port forward rail. After an exchange of bitter words between the ship's chief officer and the Italian skipper and a further long delay, the first stage of the disembarkation began. This consisted of struggling, heavily-laden into the ferry boat. For two hours nothing happened. Then the ferry boat started up and headed for the shore.

"It then became apparent why Taranto had for so long been the base of the Italian fleet. We headed straight for the shore and when it seemed that we were about to dash ourselves against the beach an opening appeared and,

ITALY

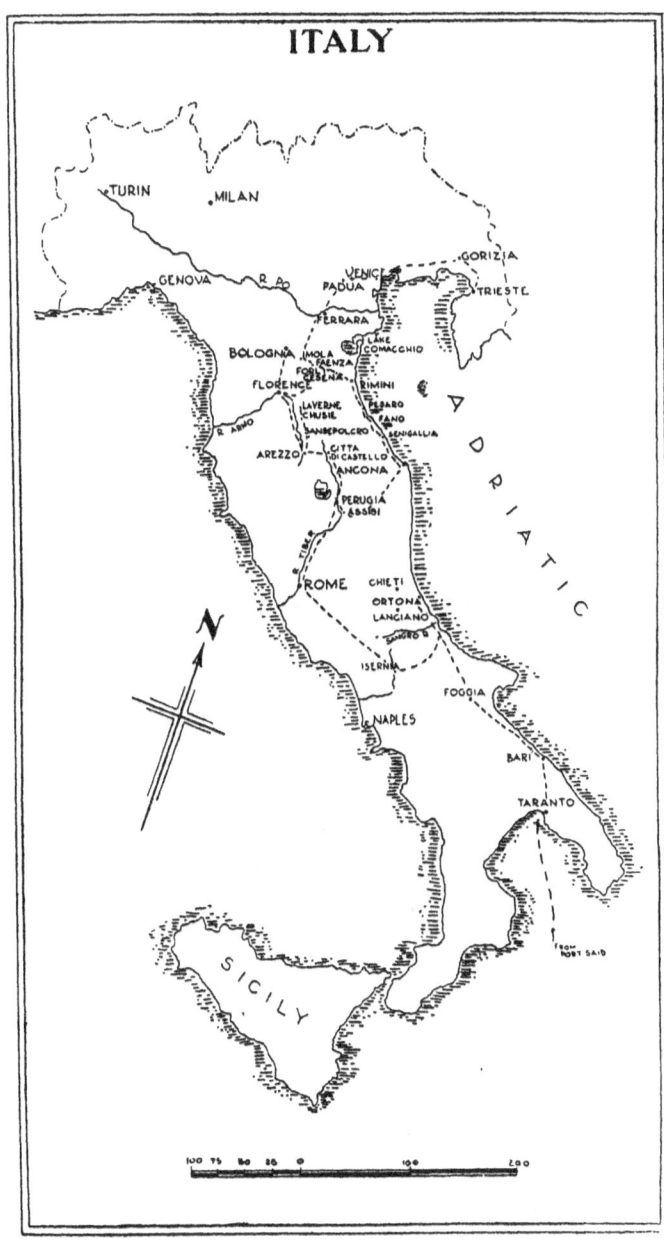

passing through a very narrow channel guarded on each side by a vast castle, we debouched on a huge inland harbour, entirely invisible from the sea, and there furthermore, anchored in rows, was the major part of the Italian fleet, cruisers, destroyers, submarines, all practically new.

"After a time we drew up alongside a dismal wharf and proceeded ashore. I might say that the wind had not abated and everyone was cold and already exhausted. We shambled ashore and huddled in a bleak and windswept field. We looked more like a collection of refugees than an invading army. I myself was wearing a sheepskin coat, had a service dress on a hanger in my right hand—I kept tripping over the braces which were hanging from it—a hurricane lamp in my left hand, a haversack and water bottle slung about my person. The C.O., in service dress, breeches and gaiters and also wearing a sheepskin coat, was suddenly seized with military fervour and the regiment being formed up, marched them off himself. This took most people by surprise. We followed just behind the R.H.Q. party, prominent amongst whom was the padre who, with the expression of an early Christian martyr, was clasping a neatly folded cassock and a small case containing his communion vessels in one hand and a distinctly pornographic American novel, which I had lent him, in the other. We walked, or rather shambled, about 6¼ miles! The pitiless wind continued and the showers became more frequent. Eventually after what seemed like a lifetime we arrived at what looked like a very muddy football field with a few bedraggled tents in it. In one corner there was a cluster of those strange modern witches cauldrons known as Sawyer stoves, round which were gathered the advance party which had left the ship early in the morning. The opportunity was too good to miss. The C.O. resplendent in sheepskin was striding ahead of our strangely assorted party. Someone started it and they all took it up. 'Baa, Baa, Baa, Baa, Baa! . . .' The Kent Yeomanry had arrived in Italy.

"Leaving the regiment huddled on the cold damp earth it might not be amiss at this stage of my narrative

ITALY

to sum up briefly the strategic situation existing in the Italian theatre of war at this time. Allied Force H.Q. was still in North Africa which was fortunately too far away for them to take any active part in the prosecution of the war. The landings in Italy had taken place the previous autumn at Salerno and Taranto. It was believed at the time that the secret armistice concluded with the Italians would ensure a rapid occupation of the entire country by our forces. Unfortunately these optimistic hopes were far from being fulfilled and the Fifth Army, after a stiff battle at Salerno had eventually captured Naples and started up the road towards Rome only to be halted at the great natural fortress of Cassino and its surrounding mountains, which came to be known as the Gustav line.

"The Eighth Army had been more fortunate and had advanced from Taranto without much difficulty capturing the Foggia Plain, with its aerodromes, on the way, but meeting with stiff opposition just south of the Sangro river. The two armies had been moving up parallel lines separated by the Apennines which are traversed by few and bad roads, so that control of the forces as a whole must have been most difficult. General Montgomery, who was in command of the Eighth Army, planned to launch an attack which he hoped would force the crossing of the Sangro. After the capture of Ortona and Pescara it was his intention to turn to the left and march on Rome from the north.

"After a desperate battle in appalling weather the Canadians crossed the Sangro and succeeded in capturing Ortona. By this time the weather was so bad that, with the troops at the last stage of exhaustion, it was decided to call a halt in order to gather strength for a Spring offensive. In the meantime in the South a force had been landed at Anjio with a view to taking the Gustav line from the rear. This venture also did not prosper although this bridgehead was found to be very valuable at a later stage.

"We learned that we were to take over from the 8th Indian Division which was under command 5th Corps in front of Lanciano. The advance parties were to go forward to do the reconnaissance practically at once. Our vehicles being still on the sea a party consisting of four officers and eight O.R.s per battery sallied forth by train and after a hideous journey arrived at Fossacesia which was the rail head at this time. We were met at the rail head by lorries and eventually fetched up with our old friends the 53rd Field Regiment (The Bolton Artillery) who received us with the greatest kindness and hospitality and made us extremely comfortable in a farm house in a valley. Even the Boche were kind to us as the shelling was unusually light. After we had enjoyed this great hospitality for one day we received orders to take over from the Canadians and not from the 8th Indian Division as originally planned.

"We drove to the right flank just south of Ortona and arrived about lunch time at the command post of the Canadian field regiment, whom we were to relieve. What a contrast to our old friends from Bolton! The Canadians, being a democratic army, seemed to have no idea whatever of how to make themselves even reasonably comfortable (incidentally the Americans are just the same). Personally I have always held the belief that any fool can be uncomfortable but that it takes a good soldier to be comfortable under difficult conditions. The Canadians had an officer's mess of sorts, but it was really just a back room to the mess cookhouse; their food was terrible and they dined at the impossible hour of 5 o'clock in the afternoon! The only arrangements which they had made for our coming was to put up a tent in a field and the B.C. then said, with the air of one doing a great favour, 'I have dumped a tent for you but I would suggest that you dig it in as we get quite a lot of shelling here at night.' Still suffering from hangovers, as we all were, we had to spend the afternoon digging ourselves a safe hole to sleep in. The Canadian gunners would stroll over every now and then to have a look at us. Doubtless the sight of a middle-aged field officer digging for dear life must have been one to gladden any truly democratic heart.

"So we spent Easter, 1944. I was much relieved when

ITALY

after two days the C.O. appeared and said that he had brought his car which had just arrived and was proposing to drive the B.C.s back to Taranto to collect the regiment. I might say that the whole of this recce, which eventually took three weeks, could have been done in 3 hours. So with great relief I joined Walter, Bert[1] and the C.O. and we returned to Taranto. At Taranto we found that most of our vehicles had arrived and after a week spent in collecting deficiencies, etc., we set off once more for the front, this time by road complete. On arrival we learnt that whilst we were to take over from the Canadian Artillery forthwith, the infantry were not due to take over for some days, so that I found myself in support of the Edmonton Regiment of the Canadian army, who were quite excellent and perfectly delightful.

"The brigade in this sector was deployed on a two battalion front and we took over three O.P.s, two in the right battalion front and one on the left. The layout was a fairly simple one and had been well established by the Canadians. When I arrived, Geoff Howell was already in Charlie O.P. with the Canadians. This O.P. was a perfectly beastly place, the top storey of a much battered house in a ruined and stinking village; the amazing part was that although it was the highest house still standing and although the village was shelled and mortared incessantly, it stood up till the end of our occupation and as far as I know is still standing.

"So we settled down to a role of defence with opportunity targets and harassing fire.

"After a few days the Garwhalis arrived and took over. Unfortunately their arrival synchronized with some very active enemy patrolling carried out by a special formation, and the Garwhalis having been out of action for some time, and indeed the majority of them having never been in action at all, the first few nights were like a Brock's benefit night at the Crystal Palace! About this time a deserter appeared in our lines and volunteered the information that an ambitious German sergeant-major, anxious for an iron cross, was organizing a raid on our

[1] Walter Prideaux and Hubert Allfrey.

lines on a house held as a strong point; unfortunately the deserter could not say which strong point. This information put every one on their toes.

"The raid eventually took place on the brigade front immediately on our right in the sector held by the Manchester Regiment, and I imagine the German sergeant-major got his iron cross, which he richly deserved as I do not think in the whole campaign I saw a better planned and executed raid. This is how it was done. A small party of Germans with a Teller mine spent the whole night working their way up to a house which was being used as a strong point. Two light machine guns were deployed covering the lines of approach. At first light the leader of the Germans called out to the section occupying the house to surrender. They refused. The Germans then touched off the mine and at the same time the machine guns opened up, thereby preventing any reinforcements coming on the scene. The whole party with their prisoners then withdrew under cover of smoke fired by mortars.

"After a short time this very active and efficient patrolling ceased and we assumed that these special troops were moved to another sector of the front. The Garwhalis, who very rapidly settled down, then began to take the initiative and scarcely a night passed without some patrol, supported by a fire plan, going out.

"So passed the month of April; a not too strenuous period with good weather and the countryside beginning to look quite lovely with masses of wild flowers, while at night nightingales and glowworms contrasted strangely with the constant harassing fire.

"We were unlucky at this time in getting very heavily shelled in the battery area by a '150 mm.', the command post receiving a direct hit and three good men being killed.

"Early in May it became evident that a very large attack was being mounted in the South with the object of breaching the Gustav line and marching on Rome. This took place on 11th May. It was decided not to attack on our sector of the front and towards the end of the month the brigade was withdrawn in order to undertake a role in

ITALY

support of the southern attack which was by this time proving most successful. The reserve brigade of 4th Indian Division took over and the 4th Indian Division was relieved by the Italian Folgore Division, who had been our enemies in the desert and were now reformed and recruited on our side. We were in support of the 3/10th Baluch Regiment but after a few days were relieved by the Poles, who, having captured Cassino, had been withdrawn from the battle.

The situation on our front was not without difficulty. We had been ordered after the relief to keep an O.P. officer and B.C. with the Poles, until they were settled in; therefore there were on our particular front, Indian troops supported by Polish artillery with two English Gunners attached to add to the confusion. That night after a day of intense artillery activity the Germans attacked in strength. Harry Wren was in the O.P. with a Polish officer who had never been in an O.P. in his life and could speak no English. I was with the Colonel of the Baluchs and the Polish B.C., whose English was confined to the words 'yes', 'no' and 'please'. Ivan Jones was with the guns. After a somewhat desperate two hours the attack was repelled, Harry having to use his pistol from the O.P. at one stage. The Baluchs sustained about 40 casualties but the enemy's casualties I should say were much heavier.

"The next morning we heard that Rome had been captured and that the invasion of Normandy had commenced.

"We proceeded to join the Brigade at Venafro on the banks of the Volturno river. The role for which the division had been earmarked was that of cleaning up the remaining Germans in the mountains in what had been the central portion of the Gustav line. But it soon became apparent that they were not going to wait to be cleaned up and the division therefore came into reserve.

"The weather being fine and dry the regiment was camped alongside the river in very low lying ground; unfortunately the weather broke and we were all nearly drowned. We had no tentage of any sort, merely the bivouacs which we had been able to scrounge, and the discomfort was acute. At one moment the Q.M. and his stores were completely under water.

"As our future role was going to be of a highly mobile character in mountainous country a period of intense training set in, and we took part in a most unrealistic divisional exercise, firing a remarkably inaccurate and ragged barrage. At the same time a new C.R.A. appeared on the scene, Brigadier Walter Goodman, who was an ex-I.G.[1] so that the disastrous barrage caused him much concern which he was quick to pass on down the line. Fortunately this time of discomfort, evil foreboding and strenuous exercise soon came to an end as we were required to take over from the 8th Indian Division to continue the pursuit of the defeated enemy.

"By now the enemy had withdrawn to the north and was fighting a rearguard action in the area of Lake Trasimene, the 8th Indian being on the right flank of the 8th Army, separated by the Apennines from the Polish Corps who had advanced up the Adriatic coast from our late sector without encountering very serious opposition.

"On the first day of our journey northward we passed through the fantastic shambles that was Cassino with the monastery like a decayed tooth standing on its hill. It was easy to see why it had proved to be such a bastion. On the second day we passed through Rome and proceeded up the Tiber valley staying that night near Assisi. The Guards brigade had just captured Perugia and the 8th Indian Division were on the right bank of the river level with the city. We took over from them the next day. During the night contact was lost with the enemy and the brigade began to advance up the valley of the river towards Umbertide.

"Meanwhile the 10th Indian Brigade were ordered to take over from the 6th S.A. Armoured Division on the left of the river. For this operation the 3/18th Garwhalis were placed under command of 10th Brigade, so that my battery was detached from the regiment.

"Crossing the river and passing through the lovely and comparatively undamaged city of Perugia we took

[1] I.G.—Instructor in Gunnery.

over from the Grenadier Guards just north of the city. They also had just lost contact with the enemy and after a rather uncomfortable night especially for the O.P. party who spent it in a house, the ground floor of which was occupied by some large and very dead oxen, we set off to try to find the enemy. One company with Geoff Howell as F.O.O.[1] occupied and searched a vast and commanding hill without finding any enemy. Another Company with Harry advanced from hill to hill and by nightfall had not found any either. Battalion H.Q. and myself also advanced without opposition. The Battery meanwhile was moving up troop by troop so that we were always covered. They had to contend with mines and demolitions.

"The next day we came up with the enemy rearguard. There was some shelling and then the forward patrol got into difficulties and had to be extricated under cover of smoke. It appeared that the enemy were holding the monastery of Monte Corona. It was decided to reconnoitre that night and attack the next evening. In the end the monastery was captured without a fight owing to a last minute withdrawal of the enemy who had been badly beaten up by the Baluchs on Monte Acuto which commanded the monastery from the left. The whole battalion then moved into the monastery and its environs in order to consolidate the position.

"I think this monastery was one of the most beautiful places I have ever seen. It was more like a walled village with a square and church in the middle and terraces of little houses all painted white and surrounded by little gardens and lavender hedges. It was filled to bursting with refugees of all sorts, one of whom embraced the Colonel calling him 'Liberatore' which embarrassed him more than somewhat.

"While we were at Monte Corona we received news of the rest of the brigade, who had run into some stiffish fighting, the Colonel and two officers of the 3/1st Punjabis having been killed. However the fall of Umbertide was imminent, and when this took place we recrossed the river and came under command of 25th Brigade once more

[1] Forward Observing Officer.

who were coming into reserve while 20th Brigade passed through them.

"A rather unsatisfactory period followed of sending companies off from the brigade to help 20th Brigade, one company of the Garwhalis being sent to the right flank where no enemy were suspected, ran into a stiff attack and being out of artillery range beat it off with their own weapons. The Company Commander won the M.C., and Peter Gordon, who was with him, had the time of his life. At this time we were subjected to one of the few air raids of the campaign, the R.S.M. being wounded.

"The next objective of the division was the town of Citta-di-Castello, which lay at the entrance to a small plain. The hills guarding either flank of the entrance to this plain were firmly held. The 4th Indian Division had come in on the left flank and were advancing from hill top to hill top and it became imperative to clear the hills on the right bank of the river. The 2/3 Ghurkas after a desperate battle captured Mount Gorgace and were hanging on to it with difficulty. It became necessary to capture the features immediately to the west of this mountain. This the brigade was ordered to do. The King's Own were to advance up the road which ran alongside the river and the 3/18 Garwhalis were to capture the ridges immediately to the left and slightly forward of Gorgace. The King's Own met stiff opposition and the Brigadier who was with them was wounded. The C.O. of the Garwhalis decided that an attack from the left flank was not possible so he proposed to the acting Brigadier (Colonel Anderson of the King's Own) that he should launch his assault from Gorgace itself. This was agreed to and a re-deployment took place.

"The reconnaissance was both hurried and difficult, the whole thing having to be done on foot and, as the right flank of the position was open, great care had to be exercised to escape observation. Shell fire was very heavy. The reconnaissance started at 5 a.m. and it was decided to put in the attack that night. The Garwhalis were to attack with all four companies. One company was to occupy a house on the right flank which was thought to be occupied by the enemy. Another company was to capture another building about 500 yards to the left of the first house and the remaining companies were to pass through this bridgehead and turn left-handed to assault the main feature. The Ghurkas then offered to move forward and occupy the first objective at dusk so that the Garwhalis would have a company in reserve. The operation would try to gain surprise and artillery fire would be on call. I had fortunately been able to register some of the features from our former position and my chief headache was therefore communications. As soon as I knew that the attack was to go through Gorgace I had a party laying a line by hand from the battery position; I also had my wireless set fetched up while I was doing the reconnaisance. As things turned out it was fortunate that I performed these wise virgin acts. We did not get back from the recce until about 6 o'clock and the battalion was due to leave their forming up area at dusk (about 9.30). I had a F.O.O. from 68th Field complete with wireless set on a mule who reported to me at this time. I also established a maintenance post at the forming up area and had a relay set as far forward as it could get (which unfortunately was not very far).

"It was very hot indeed and I had sprung a blister on each foot. Just when we were about to start a message arrived from the Ghurkas that they had found the house which they were going to occupy already occupied by the enemy and their patrol had been driven off with casualties. The C.O. therefore decided to stick to his original plan.

"It was a very dark night and it was not long before the whole battalion had got itself into the most appalling muddle. The approach march being across country and the guides supplied by the Ghurkas having no bump of locality we all got hopelessly lost. It was not until about one hour before dawn that the battalion arrived at their starting point and the attack was launched. The opposition was strong and held firm with a result that dawn found two companies pinned down, and they had to be extricated under cover of smoke. Also with the dawn it became apparent that Bn. H.Q. had established itself in full view of the enemy, which was not allowed to pass without attention from enemy artillery.

"Having extricated the two assault companies, it was decided to put in the attack again that night but on this occasion to have a strong artillery softening up programme. This was done and the two companies succeeded in attaining their objective and taking some dozen prisoners. The other two companies then passed through them. Just before dawn it became apparent that these two companies had lost direction in the night and were back where they had started from. It was then decided that the only thing to do was to commit them right away straight at the objective, that is to say instead of going round the flank, which was any way in full view by day, going straight into the valley and capturing the objective from below. This they did with spectacular success, catching the enemy, who had decided that the attack was after all not coming that night, completely on the wrong foot. A hastily put on fire plan covered them on to the objective, and the F.O.O. (Harry) who was already at the last stage of exhaustion, brought down accurate observed fire into the bargain. So what had started so badly and at various times seemed to be foredoomed to failure turned out a brilliant success. From the artillery side, although communications throughout were most difficult (the interference to the wireless at night owing to the heat and thundery weather was appalling) we were never out of touch and the firing of the two regiments (97 and 68) was accurate and unbelievably prompt. We were all a trifle exhausted as, by the time we had consolidated on the objective, we had been 84 hours without sleep.

"The 3 K.O.H.[1] then launched an extremely successful attack. Appearing in their Sherman tanks in country which would appear to be impossible for armour they took the Germans entirely by surprise and cleared them off the foothills at the approach to Citta di Castello, thereby ensuring the capture of this town which fell the next day without opposition, the enemy withdrawing up

[1] 3rd King's Own Hussars.

ITALY

the valley towards San Sepolcro with the 3 K.O.H. and the King's Own in pursuit.

"The Garwhalis meanwhile were detailed to hold the right flank of the advance, which was wide open, and they went into position at a little monastery and village called Belvedere. A quiet time was enjoyed by all and no attack developed, merely a certain amount of shelling, which was eventually silenced by our own efforts at counter battery, the divisional counter battery resources being committed on the left where 20th Brigade were engaged in a stiffish battle. The division was at this time on the extreme right flank of the advancing Eighth Army and it was decided to hold the flank lightly with various Army troops and concentrate the division on what had been up to now the left flank of the divisional front.

"The 25th Brigade were ordered to relieve the 20th Brigade. This was duly accomplished and we took over a very uncomfortable position on a ridge overlooking the valley of the Upper Tiber. Unfortunately all the positions were overlooked from a castle on a hill called Montauto, which it became imperative to capture. The Garwhalis were given this task, which seemed to be a very formidable one but in fact turned out to be comparatively easy, and a lunatic asylum, full of lunatics, a monastery, full of monks, and a large country house, full of refugees, were each occupied in turn.

"A plan to attack frontally by night after preliminary softening up by the artillery, a time being allowed to elapse at the close of the artillery programme so as to attempt surprise, was most successful. The enemy garrison turned out to be merely an artillery O.P. with about half a company of infantry and two heavy machine guns for protection. Having surprised one machine gun post and attacked it with a great deal of noise, the remainder did not wait and departed in such a hurry that they left cigarettes still burning in the castle and food still hot.

"The castle itself was not much damaged, the view was magnificent and we succeeded in making ourselves very comfortable, the only trouble being that we were shelled fairly frequently and accurately from the open flank on our right. We heard long afterwards that the enemy had expected us to continue our advance from Citta di Castello to San Sepolcro and our sidestep to the left had them completely guessing. Kesselring himself had held a conference at San Sepolcro at this time.

"Immediately to the north lay a deep valley and beyond the valley a really gigantic mountain, which was our objective. 20th Brigade, after a rest, duly launched an attack, while the sappers built a jeep track up the mountain immediately behind the advancing troops. This operation and the subsequent ones were amongst the most successful which the division accomplished in Italy. In the initial attack a foothold was obtained on the nearest peaks. These were held in spite of repeated attacks and vigorous shelling. Walter Hicks, who was assisting 20th Brigade was unfortunately captured with his O.P. party. The 2/3 Ghurkas were counter-attacked when they were short of ammunition and beat off the attack with the khukri, killing, it is said, 190 Germans.

"Meanwhile 25th Brigade, having been ordered to take over from 4th Indian Division on the left, were relieved by the Lovat Scouts. The relief, which was a difficult one, was accomplished in torrential rain and inky darkness.

"The position was a very awkward one, observation was difficult, shelling was very heavy and the battery lost 5 signallers wounded, one seriously. Gnr. Prout was hit at the O.P. and the Garwhalis carried him down on a stretcher by night a distance of three miles over appalling country and undoubtedly saved his life by so doing. Otherwise the position was not unpleasant, particularly after Bn. H.Q. had moved to a nice position by a little stream with a magnificent view southwards over Arezzo and the Arno valley. This move was expedited by the officers mess sustaining a direct hit, the officers' latrine being severely damaged. It was rightly considered that war is war and fair is fair, but such happenings are too much of a good thing.

"We remained in this position for some ten days and then took over from 20th Brigade on Monte Castello, on which vast height they were having a fairly sticky time as the enemy were hanging on to an adjoining peak called Regina. The move being completed it became incumbent on the brigade to capture Regina, which after a number of false starts they eventually did. The Garwhalis meanwhile were planning to capture a hermitage which was located on slightly lower ground immediately to the north of Castello. This attack was remarkably successful. The regiment brought down such accurate fire that the defending forces withdrew for safety into the building, thus enabling the Garwhalis to get right up to them and capture the entire holding force.

"The next morning a party of Germans, dug in on the northern slopes of the hill on which the hermitage was situated, launched a determined counter attack. In this engagement Peter Gordon, who was our F.O.O., went forward alone with a small W/T set and ranged the battery so accurately on the enemy's positions that not only was the counter attack dispersed but they were forced out of the position altogether.

"The hermitage was a lovely place with the most beautiful views in all directions. Its immediate surroundings were rather like a typical village common, with beautiful green turf, gorse bushes and blackberry bushes, on which the fruit was ripe. Not unnaturally it soon became a great vantage point for senior officers to make their plans and air their views, and scarcely a day passed without some of the Big Shots holding forth and gathering blackberries for all the world like a spinsters' outing; all this in full view of what was considered to be the much heralded 'Gothic Line'.

"Immediately to the north and across a valley there was a round hill with a monastery nestling in its side and trees of great height and antiquity growing right up to its summit. This was the famous Monastery of La Verna, one of the show places of Italy and now considered to be a bastion of the Gothic Line. This ripe plum was most tempting to the mighty ones who, observing it from afar, all agreed that we must have La Verna. Unfortunately our forces were considerably weakened as the big attack, which was confidently intended to drive the Germans out of Italy, had been launched and, although the Gothic Line had been breached, the 'unleashing of the armour' had by no means gone according to plan. The 1st Armoured Division was already in difficulties on the Coriano ridge. Forces therefore had been withdrawn from our sector and our plan was only to 'lean' on the enemy. Constant patrols showed La Verna to be held in strength. However constant harassing fire was kept up and two 'chinese attacks' delivered with the result that the enemy eventually withdrew and we occupied it without opposition.

"The regiment, who had been following the advance up the Arno valley, came into position in the village of Chiusi about a ½-mile from the monastery, where it was discovered that we were indeed up against the Gothic Line at its most impassable and no further progress could be made.

"We remained in Chiusi for about 10 days and then were ordered over to the east coast to assist 5 Corps in their advance.

"Then began the most exhausting and gruelling fighting which the regiment experienced in the whole campaign. In the first place it was now late September and almost immediately the weather broke and the wettest autumn in living memory set in; secondly the original attack, after initial success, had lost momentum and had failed to break through on the plain in time for the armour to be deployed successfully on comparatively dry ground. Furthermore a large proportion of the armour had been written off through being unleashed too soon and with some confusion at Coriano.

"After a week at Senegalia we were detailed to take over from 4th Indian Division who having cleared San Marino had crossed the Rubicon and were the left flank of the corps. Meanwhile on the right flank the Greek brigade had captured Rimini while the 4th and 46th Divisions were fighting up route 9 which connects Rimini with Bologna.

"The hand-over took place in the most appalling weather. The Rubicon was in full flood and the regi-

ITALY

ment just got over the Bailey bridge before it was washed away. It was not long before the division was once more attacking, this time to force the crossing of the Fiumincino river. The Kings Own supported by 470 Battery captured San Martino, which was overlooking the left flank, and three days later the Garwhalis crossed the Fiumincino and captured San Lorenzo.

"This was a very difficult and trying operation as, apart from the fact that it rained pitilessly for three days and nights, it was one of those operations which are a B.C.'s nightmare, i.e. those that entail a long approach march. This particular one was specially trying as we ran into the enemy defensive fire on the march and the wireless sets, which were being carried, became damaged and parts lost in the dark so that it became impossible to make up more than two sets. Furthermore the river rose to such an extent that it became impossible to maintain the telephone line across it. Being so wet wireless communication at night was most difficult. However, in spite of grave difficulties the attack succeeded, prisoners were taken and gains consolidated.

"The next night the 3/1st Punjabis (385 in support) captured Roncofreddo. We were then relieved by 46th Division who were on our right. However there was no rest as we were put into the line again at once on the left flank to assist 10th Brigade who were clearing the remainder of the ridge at a place called San Paulo.

"Meanwhile the Division had been joined by 43 Lorried Infantry Brigade (Ghurkas) who, with 20th Brigade on the left flank, were advancing rapidly against tough opposition. The 10th Brigade having captured Sorrivoli, the regiment moved into action in that area along what were practically impassable roads. So bad in fact were the roads that ammunition supply had to be by jeep.

"Having driven the enemy from the Bora-Della Vache ridge the Punjabis captured Monte Reale and the stage was set for the crossing of the Savio river. In this operation which was undertaken as usual in torrential rain the entire division was committed and when morning came although the river had been crossed (it was by now in full flood and a number of men were drowned) the net gains were nil. However, after a desperate battle the enemy was outflanked the next night, by 20th Brigade with 43rd Brigade on the left flank, and withdrew. The regiment then crossed the Savio and prepared to follow up the advance. The enemy however withdrew rapidly to the river Ronco and 25th Brigade eventually passed through 43rd Brigade and, crossing the Ronco by an aquaduct left behind by the Germans in their retreat, succeeded in patrolling as far as Forli airfield and the Rabbi river. We then handed over to 46th Division and withdrew for a rest at Viserba just north of Rimini.

"All these operations had taken about six weeks in the most appalling weather imaginable and the guns had come into action in places one would have thought impossible; also the gunners had been in action the entire time and had fired thousands of rounds, so we all felt that we had perhaps earned a slight rest.

"We were at Viserba for a fortnight. During our stay most people had a little leave and there were E.N.S.A. shows and a dance and a cinema. It was a very pleasant break for everyone, my own enjoyment being clouded at the end by the tragic death of Zinkie Leask, the C.O. of the Garwhalis, in a bomb outrage at his H.Q.

"The 46th Division's attack being successful we were moved to a position just west of Forli on the banks of the Montone river in order to support an attack by 20th Brigade. This attack was successful and the regiment was pulled out to support 25th Brigade who were to come under command of 46th Division, whom our own division was eventually destined to relieve.

"By this time it was well on in December and the days were short. The take-over was done in under 24 hours without proper reconnaissance, using the most awful tracks which were in places almost impassable. The brigade which we were relieving was in the middle of a battle with the enemy; and scarcely had the take-over been accomplished when the enemy, our old friends the 90th Light, attacked with vigour. For a time the situation was critical and we lost one F.O.O. (Bill Birbeck), and his party and even Brigade H.Q. was directly threatened, the Brigadier himself armed with a tommy gun preparing to sell his life dearly. However, the artillery which was fairly thick on the ground (two divisional artilleries plus an A.G.R.A.[1]) hurled a great deal of metal through the air and eventually the situation was restored.

"A few days later the rest of the division came into action and an attack was planned as follows: the Polish Corps on the left flank was to capture the high ground, the 10th Indian Division the ridge dominating the Senio river and the New Zealand Division was to advance under a barrage to the banks of the river on the plain. The initial stages were successful against really tough opposition, the Poles attaining their objectives, as did the Garwhalis on the left flank of the division. The New Zealanders were also successful but 10th Brigade, in the centre, met very strong opposition and it was not until the following night that all objectives were gained.

"This turned out to be the toughest battle in which the regiment took part. Both Jack Bazzard and Jimmy Baird received M.C.s for extreme gallantry under very trying circumstances. As usual it rained in torrents and the whole countryside became a quagmire. Jimmy Wigginton of 470 was killed in his O.P. in this battle and the infantry casualties were very heavy. The Garwhalis having captured Zola and Monte Coralli succeeded in putting a platoon across the river and establishing a small bridgehead. The next night 25th Brigade handed over to 10th Brigade and withdrew to rest, the regiment however moved forward to support the further advance and came into action in a position which was not only within mortar range of the enemy but, in clear weather, was well in view. It was in this position that we spent Christmas. Further attacks were put off several times and eventually abandoned owing to unfavourable weather.

"The Higher Command then decided to form a winter line. With this in view the regiment withdrew to the

[1] Army Group Royal Artillery.

valley of the Lamone while the infantry was established on the line of the river Senio.

"The next few weeks were taken up with the usual static tactics, harassing fire, fighting patrols, small raids, etc. At the beginning of February the division was relieved by the Poles and 10th and 20th Brigade went over to Monte Grande on the central sector, whilst 25th Brigade withdrew to San Sepolcro for a rest. The weather took a turn for the better and a most pleasant time was had by one and all.

"At the beginning of March the Brigade took over from the 85th U.S. division on Monte Grande. This was a truly remarkable experience. I had never before realised quite how much we differ in practically every way from our great allies. Not only in organisation methods but in outlook and manner are we poles apart. The 85th U.S. division was a first class one and everyone we met was perfectly charming, but oh so earnest and serious! They seemed to live their war like a page of the *Saturday Evening Post* and their officers were a cross between cowboys in Western films and 'executives' in financial pictures. I imagine that they found us quite as extraordinary.

"Having completed this take over I personally withdrew to England on leave on 17th March and by the time I returned the war was over.

"Looking back on this campaign I regard it as one of the happiest times which I have ever spent. To the ordinary civilian this no doubt would seem odd but an old soldier I am sure would understand this feeling. I see it all now in a series of little incidents, all lit by the clear blue of the Italian sky with the monasteries on their little hills with their cypress trees around them. I taste again the many delicious cups of tea drunk at all sorts of funny times; just before dawn during an attack; in the command post in the morning. I see again my magnificent F.O.O.s Jimmy Baird, Harry Wren and Ivan Jones with their parties, those wonderful signallers laden with their wireless sets waiting patiently to go out into some awful battle. I see again the detachments round the

ITALY

guns, with the brew tin sizzling on the fire and hear the order 'fire' and smell again the smell of cordite. I see the welcome figures of the line signallers plodding along in all weathers laden down with line and always willing and cheerful. I sit again on a hillside with Zinkie Leask and watch the light fade over the valleys and see Arezzo church tower in the distance sink into the dusk. Gone are the awful anxieties, waiting for news, faulty communications, coldness, hunger and thirst. I just remember the happy things and there were many of them. And when I think of these things, I know why we won the war, which we ought by all account to have lost and I know why we will win all future wars. The reason is just this: there is something in the character of all these people to whom success and adversity come alike but defeat is unthinkable. For after all is not 'Invicta' the motto of the Regiment?"

II

The following account of the part played by the regiment during the summer of 1944 is by Gunner Highfield:

"In Italy the particular phase of the campaign which lasted from 29th June to 16th September, 1944, covers the pursuit of the enemy armies which Field Marshal Alexander had initiated after the capture of Rome, and which came to an end in mid-September when the enemy halted once more to stand and fight behind his main defences known as the Gothic Line. From the point of view of the regiment this pursuit of a beaten enemy marks the end of a long period of waiting, of rumours and expectations, of hopes and doubts and fears. Since the battle of El Alamein in October and November, 1942, the regiment had seen no active service. A proportion of old soldiers who had fought in Africa, and a smaller number of those who remembered Dunkirk and St. Valery, still remained, but there were a very large number of soldiers who had seen no fighting at all and to whom the war up to date had meant nothing more than training and fatigues repeated ad nauseam. The 29th June, the date the regiment went into action in the area of Perugia, may be said to mark the end of this period of waiting and the beginning of a long series of battles and minor actions which were not to end until the conclusion of the war.

"The part of Italy through which the regiment marched and fought lies in the provinces of Umbria and Tuscany, in some of the most beautiful country in the peninsula. The valley of the Tiber, running North from Perugia, is particularly fine. The valley bottom, gradually narrowing, is filled with rich farmland, small villages, isolated villas, and farmsteads. Hills, often thickly wooded, and rising to heights of over 2,500 feet, guard its flanks all the way up. Just north of Citta di Castello, it makes an oval upland plain, surrounded by the southern ridges of the Apennines, among which it rises. The Arno Valley is similar, the country varying from a rich agricultural plain at Arezzo, to pine-clad slopes and mountain villages further north.

"Historically too, the country is rich. The Kent Yeomanry were fighting over what, in the fourteenth and fifteenth centuries, was one of the main battlefields in the struggles between the Pope and the communes of Florence and Perugia. The castle of Solfagnano, north of Perugia, had been the fortress of the Duke Orsini, while the towns of Arezzo, Citta di Castello, Assisi and Perugia, had all been medieval communes, and retaining much of their original character, were good rest centres for sight-seeing when this was possible.

"Tactically and geographically, however, the country was far from ideal. Almost every bridge over the tributaries of the main rivers was demolished before our infantry reached it. The wooded hills, which in England would have been called mountains, meant long and exhausting marches, for O.P. parties and infantry alike. Practically every track entrance was mined; the valleys were malarious, while what we learned later were at times 'the elements of five German Divisions', defended obstacles like the fortress village of Montone, with as much stubbornness and trickery as ever their medieval defenders had shown.

ITALY

"At first all went well. Opposition was slight and within a week the enemy had been driven back behind Umbertide, a distance of over twenty miles. It was not until the 7th July that the enemy made any determined effort to stem our advance and to gain time for his engineers to complete the defences of the Gothic Line in his rear. He chose his ground carefully. To the north, west of Umbertide, the village of Montana stands on a spur which commands the whole valley and it was here he decided to make a stand.

"A frontal attack on the village failed and the planning and execution of a second attack was then entrusted to Lt.-Colonel Anderson of the King's Own, who decided upon an attack from the rear, involving a long and difficult night march through enemy country.

"Mount Cuckoo, the battalion's first objective was some two thousand yards north of the village. Lt.-Colonel Anderson and Major W. A. Prideaux of 470 Battery led the column which started out at nine o'clock on a moonless night. The route had been previously reconnoitred by the intelligence section but a small amount of rain had fallen during the day sufficient to make the going extremely difficult. For fourteen miles over ditches, valleys and hills the long column wound its silent way and at length reached the foot of Mount Cuckoo. Halting the remainder Colonel Anderson and Major Prideaux led a small reconnaissance party to the top. On reaching the summit they were startled to observe a group of figures, mere shadows in the dark. The patrol, immediately on the alert, took cover, and were about to open fire when a voice came from the darkness.

" 'Cor!' remarked the voice. 'What a bloody march!' It was the intelligence section who had preceded them up the hill and found it unoccupied.

"It was then four o'clock in the morning and a divisional 'stonk'[1] was due to come down on Mount Cuckoo at half past. Wireless communication was established

[1] Rounds of gunfire from all available guns concentrated on the same target at a given time.

with the guns just in time to prevent this, one troop having already taken post ready to open fire when the news that the first objective was already in our hands came through. The main attack on the village itself took place shortly afterwards and was completely successful. Early in the battle a lucky round from 470 Battery made a direct hit on an enemy strong point at the entrance to the village. The infantry poured in and hand-to-hand fighting ensued which lasted for some three hours. About 100 Germans were killed and 70 captured.

"The success of Montone put great heart into the infantry and from then on events moved rapidly. The enemy, who had reckoned on holding this position was temporarily disorganised, and prisoners kept coming in on an ever increasing scale. Communication between batteries and O.P.s were more than ever difficult to maintain and the signallers had to work ceaselessly to keep things going as the tempo of the advance quickened.

"It took a fortnight to cover the ten miles on to Citta di Castello, but most of this was spent in the final positions before the town where the enemy put up a lively defence among the wooded hills and on a small water line. For the last stages of the attack tanks of an armoured brigade were brought up. Captain T. A. Bowring acted as F.O.O. with the 3 King's Own Hussars. His tank was destroyed and a signaller killed in an action in which the Hussars accounted for over seventy of the enemy.

"With the fall of Citta di Castello the general plan was changed. It was decided to make no further attempt up the Tiber valley but to concentrate in the Arno valley further west. The 10th Indian Division moved forward to occupy the high ground between the valleys and was responsible for the right flank of the Eighth Army. To assist the infantry advance the Divisional Commander planned to drive a jeep track over the mountains behind them. It was an ambitious plan as the peaks here rise to over 6,000 feet. Heavy summer rains had started which greatly added to the difficulties.

"While the infantry were making superhuman efforts on the mountain slopes and the engineers were struggling with the track the regiment supported them from positions in the little village of Anghiari. These positions which were well forward, in the case of two of the batteries virtually in the F.D.L.s,[1] were heavily shelled. Shortly after the guns had been moved a strong German patrol occupied the area.

"On the 10th August the Division extended its front still further west. It was now covering a ten mile frontage forward as well as the unprotected right flank, and communications were stretched to the utmost. In order to give closer support gun positions were chosen in the Arno valley north of Arezzo. With the O.P. parties well forward up the jeep track this meant a round of over thirty miles for the signal lines.

"Slowly but surely the whole mountain massif was cleared of the enemy. One of the last peaks to be occupied was Monte Foresto which was captured by the Royal Garwhal Rifles after stiff fighting. Anticipating the inevitable counter-attack Lieutenant P. O. Gordon of 387 Battery moved forward to a slit trench a hundred yards in front of our own F.D.L.s. Close defensive fire tasks were carefully registered while the actual preparations for the counter-attack were being observed. When it was finally delivered, deadly and extremely accurate fire was brought down within fifty yards of the O.P. and the counter-attack broken up.

"The regiment now left the main Arno valley to spend the rest of the period in the Apennines. The mountain valleys were small and steep, covered with woods of acacia, oak and Spanish chestnut. The mountain tops were bare outcrop and often precipitous. It was 'Partisan country' too, and information was continuously being brought in by friendly peasant folk. The regimental recce parties, when they entered the village of Chitignano on the 29th, found a warm welcome awaiting them, as they were the first British troops to reach there. For the first time the Kent Yeomanry found themselves as liberators. Civilians brought out glasses of the local fire-water into the street, and every one seemed delighted to see the English troops.

[1] Forward Defence Lines.

R.H.Q. was established in what had been the local H.Q. of the Fascists, and the regiment as a whole settled in among people who will long be remembered by Kent Yeomen as some of the most hospitable in Italy. It was even found possible to organise a local dance for those off duty, and with fifty local village belles as guests this proved a great success. Much work however of a more serious nature continued to be done.

"The country in which the O.P.s and infantry were working was difficult in the extreme, resembling the bluffs of Sutton Bank or the Cheviot country. The defence positions here formed part of the Gothic Line, and were pivoted on a wooded mountain on whose southern slopes stood the small Franciscan monastery of La Verna, rich in ceramics of the Dalla Robbia Brothers. This monastery was unfortunately for some time defended strenuously by German machine-gunners, and suffered accordingly. Heavy harassing fire was put down and eventually the enemy withdrew on 4th September, making it possible for the regiment to occupy positions near the monastery, around the village of Chiusi, while O.P.s went beyond La Verna.

"For another fortnight these positions were occupied, and were frequently shelled by the enemy.

"The weather now became very cold, with intermittent rain, and in the absence of any roads northwards it became evident that further progress would be difficult. The division had at the time made the greatest penetration into the outer-Gothic Line defences, and could expect no enemy withdrawal as a result of outflanking threats. It was with no surprise therefore, in view of this and of the opening of the main assault in the Adriatic sector, that we learnt on 10th September that we were to be switched over to the east to join in the attempt to penetrate the enemy defences there.

"The summer campaign was over, the regiment had been continuously in action for more than ten weeks. Thirty different positions, many of them up mountain tracks, and all within five thousands yards of the F.D.L.'s had been occupied. Nearly a hundred thousand rounds had been fired on targets of every description. The advance of over fifty miles through most difficult country was a tremendous achievement for the British and Indian infantry of the brigade, and the regiment was proud to have had the opportunity of contributing to their success by giving them the close and continuous support of their guns."

CHAPTER VIII

THE SECOND LINE
143 FIELD REGIMENT R.A., KENT YEOMANRY

I

THE following short history of the 143rd Field Regiment R.A., Kent Yeomanry, is by Major E. R. H. Bowring, M.C.:

"The regiment began its career as an Army Field Regiment and concentrated at Maidstone in September, 1939. From there they moved to Tunbridge Wells and in April, 1940, joined the Corps Artillery of the 4th Corps, then preparing to go to France. In May the regiment mobilized and in June the advance parties were in Southampton preparatory to embarking, when France fell and the regiment found itself one of the only fully-equipped regiments in England ready to resist the threatened invasion. 386th Battery was put under command of the 50th Division and dug themselves in near Bridport for the defence of a large stretch of the Dorset coast, while 388 Battery were kept in 5th Corps reserve. When other units became re-equipped the whole regiment was put in Corps reserve and moved first to Blandford and later to Winchester. By the end of the first year of the war the regiment had visited almost all the southern counties.

"In October, 1940, the regiment embarked for Iceland, where they joined the 49th Division. 386th Battery remained near Reykjavik in support of 70th Brigade, and 388th Battery moved to the North-West Sector with their battery headquarters at Borganes and sections at Blondos and Reykjaskoli. In early 1941, when the 70th and 147th Brigade changed their roles, the regiment was put in support of 147th Brigade and began a long and happy association with that brigade which lasted till the end of the war. In the summer of 1941 the third battery, the 507th, was formed.

"After eighteen months of monotonous and chilly vigil the regiment handed over to the Americans and

143 FIELD REGIMENT R.A.

returned to England in April, 1942. The next fifteen months were largely spent in or near Pontypridd in South Wales, a town for which the regiment will always have a lasting affection. During this period 386th Battery left the regiment to assist in forming the 185th Field Regiment, R.A., and a new battery, the 190th, was formed.

"In July, 1943, the regiment moved to Newmilns in Scotland, was converted to an S.P. regiment with American 105 mm.s (Priests) and took part in some strenuous combined operations, training at Inverary and Rothsay. In January, 1944, they moved to Hemsby, near Yarmouth, and remained there till just before D-Day. While at Hemsby they were re-equipped with 25-pounders.

"The regiment embarked at Victoria Docks, Tilbury, on 8th June, and landed at La Riviere four days later. The early days in Normandy were a period of very intense firing, and from the time the regiment landed till the advance to the Seine in August they fired over 150,000 rounds, or more than 100 rounds a gun a day. Sometimes guns fired as much as 500-1,000 rounds in twenty-four hours, for even when there were no fire plans, there was always a steady programme of harassing and counter-battery fire, so that in those early days there was little difference between night and day, and very little rest for the gun crews.

"The regiment fired their first barrage in support of the K.O.Y.L.I. in their attack on Cristot on 16th June, and the following day they fired another in support of the 6th D.W.R.'s attack on the Parc du Bois Londe, where both O.P. parties, in support of that battalion, were blown up on mines within a few minutes of each other. A day later the regiment supported the 7th D.W.R. in their famous attack on Point 102.

"From 25th June to 1st July the regiment saw a period of particularly intense activity. The guns were in action between Audrieu and Ducy St. Marguerite, and fired continuously in support of the three brigades of the division in their battles around Fontenay, Rauray, and Tessel Bretteville; and also in support of the 50th Division on their right, and the 15th (S.) Division on their left. The regiment will long remember the attack of the 11th R.S.F. on Fontenay-le-Pesnil, where despite the thick fog, it was necessary to bring down 'U' targets very close to our own troops in order to dislodge the Germans from their positions. The day the Tyneside Scottish were counter-attacked at Rauray was another day of almost continuous firing.

"The regiment left the division on 6th July for a short spell, and went to Caen to support 1st Corps in their successful attack on that pivot of the enemy's position. The regiment came into action near Lion-sur-Mer which they were later to know as a rest centre. On 10th July they returned to Audrieu, and a few days later moved up to Fontenay to support the 59th Division's attack on Noyers. While at Fontenay they came under some unpleasant bombing of the gun positions, although few casualties were caused as the regiment was well dug in.

"On 23rd July the regiment moved with the rest of the division to the Caen sector and again came under command of 1st Corps, this time more permanently. The guns came into action at Gibberville and O.P.s were established at Frenouville and Cagny. The country was more open than it had been previously and the regiment was able to carry out considerable observed shooting, not to mention innumerable counter-battery and counter-mortar targets and 'stonks' on Star Wood and elsewhere.

"It was not, however, a pleasant period, for the Boche had more guns and bombers than they ever had subsequently and concentrated them on this end of the front, while the mosquitoes were an added nuisance. Also 507th Battery lost their first issue of fresh rations by a direct hit on their cook's lorry. Casualties at the gun end were higher at this period than any other time during the fighting.

"When 147th Brigade moved to Vimont the regiment moved to Frenouville and remained there for a few days until the big advance began on 16th August. Once the advance was under way the regiment changed gun positions daily and sometimes two or three times in a single day. In a period of ten days most batteries occupied no fewer than fourteen different positions.

"These were an exciting and breathless ten days, full of the thrill of victory, and made more enjoyable by the enthusiastic welcome of the civilians with their 'Calvados' and cider. Alternatively F.O.O.s supported the Recce Regiment, tank squadrons and advance guard battalions, and some good shooting was enjoyed during brief but fierce encounters with enemy rear-guards on the rivers, Vire, Touques, and Risle. On 28th August the regiment reached Bourneville on the east of the River Seine and supported the Recce Regiment in their ferrying operations across the river. One O.P. carrier is still at the bottom of the River Seine, owing to the capsizing of the ferry. The troop commander was rescued clinging to his valise in the middle of the river.

"On 2nd September the regiment crossed the Seine by night over the precarious bridge at Rouen and came into action outside Le Havre. During the preliminary softening they assisted in neutralizing enemy A.A. guns while the R.A.F. bombed the town, and on 11th and 12th September they supported the division during the highly-successful attack on the port. Among other booty, Lieutenant Richards captured a German Admiral.

"After Le Havre the regiment had a short rest, firstly outside Bolbec and then outside Dieppe, and on 22nd September they moved into Belgium and came into action south of the Albert Canal at Zoerle Parwys. On the 23rd Herenthals was liberated and the following day 507th Battery supported the 11th R.S.F. in their advance at Turnhout. The regiment came into action west of Turnhout and from there supported the 146th Brigade crossing of the Turnhout canal, which was followed by some stiff fighting round Ryckevorsel and the Depot de Mendicité. On 5th October they supported the Polish Armoured Division in their attack towards Baarle-Nassau and shortly afterwards they took over gun positions from the 69th Field Regiment south-west of Poppel.

"On 19th October the regiment moved to St. Leonards and supported 56th Brigade in their crossing of the canal the following day. They then moved up to Wustwezel and were able to assist the 1st Leicesters and 11th R.S.F. when they were counter-attacked by Boche infantry and S.P. guns there.

"When relieved by the artillery of the American 104th Division they moved to Wildert, and then to Eschen, following closely on the heels of 'Clarkforce', for whom they provided several F.O.O.s. On the 29th they supported 147th Brigade group in their attack on the Boche outside Roosendaal, and the following day that town was liberated. For their part in the liberation of Roosendaal the regiment was invited to accept a flag from the inhabitants of the town on behalf of 147th Brigade group. Two days later the regiment moved on to Oud Castel and provided support for the final clearing of all the ground south of the River Maas.

"In November, a short interlude was spent with 12th Corps, and the regiment alternately supported 53rd Division, 51st Division, and 49th Division in their drive towards Venlo. While in positions west of Blerick they fired their first shells on to German soil. On 29th November, with the rest of the division, they moved on to the 'Island' between Nijmegen and Arnhem, and took over gun positions near Lent from artillery of the 50th Division.

"While on the Island ammunition was severely rationed, often to a maximum of only 7 rounds a gun a day. However, any worth-while targets were always engaged and there was a harassing fire programme every night—although, after so many 'U' and 'M' targets in the past, troop targets scale 1 didn't raise much enthusiasm among the gun crews. On 4th December the regiment were able to give the 7th D.W.R. some useful assistance during their battle of Halderen, particularly in discomforting the enemy's reserve companies, and for an hour or two forgot the ammunition restriction.

"Like all other units of the division the regiment moved around during the winter of 1944/45 and while O.P.s did the circuit of Bemmel, Halderen, Elst, Valberg and Zetten, the guns took over various positions on either side of the river. The chief discomfort on the Island was the flooding of the gun pits, though when the ground froze this problem was solved. The regiment was able to do some good shooting on various occasions, notably when the Leicesters were attacked at Zetten and, later, when 56th Brigade put in their counter-attack, and again when D Company of the 11th R.S.F. made their highly successful waterborne raid on the enemy east of Halderen.

"On 30th March the regiment moved to Cleve and supported the 3rd Canadian Division in their attacks near Emmerick on the east of the Rhine, and on 1st April they returned to the Island in time to assist in its clearing, which was done successfully during the following two days while the guns fired from Bemmel. The regiment's final big barrage was fired for the attack on Arnhem and they were proud to assist in liberating that town, made famous by the 1st Airborne Division. On 16th April the regiment took up positions in Arnhem and the following day, after a rapid advance west, were able to assist the 11th R.S.F. in their capture of Ede.

"Between 18th and 21st April 507th Battery assisted the Recce Regiment in the enjoyable operation of clearing the area between Appledoorn and the Zuider Zee, where they were greeted with great enthusiasm by the populace.

"The regiment finally ended the war at Lunteren, short of the Grebe Line. They supported 147th Brigade in their advance towards Renswoude and assisted the 1st Leicesters in throwing back an abortive enemy counter-attack in that area, which was proceeded by one of the heaviest enemy artillery concentrations fired for some time.

"During the whole campaign the regiment fired between 350-400,000 rounds of ammunition."

II

The following are some individual experiences:

Among gunners, F.O.O.s and their crews usually have the thinnest, if also the most heroic time, and on 21st October, 1944, three different O.P. parties had exciting experiences. On the morning of that day the 1st Leicesters took over Stone Bridge from "Clarkeforce", intending to spend a peaceful day holding a flank of the divisional advance.

The guns of the regiment came into action in the village of Wustwezel about 2,000 yards from the forward troops. The Boche, however, had more ambitious ideas, and at about 11.00 hours they attacked the Leicestershire positions with infantry and S.P. guns, and overran the forward platoons, penetrating as far as battalion H.Q.

Lieutenant Marriott, of 388th Battery, who had an O.P. with a forward section of C Company, suddenly finding himself confronted by advancing infantry and S.P. guns, engaged them with heavy concentrations of fire until they got within 100 yards. When the forward section was ordered to withdraw, he withdrew with it to platoon headquarters which was a small cottage nearby. Life there was not much healthier because an enemy S.P. gun came up to within 20 yards of the cottage, and, putting several rounds into it, set it ablaze. The platoon commander, Lieutenant Gaunt, got permission to withdraw the remnants of his platoon, and Lieutenant Marriott arranged a smoke-screen to assist the withdrawal.

The smoke-screen had not arrived when the platoon attempted to withdraw and Boche infantry, charging the house, captured the survivors of this gallant platoon. Lieutenant Marriott and his signaller, in some trepidation, lay still on the ground and the Boches, though practically stepping on them, left them as dead. Shortly afterwards the smoke came down and blanked everything out. Lieutenant Marriott and his signaller were able to crawl back to Company H.Q. From there they continued to shell the enemy with good effect, for Lieutenant Marriott had fortunately left his carrier at Company H.Q.

During the same battle Captain Frost was F.O.O. with A Company, the other forward company, and he also spent a busy day engaging enemy infantry and S.P. guns at short range until he was compelled to withdraw with the infantry and had to abandon his carrier, much to his disgust.

The third F.O.O., Captain Whitehouse, of 507th Battery, with his signaller, Bombadier Ward, had a most unusual experience for a gunner. He was in an O.P. tank supporting C Squadron 147 R.A.C. and when the Leicesters called for assistance from the tanks he went forward with the squadron to engage the enemy S.P.s. It was only the second time either he or his signaller had been in a Churchill tank and when separated from the rest of the squadron they were aghast suddenly to see an enemy S.P. gun only 50 yards away. With considerable promptness Captain Whitehouse laid the Churchill's 6-pounder, Bombardier Ward loaded it, and the R.A.C. Sergeant fired it, with the result that before the S.P. had time to swing its own gun it had received a direct hit. Almost immediately afterwards another S.P. gun appeared and Captain Whitehouse and his crew, emboldened by their first kill, suitably accounted for that one too.

During the day of this action the regiment fired over 5,000 rounds, mostly at ranges around 2,000 yards. The gun crews worked like niggers all day and greatly helped in breaking up the enemy attack.

EPILOGUE

ON 6th September, 1946, a party of civilians sailed from Dover in a small cross-channel steamer chartered by the War Office to take military personnel to and from the occupied countries of Germany and Italy. The party consisted of five officers and nine men of the 97th Field Regiment, R.A., Kent Yeomanry, who, at the invitation of the Mayor of Pérenchies were returning to France to receive from his hands the band instruments they had left in the town on 10th May, 1940, the day that Hitler marched into Belgium. For over six years the citizens of Pérenchies had kept hidden the drums and trumpets of the regiment and now they were anxious to return them and with true Gallic hospitality to express their pleasure at seeing once again their old friends who had been billetted on them in days gone by.

All the members of the party might with justice be described as veterans of the regiment, their combined service in the Kent Yeomanry amounting to not less than 160 years, and all of them had been actually serving with the regiment on the historic date that marked the end of the "phoney" war and the beginning of the real one.

After a somewhat heated argument with the E.S.O. at Calais they were eventually allowed off the boat and, their credentials having been examined and approved, were taken to the Transit Camp to spend the night.

On Saturday morning the party travelled to Pérenchies and after greetings, and a short discussion on the plans for the ceremony next day, were taken on by the Mayor to Lille where billets had been reserved for them. The afternoon was spent visiting old haunts. The men went to Monchaux where most of them had been billetted in 1939/40, the officers to Auchy and Visterie, the two villages occupied by the regiment before they moved to Pérenchies.

By a happy chance the day selected for the return of the band instruments was also the second anniversary of the liberation of the town from the Germans. By a less happy chance it also happened to be a day of pouring rain. The first half of the proceedings took place inside

EPILOGUE

the Mairie. At one end of the large bare room was a table on which the trumpets and side drums, the big drum and the big drummer's leopard skin had been arranged. In the public gallery the town band mingled with the crowd of sightseers. The members of the British party gathered somewhat self-consciously by the table were then introduced to the Mayor of Pérenchies and his town council, to his colleague the Mayor of Armentiéres, to M. le Colonel Hézard, chef de résistance, and to another French Colonel who was going to present medals to the members of the Resistance Movement.

While this was going on the room was filling up and a number of men with banners had taken up their position down one side, while on the other those who were going to receive medals were being lined up. A fanfare on the trumpets and three little girls advanced down the empty space in the centre with an enormous bouquet of flowers which, much to his embarrassment, they presented to Lt.-Colonel Lushington, the leader of the party. The Mayor of Armentiéres then stepped forward and made a long and impassioned speech in which "La Gloire" and "La Patrie" and "La France" and "Les Anglais" occurred at regular intervals. Still clutching the bouquet in both arms, in a manner reminiscent of a newly-made father with his first baby, Colonel Lushington made a halting reply. Taking pity on him the Mayor then summoned the three little girls to take the flowers back at the same time ordering them to follow M. Le Colonel Anglais wherever he went and on no account to let him out of their sight even for a moment till the proceedings were over.

The band then struck up the "Marseillaise", followed by "God Save the King", with a special French twiddle at the end, the banners were lowered and raised, and a young French officer in uniform read out the names of the members of the resistance movement alive and dead who had been granted the Croix de Guerre for gallant and distinguished service. Each name was followed by a fanfare on the trumpets and the French Colonel then stepped forward and after kissing him on both cheeks

pinned the medal on the recipient's breast. In the case
of "les victimes", the mother or father of the dead man
received the medal and it was a touching sight to see
some little old lady in her Sunday black crying bitterly
while the name and memory of her son was honoured.

Outside in the main square a big crowd had gathered.
It was still raining but nobody minded except perhaps the
notables standing on the steps of the Mairie who were
forced to discard umbrellas, coats and even hats in the
interests of the town photographer. A stickler for form,
he insisted on the British visitors alternating with the
French, the Colonels and Mayors standing on the bottom
step in front and the rest in strict order of precedence
on the steps above till they disappeared through the
doorway.

It was now necessary to adopt a new formation in
order to lay a wreath on the War Memorial, and a good
deal of time was spent while the town clerk and other
functionaries bustled about in the rain herding people
into their places while the small boys of the town ran
wildly about, making excited remarks in French and
getting in everybody's way, and the three little girls
with their bouquet stuck grimly to their post.

Eventually all was organized and arranged, the
Mayors and Colonels, British and French, in a row in
front, then the three little girls, then the rest of the British
delegation followed by the town council in column of
fours with the band on the flank. At a given signal the
band struck up the "Marseillaise", followed by "God
Save the King", followed by the peculiar French twiddle
which, not being a musician, I am unable to describe in
any other way—and in due course the wreath was laid.

The next item on the agenda was the march to the
cemetery behind the band. The cemetery was a mile
away at exactly the other end of the town. It was still
raining and it was not considered correct to wear a hat.
At least one presumed not as nobody did except the two
French Colonels who, fortunately for them, were in
uniform. At the cemetery the graves of "les victimes de la
Résistance", were decorated with French flags; and again

some time elapsed before the marching column could be made to adopt the correct formation and again the proceedings were somewhat hampered by crowds of little boys who wanted to see what was going on. Also whereas before it had been merely raining it now came down in torrents so that it seemed hardly the opportune moment for the band to play a long, slow funeral dirge. The dirge was followed by the "Marseillaise", which was followed by "God Save the King", not forgetting the twiddle at the end, and in due course the wreaths were laid, and the three little girls handed over their bouquet again. Conscious of duty well done they seemed totally unaware of the fact that they were wet through.

Those who thought thankfully that this was the end were mistaken for there were still the graves of "deux soldats anglais" at the other end of the cemetery on which flowers must be laid and where the whole performance must be gone through again. After which there was the march back to the Mairie in the rain with two bands this time, one in front and one in rear, both playing alternately with admirable spirit in spite of the handicap of the weather.

Back in the Mairie again we gathered once more round the British drums, whilst the Mayor made a speech describing some of the horrors of the occupation, of how the Gestapo had three times searched every house in the town from cellar to garret, but had never found the band instruments, which were hidden under a pile of gasmasks and anti-gas clothing in the secretary's office, nor had they found his friend the head of the Resistance who had concealed himself in a well in the garden on the cover of which he had thoughtfully sprinkled some pepper to deceive the German "chiens de chasse". Replying in suitable terms Colonel Lushington presented the Mayor with a silver salver inscribed in English "To our friends and allies in Pérenchies as a token of admiration and gratitude from all ranks of the 97th Field Regiment, R.A., Kent Yeomanry" with the two dates 10th May, 1940, and 8th September, 1946.

From then on the sequence of events is less clear. Wine

was produced, healths were drunk, the three little girls kissed everyone and were kissed in return, those people in the town who had had members of the regiment billetted on them in 1940 insisted on their coming to their houses to drink more wine, the members of the Resistance held an impromptu party in the local "Debit du Buissons" where souvenirs in the shape of home-made grenades and other lethal weapons were produced and the visitors pressed to take them home. Finally M. le Colonel Hézard swept all the officers off to Lille where they ate the largest luncheon that any of them had seen since the days before the war and consumed quantities more wine. In the evening a special dance was held for the men and all day long and all night the hospitality went on so that by next morning when the party rose early to catch the train to Calais even the strongest felt it was just as well they were not staying another day. It had been a wonderful experience, we had enjoyed every moment of it, but the human frame is only capable of standing a certain amount, either of pleasure or pain, and the limit of endurance is soon reached. And so with many protestations of undying friendship and demands on the one side that they should come again and stay longer, and promises on the other that they most certainly would, the men of the Kent Yeomanry said good-bye to their kind hosts and steamed away.

This visit to old haunts left one member of the party at any rate with the firm conviction that it is only by the daily common intercourse of the common man of one nation with the common man of another that friendship between nations can be achieved, misunderstandings ironed out, suspicions proved unfounded, and unity and concord, peace and happiness made the rule instead of the exception.

Mr. Churchill in a recent speech (September, 1946) has thus described the present state of Europe:

"Among the victors there is a babel of voices, among the vanquished the sullen silence of despair. ... Is the only lesson of history to be that mankind is unteachable?

EPILOGUE

Let there be justice, mercy and freedom. The people have only to will it and all will achieve their hearts' desire."

He might have added "Let there be love and friendship among the people". Surely it does not need a world war for these qualities to be born and to find expression among the widely different nations of which Europe is composed? If a tithe of the goodwill and friendship shown by the people of Pérenchies for their British guests was shown by the people of the world, not necessarily for their enemies, but even for their alleged friends, there would be no need for Peace Conferences with their "babel of voices", no cause for the sullen silence of despair among the vanquished.

Just as in war the men in a regiment, thrown together from different places and from widely different spheres of life, by enforced proximity learn mutual tolerance and mutual understanding, which, as time goes on, blossoms into what is known as "the spirit of the regiment", a mixture of comradeship and pride and love, so in peace the men and women of different nations must somehow learn the value and worth of these qualities, not only within the family circle, but within the circle of the world at large. And how can they learn them except by personal contact, by a proximity free and unenforced? Let us abolish visas and passports and all the maddening restrictions on travel, open up the frontiers and let every man see for himself how his neighbour is living and discover what he is really doing and thinking and feeling instead of reading highly-coloured and distorted accounts in the newspapers. Finally "Let there be justice, mercy and freedom, love and understanding and friendship. The peoples have only to will it and all will achieve their hearts' desire."

By a coincidence I finished writing this short history on the fourth anniversary of the battle of Alamein. I feel I cannot do better than conclude with the words of two men blinded in the battle who sat near me that night in a box at the Albert Hall:

"We have learned something from our wounds. We do not think we have lost anything if people have learned a lesson and decide that they will try to live together, work together and never engage again in killing each other."

Pigeon Hoo, Tenterden, Kent.
24th October, 1946.

APPENDIX A

Commanding Officers, 97th Field Regiment R.A., Kent Yeomanry

Sept., 1921–Sept., 1925, Lieut.-Col. N. I. E. Twistleton-Wykeham-Fiennes, D.S.O.
Sept., 1925–Sept., 1930, Lieut.-Col. Halford H. Dawes, O.B.E., T.D.
Sept., 1930–Sept., 1936, Lieut.-Col. C. E. Ponsonby, T.D.
Sept., 1936–Dec., 1939, Lieut.-Col. H. W. Lucy, O.B.E., T.D.
Dec., 1939–Apr., 1943, Lieut.-Col. F. Lushington.
Apr., 1943–Sept., 1945, Lieut.-Col. W. J. H. de W. Mullens, D.S.O.

Commanding Officers, 143rd Field Regiment R.A., Kent Yeomanry.

Outbreak of War–Aug., 1942, Lt.-Col. F. N. Richardson, T.D.
Sept., 1942–May, 1943, Lt.-Col. W. J. N. Norman Walker, M.B.E.
May, 1943–July, 1944, Lt.-Col. D. S. Hamilton, D.S.O.
July, 1944–Sept., 1944, Lt.-Col. E. H. N. Rees-Webb
Sept., 1944–July, 1945, Lt.-Col. D. S. Hamilton, D.S.O.
July, 1945–March, 1946, Lt.-Col. C. D. T. Pope

APPENDIX B

R.A. 5 Div Operation Order No. 15.   SECRET.,
                                     Copy No..........
Ref Map. 1/250,000.   28 May 40.

INFORMATION

1. B.E.F. is withdrawing to a bridge head covering NIEUPORT and DUNUERQUE.

2. 5 Div is withdrawing after dark tonight to a posn facing S.E. between NOORDSCHOTE H 57 and DIXMUDE.

3. A lager for surplus personnel is established in the area BULSCAMP H 48—HOOGSTADE H 47—BEUEREN H 47—HOUTREM H 48—5 Div personnel should report to either BEUEREN or HOOGSTADE.

METHOD

4. Units will move in the lightest possible order. Equipment and vehicles left behind will be systematically destroyed as far as possible, but in the interests of secrecy will NOT BE BURNT.

A suggested list of vehicles to be left behind etc. is in Appx "A".

5. *Guns.* All guns will move with one trailer between gun and tractor. The tractor and trailer will be full of amn (H.E. only). One spare tractor will move at tail of each regt, remaining tractors will be destroyed. A.P. shot will be taken.

6. *Baggage.* The following will be left behind—

        Officers' Mess.
        Officers' Kits.
        All unit equipment.
        Cooking gear.
        Gas stores.

The only exception will be what officers and men stand up in plus sufficient gear to make tea for the men, and the minimum possible equipment to fight the guns.

7. *Rations.* Personnel will carry one day's preserved rations on the man.

8. *18-Pr. Equipments.* All 18-pr. equipments will be destroyed on present posns before withdrawing and 18-pr. btys will take away personnel only.

9. *Communications.* W/T sets will be retained. All other signalling equipment will be destroyed and left. R.A.F. sets will be destroyed.

10. *Weapons.* All small arms and a normal echelon of amn for them will be taken.

11. *Papers.* All papers will be burnt and all maps not required for the move will be buried.

12. *Personnel.* After unloading on lines of Appx "A" units will load emptied 30 cwts with remaining personnel as full as possible.

Any surplus 30-cwt or 3 ton lorries remaining after para 13 has been complied with will be reported immediately to this H.Q. as they will be wanted for other personnel.

13. *Lorries.* 3 ton lorries for carrying wounded will be dispatched as follows:—

    18 Fd Regt—4 to M.D. 3 LOCRE 5054.
    97 Fd Regt—2 to A.D.S. 556501.
    9 Fd Regt—2 to A.D.S. WYTSHAETE 5854.
    91 Fd Regt—2 to A.D.S. VIERSTAAD 5655.
    All to report by 14.00 hrs.

14. *Spare personnel* not wanted for fighting the guns will be sent FORTHWITH to the spare personnel lager.

15. *Evacuation of present posns.*
Further orders will be issued. All Gun amn except that mentioned in para. 5, may be expended by 21.30 hrs. tonight.

16. *Route*—later.

17. The present posn must be held until the time given as the safety of the B.E.F. entirely depends on this.

                                            Capt. R.A.,
ACK.   B.M.R.A. 5 Div.,
Issued to Sigs at .... 11.15 hours.
Distribution—Copy No.   etc.   etc.

APPENDIX C

97TH FIELD REGIMENT, R.A.
HONOURS AND AWARDS

D.S.O. and Bar
Lt.-Col. W. J. de W. Mullens	385 & R.H.Q.

D.S.O.
Capt. M. C. Allfrey	385

M.C.
Major H. M. Allfrey	387
„ P. C. Mills	387
„ W. A. Prideaux	470
Capt. J. R. G. Baird	387
„ T. A. Bowring	470
„ C. A. W. Dawes	385
„ P. C. Mills	385
„ J. Watt, R.A.M.C.	R.H.Q.
„ H. M. Wix	385
Lieut. J. C. Bazzard	385

M.B.E.
Major P. C. Eliot	R.H.Q.
Capt. (Q.M.) W. E. Walker	R.H.Q.

D.C.M.
B.S.M. E. Janes	385
Sgt. J. R. Romaines, R.C.S.	R.H.Q.

M.M.
R.S.M. P. E. Baker	R.H.Q.
Sgt. A. H. Crouch	385
Bdr. J. Crowe	
Gnr. J. H. Grave	
Sgt. E. G. Harris	385
Bdr. R. Herdman	385
R.S.M. H. R. Peters	385
L/Sgt. J. G. Willmott	385

APPENDICES

Mentioned in Despatches

Lt.-Col. F. Lushington	R.H.Q.
Lt.-Col. W. J. de W. Mullens	385
Major D. B. H. Warner	R.H.Q.
Major C. W. Johnson	385
Capt. N. A. Campbell	R.H.Q.
Capt. A. A. Hicks	R.H.Q.
Capt. T. A. Bowring	470
Lt. J. R. Romaines, R.C.S.	R.H.Q.
L/Bdr. L. Streeting	385
L/Bdr. J. Mitchell	387
Gnr. R. Bower	387

143 FIELD REGIMENT, R.A.

HONOURS AND AWARDS

D.S.O.

Lt.-Col. D. S. Hamilton

M.C.

Major E. R. H. Bowring
Capt. D. J. Brabin (while with the 185 Field Regiment, R.A.)
Capt. P. R. R. Coad
Capt. D. R. Frost
Lieut. D. H. Marriott

M.M.

Sgt. W. G. Stace

M.B.E.

R.S.M. J. Burr

Croix de Guerre (Gilt Star)

Capt. R. F. G. Roberts, R.A.

Croix de Guerre (Bronze Star)
Gnr. M. J. Wood,

Mentioned in Despatches
Lt.-Col. D. S. Hamilton
Major E. R. H. Bowring
Major S. B. Childs,
Major E. H. N. Rees-Webbe
Capt. H. H. K. Woodman
Capt. D. R. Frost
Capt. R. J. Whitehouse
Capt. P. H. Williams,
B.S.M. C. W. Woodhouse
Sgt. H. T. Sargent
Sgt. W. G. Stace
Sgt. S. G. Thomsit
Cpl. L. W. Smith
Gnr. F. H. Chapman
Gnr. F. J. Richardson

Commander-in-Chief's Certificate
R.S.M. J. E. Rycroft
Sgt. D. N. Meneaud-Lissenburg
Sgt. W. R. Richards
L/Sgt. C. E. Broughton
L/Sgt. W. E. Tanner
L/Sgt. G. Weedon
Bdr. J. E. Andrews
Bdr. D. E. W. Kerley
Bdr. H. P. Morgan
Bdr. A. A. P. Vine
Bdr. J. C. Ward
L/Bdr. J. E. W. Hamilton
L/Bdr. R. T. Lawrence
L/Bdr. D. Waters
Gnr. B. Beeston
Gnr. R. Brown
Gnr. S. G. Smee

APPENDIX D

Extract from speech by Mr. Churchill to the 7th Armoured Division in Berlin, 21st July, 1945:

"Dear Desert Rats, may your glory ever shine. May your laurels never fade. May the memory of this glorious pilgrimage which you have made from Alamein to the Baltic and Berlin never die. A march—as far as my reading of history leads me to believe—unsurpassed in the whole history of war. May fathers long tell their children the tale. May you all feel that through following your great ancestors you have accomplished something which has done good to the whole world, which has raised the honour of your country and of which every man has the right to feel proud."

APPENDIX E

ROLL OF HONOUR

(97th Field Regiment Kent Yeomanry)

Allfrey, M. C.	Captain
Anderson, W. T.	L/Bdr.
Angus, L. D.	Gnr.
Austen, D. S.	Gnr.
Austen, E. J. C.	Gnr.
Biggleston, D. H.	Lieut.
Burgess, L. G.	Sergt.
Brown	Sergt.
Bingham, W. H.	L/Sgt.
Bourne, A. B.	L/Sgt.
Birch, R. A.	Bdr.
Bewsher, J. D. H.	L/Bdr.
Barron, W. A. W.	Gnr.
Bartlett, S. J.	Gnr.

ROLL OF HONOUR

Bassett, H. F.	Gnr.
Bint, F. W.	Gnr.
Bloomfield, K. G.	Gnr.
Brooks, G. A. A.	Gnr.
Bowerman, D.	Gnr.
Butler, L. R.	Gnr.
Basterfield, J. R.	Gnr.
Connell, H. A.	Lieut.
Collard, S. J.	Bdr.
Crown	L/Bdr.
Clarke, A.	Gnr.
Cotter, J. H.	Gnr.
Cole, R. D.	Gnr.
Cronshaw, J.	Gnr.
Dines, S. J.	Gnr.
Emery, G. F. S.	Gnr.
Epps, S. C.	Gnr.
Etheridge, R. E.	Gnr.
Euesden, G. C. W.	Gnr.
Evans, G. L.	Gnr.
Frost, W. A.	Bdr.
Ferguson, R. A.	Gnr.
Flisher, G. W.	Gnr.
Fincham, J. R. F.	Gnr.
Gawler, H.	L/Bdr.
Green, H. G.	L/Bdr.
Goody, F.	Gnr.
Griffin, A. J.	L/Bdr.
Groom, C. W. E.	Gnr.
Harris, P. G.	B.S.M.
Hills, G.	Sergt.
Hobbs, A. G.	Sergt.
Hague, R. W.	L/Sgt.
Haste, A. V.	Bdr.
Hamill, J. M.	Gnr.
Hammond, A. S.	Gnr.
Harvey, D. V.	Gnr.
Howlett, G. J. H.	Gnr.
Hughes, J. G.	Gnr.

APPENDICES

ROLL OF HONOUR

Hullis, L. B.	Gnr.
Janes, D.	Gnr.
Jenkins, C. T.	Gnr.
Jillians, L. W. J.	Gnr.
Jones, C.	Gnr.
Jones, E. S.	Gnr.
Jones, R.	Gnr.
Kay, N. D.	L/Bdr.
Kelly, G. W.	Gnr.
Lambourne, G. A.	Gnr.
Liddiatt, F. T.	Gnr.
Marsh, F. P.	Bdr.
Macleod, K. M.	Gnr.
Marshall, B. M.	Gnr.
McCullin, J.	Gnr.
McGarva, D.	Gnr.
Meekings, A. J.	Bdr.
Molineux, R. D.	Gnr.
Murrell, B. W.	Gnr.
Murphy, T. I.	Gnr.
Morrison, H.	Gnr.
Marr, T. M.	Gnr.
Neal, J. B.	L/Sgt.
Neale, D. W. T.	Gnr.
Norrington, A. W.	Gnr.
Oxley, L. W. F.	Gnr.
Piddock, C. H.	Staff Sgt.
Phillips, P. W.	L/Bdr.
Palmer, C.	Gnr.
Parr, H.	Gnr.
Parkinson, R.	Gnr.
Parsons, J. H.	Gnr.
Parsons, W.	Gnr.
Perkins, G. A.	Gnr.
Poole, E. G.	Gnr.
Potter, F. E.	L/Bdr.
Pullen, J.	Gnr.
Rintoul, D. F.	Bdr.
Ralph, H.	Gnr.

ROLL OF HONOUR

Relf, C. T.	Gnr.
Roberts, E.	Gnr.
Rogers, K. J.	Gnr.
Robinson, J.	Gnr.
Smith, J. E.	Sergt.
Stroud, C. A.	Gnr.
Sergeant, A. A.	Gnr.
Scott, G. E.	Gnr.
Sims, N. E. G.	Gnr.
Sladen, N. D.	Gnr.
Sloman, S.	Gnr.
Smith, E.	Gnr.
Snowball, T. P.	Gnr.
Stafford, J. T. G.	Gnr.
Sullivan, P.	Gnr.
Turnbull, A. D.	L/Bdr.
Tew, J. D. F.	Gnr.
Thomas, D. C.	Gnr.
Thompson, H.	Gnr.
Thompson, W. A.	Gnr.
Turner, J. J.	Gnr.
Vertue, K. R.	Gnr.
Wix, H. M.	Captain
Wigginton, J. E.	Lieut.
Waterman, E. H.	Sergt.
Weir, G.	Sergt.
Webb, G. H.	Sergt.
Willis, L. J.	Bdr.
Welch, M. C.	Gnr.
Welch, W. C.	Gnr.
Wesley, A. C.	Gnr.
Wellard, E. C.	Gnr.
Whatford, Dr. R.	Gnr.
White, T.	Gnr.
Wilson, G.	Gnr.
Williams, J. J.	Gnr.
Wright, J.	Gnr.

APPENDICES

ROLL OF HONOUR

Wood, R. T. Gnr.
Yates, H. G. Gnr.

NOTES 1. The above list is subject to corrections and amendments. It is the best that could be obtained before going to press.
2. It is regretted that no similar list has so far been made available for 143rd. Field Regiment.

APPENDIX F

HISTORY OF 97TH FIELD REGIMENT IN DIARY FORM, 1939–1945

1939
Sept. 3 Outbreak of war finds Regiment embodied at its Drill Halls in Maidstone, Bromley, Ashford and Canterbury.
„ 9 Concentrate Mote Park, Maidstone, and mobilize for foreign service.
„ 18 Advance party leaves for France.
„ 25 Main body embarks at Southampton.
„ 26 Disembark Cherbourg. Move by rail to La Hutte.
27 Concentrate Le Mans area. Joined by guns and vehicles which had travelled separately to Nantes.
Oct. 4 Move by road to Belgian Frontier and attached to I Corps Artillery under command Brigadier Pratt.
R.H.Q. established La Planque near Auchy. 385 at Visterie, 387 and Waggon Lines at Moncheaux.
Oct.–Nov. Dig gun pits in frontier defence line.
Dec. 1 Lt.-Col. F. Lushington takes command vice Lt.-Col. A. W. Lucy who returns to U.K. sick.

Dec.	6	Practice Camp at Sissons.
	28	Move to Somme area for mobile training. R.H.Q. and 385 at Marieux. 387 at Louvencourt.
1940		
Jan.	1	Visit Somme War Memorials.
,,	13	Move to Auchy at short notice. 385 again occupy Visterie.
Mar.	15	Return to Somme area for further training. R.H.Q. and 385 in Toutencourt and 387 in Pushevilliers.
Apr.	9	Return to Lille area and come under command III Corps Arty. Brigadier W. Duncan. R.H.Q. and 387 in Perenchies, 385 in Premesques.
,,	25	385 leave for Saar area and come under command 1st R.H.A. in support 51st Highland Division.
May	10	Germany invades Holland and Belgium. 12th Lancers occupy the line of the River Dyle.
,,	12–14	I Corps and II Corps B.E.F. in position on the Dyle. Regiment joins 5th Division G.H.Q. reserve.
,,	15	Arrive Ghoy in Belgium.
,,	16	Ordered forward to line of Mons Canal in support of 13 Inf. Bde.
,,	17	Arrive Brages.
,,	18	Return Ghoy. Ordered to St. Sauveur. Continue retreat to Seclin.
,,	19	Seclin.
,,	20	Move to Estevelles.
,,	21	Move to Oppy and Neuvreuil and later to Fresnes.
,,	22	Move back to Neuvreuil.
,,	23	Advance R.H.Q. established Gavrelle. Enemy attack; 13 Inf. Bde. withdraw.
,,	24	Arrive Verlinghem.
,,	25	Recce parties go to Cantin and return, meeting regiment on the road at Pont-a-Marc.

APPENDICES

May	26	Ordered Ploegstreet. 387 in action Warneton.
,,	27	Enemy attack. Grenadiers counter-attack.
,,	28	Withdraw to Rossignol.
,,	29	Arrive Eikhoek on Yser Canal.
,,	30	Arrive Moeurs inside Dunkirk perimeter.
,,	31	Embark Dunkirk.
June	1	Disembark Dover.
,,	7	Concentrate at Oakhampton and Inverurie, Scotland.
,,	14	Move to Abergele, N. Wales.
,,	16	385 rejoin. France sues for peace.
July	1	385 take over anti-tank defences in Wirral Peninsula.
,,	9	R.H.Q. established Swansea. 387 take over defences Swansea area.
Aug.	1	385 take over defences Carmarthen.
Sept.	16	Defences manned on receipt of code word "Cromwell".
Dec.	1	R.H.Q. and 385 move to Builth Wells, 387 to Llangammach. Mobilization and training as mobile Field Regiment begins again.
1941		
Feb.	20	Leave Wales. Billet for the night at Agricultural College, Cirencester.
,,	21	Halt for night at Stevenage.
,,	21	Arrive Harwich-Clacton area.
,,	23–25	Take over from 111 Field Regt. R.A. in support of 223 Inf. Brigade, Essex Division, under command Brigadier Sir A. Stanier. R.H.Q., at Great Bentley, 385 at Harwich, Great Oakley, and Thorpe le Soken, 387 at St. Osyth and Clacton.
Mar.	8	Ordered to mobilize for overseas service 8th April.
,,	15	Inspection by M.G.R.A.—Major General Otto Lund.
,,	17	Move to Great Baddow. Regiment changes to three battery basis. Date of formation of 470 Battery.

Apr.	8	Return to Harwich peninsula. Orders for overseas service cancelled.
,,	17	Inspection of regimental area by H.R.H. the Duke of Gloucester.
,,	22	Inspection by Lieut.-General Massey comd. XI Corps.
,,	29	Move to West Down Practice Camp, Salisbury Plain.
May	3	Return from West Down.
,,	6	Inspection by M.G.R.A.
,,	20	Inspection by Army Commander and Corps Commander.
June	1	Anniversary of return from Dunkirk. Parade on Great Bentley Green followed by thanksgiving service.
,,	18	Advance party move to Skreens Park near Chelmsford.
,,	22	Hand over to Devon Yeomanry. Move to Skreens Park.
Aug.	11	Major C. W. Johnson takes command 387 vice Major D. B. H. Warner promoted second in command.
,,	14	Visit by Hon. Colonel and other members of the Regiment.
,,	19	All vehicles sent to Wales for embarkation.
,,	22	Inspection by Brigadier C. B. Findlay, Inspector General of Artillery.
,,	27	Entrain Chelmsford for Glasgow.
,,	28	Embark SS. *Orontes* at Glasgow.
,,	30	Convoy sails.
Sept.	13	Arrive Freetown.
,,	17	Leave Freetown.
,,	30	Arrive Capetown.
Oct.	3	Leave Capetown.
,,	23	Arrive Bombay and tranship to H.M.T. *Devonshire*.
,,	24	Leave Bombay.
,,	30	Disembark Basra.
,,	31	Arrive Zubair.

APPENDICES

Nov.	6	Visited by Brigadier J. Halifax, B.R.A. 10th Army.
,,	12	Leave Zubair.
,,	17	Arrive Lancer Camp, Baghdad.
,,	20	Visited by Russian Mission at Lancer Camp.
,,	21	Arrive Habbaniya. Join 10th Indian Division—Maj.-Gen. W. J. Slim.
Nov.–Dec.		Train for desert warfare.

1942
Jan.		Construct gun pits and defence positions at Hindiya Barrage.
Feb.	2	Return from Hindiya. Training continued.
Mar.	1	Take part in Divisional Exercise near Ramadi.
,,	9	Inspection by General Auchinleck, C. in C. Middle East.
,,	11	Leave Habbaniya staying night at Sumaika.
,,	12	Arrive Beiji attached 20 Indian Infantry Brigade—Brigadier Macgregor.
Mar.–Apr.		Intensive training with affiliated infantry.
Apr.	7	Take part in Divisional Exercise in Sumaika area.
May	18	Leave Baiji.
,,	19	Arrive Taji near Baghdad.
,,	23	Leave for Western Desert staging first night at Majara.
,,	24–27	Cross desert into Palestine via LG5, H3, H4, and Mafracq.
,,	28	Arrive Tulkarm.
,,	30	Leave Tulkarm stage night Asluz.
,,	31	Stage night Canal area.
June	1	Pass through Cairo. Stage night Wadi Natrun. 470 are left behind in Cairo to form part of newly-formed 164 Field Regiment.
,,	2	Leave heavy baggage at Amriya. Short halt at Daba. Travel on all night to Mersa Matruh.

P

June	3	Arrive Matruh 04.00 hours and leave again 07.30 hours. Halt for night at Sollum.
,,	4	Join 20 Ind. Inf. Bde. at Bir-Amud.
,,	6	Occupy defensive positions at Ed Duda, Sidi Resegh and Belhamed.
,,	13	Support night attack on enemy positions at El Adem.
,,	16	Sidi Resegh attacked and over-run. 385 withdraw after losing two guns.
,,	17	Belhamed evacuated.
,,	18	Occupy Sollum defensive positions.
,,	22	Evacuate Sollum.
,,	25	Take over from 4 N.Z. Field Regiment in Matruh area.
,,	26–28	385 go out on column with 12th Lancers.
,,	28	10th Indian Division and 50th Division, surrounded at Matruh, break through enemy lines during the night.
,,	29	Arrive El Alamein.
July	1	Occupy Deir el Shein in Alamein defence line. Position attacked in the afternoon and over-run by German tanks.
,,	2	Remnants, less guns and equipment, concentrate at Amriya.
,,	3	470 Battery rejoin.
,,	4	Leave Amriya for R.A. Base Depot, Almaza, Cairo.
,,	5–20	Regiment reforms as two batteries, 385 and 387. Major D. B. H. Warner leaves to command 87 Field Regiment.
,,	20	Move to Cowley Camp, Mena. Join 50 Division R.A., Brigadier C. Eastman.
,,	27	Brass KY title badges adopted.
Aug.	24	Return to the desert. Concentrate El Hamam in support 8th Armd. Bde.
,,	28	In action El Huweija. Enemy attack expected.
,,	29	Visit by Army Commander, General B. L. Montgomery.

APPENDICES

Sept.	1	8th Armd. Bde. are attacked by 15 Panzer Div.
,,	2	Enemy halted at Deir el Agram.
,,	4	Regiment forms part of a column in pursuit of enemy withdrawal.
,,	9	Column disperses. Regiment moves into rest and training area.
,,	11	In support 22nd Armd. Bde. 7 Armd. Div. in area Deir el Tarfa.
,,	19	Inspection by Commander XIII Corps, Lt.-Gen B. Horrocks.
Sept. to Oct.	19 ⎫ ⎬ 3 ⎭	Period of intensive training and preparation for coming offensive.
Sept.	24	Visit by Army Commander.
,,	26	Cadre leaves for R.A. Base Depot, Cairo, to reform 470 Battery under command Major W. Prideaux.
Oct.	23	Battle of Alamein.
,,	30	Move back to Pepsodent position behind firing line.
,,	31	Take over from I R.H.A. in northern area.
Nov.	1/2	Final attack by New Zealand division supported by barrage.
,,	3	Attack successful. Rejoin 22nd Armd. Bde. and leaguer behind F.D.L.s.
,,	4	The break-through and the pursuit. In action near Tel Accakir.
,,	5	Advance seventy miles across desert.
,,	6	Action with 15 Panzer rear-guard near Sidi Haneish.
,,	7	Heavy rain delays pursuit.
,,	8	Move forward sixty miles. American and British forces land in French North Africa.
,,	9	Move forward sixty-two miles.
,,	10	Cross frontier wire into Libya.
,,	11	In action with German rear-guard near Capuzzo.
,,	12	Capture Tobruk and halt near El Adem.
,,	15	Victory thanksgiving service near El Adem.

Nov.	25	Leave 22nd Armd. Bde. and start march back to Cairo.
,,	29	Arrive Base Depot, Almaza. 470 Battery joins regiment.
Dec.	9	Inspection by M.G.R.A. Advance party leave for Cyprus.
1943 Jan.	15	Leave Almaza by train for Beirut.
,,	17	Embark on H.M.S. *Welshman*.
,,	18	Disembark Famagusta. Join 10th Indian Division.
Apr.	12	Lt.-Col. W. J. Mullens takes over command vice Lt.-Col. F. Lushington. Exercise "Tough".
May	15	Move to seaside camp at Boghaz.
June	14	Embark H.M.S. *Manxman* for Palestine.
,,	15	Concentrate at Arama in Safad area.
June to July	28 3	Take part in exercises and training in Galilee area.
,,	5	Move to Afula for Combined Operations training.
,,	24	Move to Combined Ops. Training Centre, Kabrit on Great Bitter Lake.
Aug.	11	Return to Arama.
,,	23	Move to Demeir near Damascus for Div. Arty. Practice Camp.
Sept.	3	Div. Arty. Sports meeting at Damascus Stadium.
,,	5	Move to Bayada.
,,	27	Malaria epidemic.
Oct.	1	C.O. and skeleton staff join III Corps in Cairo.
,,	2	Move to Sidon.
,,	16	C.O. returns from Cairo.
,,	24	A cadre including F troop leave for Haifa to join 805 Defence Regiment detailed for service in the Aegean.
Nov.	12	Regiment is represented at visit of King Peter of Yugoslavia to Royal Yugoslav Guards.

APPENDICES

Nov.	18	Leave Syria and move into winter quarters at El Bureij near Gaza.
,,	21	Stand by to quell riots in Tel Aviv.
,,	24	Move to Asluj in Sinai desert for Div. Arty. Practice Camp.
Dec.	5	Practice Camp ends. Return to El Bureij.
,,	7	805 Defence Regt. disbanded and cadre returns.
,,	9	Move to camp at Isdud, Palestine.
,,	13	Take part in demonstration exercise at Middle East Training Centre, Gaza.
,,	30	Move to Julis.
1944 Jan.		Course shooting at Asluj in Sinai Desert on various dates.
Feb.	3	Distribution of Africa Star ribbon.
,,	10–11	River crossing exercise.
,,	12–19	R.H.Q. and party take part in Exercise "Token" at Abbassia Barracks, Cairo.
,,	23–26	Divisional Artillery firing exercise at El Auja in Sinai Desert.
Mar.	1–8	Ninth Army Exercise "Crocodile" in Jordan Valley near Jericho. Regt. supports 25th Ind. Inf. Bde. in crossing of Jordan and advance to Es Salt against troops of 31st Ind. Armd. Div.
,,	11	Return to Julis.
,,	14	Move to Ter-Hag in Egypt to mobilize for overseas.
,,	22	Move to Port Said.
,,	23	Sail for Italy in SS. *Franconia*.
,,	28	Disembark Taranto.
Mar. 28 to Apr. 19		Concentrate near Taranto.
Apr	6	Inspection by Maj.-Gen. C. W. Reid, commanding 10th Ind. Div.
,,	19	Move to Cerignola.
,,	20	Move to Termoli.
,,	21	In action in La Torre—San Leonardo area.

June	5	Relieved by Carpathian Div., Polish Corps.
,,	6	D Day. American and British forces land in Normandy.
,,	7	Concentrate at Monte Aquila on River Volturno. Rejoin Eighth Army after absence of eighteen months.
,,	27	Move by Route 6 past Cassino to staging area ten miles S.E. of Rome.
,,	29	Div. relieves 8th Ind. Div. east of Perugia. Regt. comes into action near Ripa.
,,	30	Advance up the Tiber valley begins.
July	1	Move to Colombella.
	2	Advance continues.
,,	3	Advance continues.
,,	5	Move to San Lucia and on to Umbertide.
,,	6	Move north of Umbertide.
,,	8	R.H.Q. and 385 dive bombed.
,,	10	Advance continues.
,,	13	Move to Promano. Contact with enemy is lost.
,,	15	Advance continues.
,,	26	Visit by H.M. the King.
,,	28	Cross the Tiber and move fifteen miles to Monterchi by night.
,,	29	Further night move to Castella Soccio.
Aug.	1–2	Anghiari captured.
,,	4–13	Pause for consolidation.
,,	14–21	Move westwards over the ridge from the Tiber into the Arno valley.
,,	22	Advance past Subbiano to Villa Giuseppe.
,,	23	Paris and Marseilles taken by the Allies.
,,	25	Monte Forresto captured.
,,	27	Move to Chitignano. Capture of La Verna.
Sept.	6–17	Move to Chiusi.
,,	18	Move to Foligno.
,,	19	Move to Sennegallia.
,,	26	Concentrate at Coriano.
Oct.	1	Move through state of San Marino to Trebbio.
,,	2	In action at Cornacchiara.

APPENDICES

Oct.	10	Roneofreddo captured in night attack across Rubicon.
,,	11	Night march through Sagliano to San Paola.
,,	15	Move to Sorrivoli.
,,	18	Capture of Montereale.
,,	21	Capture of Taverna and S. Carlo.
,,	24	Move to Gallo; Cesena falls.
,,	31	Move to La Fratta.
Nov.	3–18	Rest area at Viserbo.
,,	19	In action at Villagrappa.
,,	20	Capture of Forli.
,,	23	In action at Villafranca.
Dec.	7	Move to Marzeno.
,,	8–16	Series of stiff battles across the River Lamone culminating in the capture of the Pideaura Ridge.
,,	17	Move to Pergola.
1945		
Jan.	4	Move to area west of Faenza.
Feb.	10	Relieved by 2 Carpathian Bde.
,,	12	Move to Fano.
,,	13	Move to Assisi.
,,	14	Rest area at San Sepulchro.
Mar.	11	Move to Vechio.
Mar. to Apr.	13 } 14	In action Sillaro Valley near San Clemente. The end of the valley blocked by permanent artificial smoke screen.
Apr.	14	Relieved by the Italian Folgore Division.
,,	15	Concentrate at Sassaleone.
,,	16	Move to Lugo on Adriatic front.
,,	17	Concentrate at Massa Lombarda.
,,	18	In action near Medecina. Fire barrage of 480 r.p.g. in support attack by 2nd N.Z. Div.
,,	20	Move forward to Selva.
,,	22	Pursue retreating enemy to Minnerbio.
,,	23	Move to Altedo.
,,	27	Move to forward concentration area near Ferrara.
May	2	End of Italian Campaign.

APPENDIX G

HISTORY OF 143RD FIELD REGIMENT IN DIARY FORM, JUNE, 1944–MAY, 1945

1944

June	12	Landed at La Riviere, concentrated near Brecy and came into action at Coulombs.
,,	16	Supported 1/4 K.O.Y.L.I. attack on Cristot Moved to Audrieu.
,,	17	Supported 6 D.W.R. attack on Parc du Boislonde.
,,	18	Supported 6 D.W.R. during counter-attack at Parc du Boislonde and 7 D.W.R. attack on Point 102.
,,	25	Supported Divisional attack on Fontenay and Tessel Brettville.
,,	26	Supported 15th (S) Division attack on Cheux.
,,	30	Supported 1 Tyneside Scottish during counter-attack at Rauray.
July	6	Moved to Hermanville sur Mer near Caen.
,,	8–9	Supported attack by 1st Corps on Caen.
,,	10	Returned to Audrieu.
,,	14	Moved to Fontenay.
,,	16–17	Supported attack by 59 Division towards Noyers.
,,	23	Moved to Gibbeville.
Aug.	10	Moved to Frenonville.
,,	16	Moved to Bernaville La Compagny.
,,	17	Moved to Pedouzes.
,,	18	Moved to Magny.
,,	19	Supported 11 R.S.F. crossing of the River Vire at St. Crispin.
,,	20	Moved to Mezidon.
,,	21	Moved to Cambremer.

APPENDICES

Aug.	22	Moved to La Closseterie.
,,	23	Supported 11 R.S.F. and 1st Leicesters crossing of the River Tooques at Villy La Vicomte.
,,	24	Moved to Le Pins.
,,	25	Moved to Lieurey.
,,	26	Moved to Compigny.
,,	27	Moved to La Vieville.
,,	28	Moved to Bourneville.
Sept.	2	Crossed Seine at Rouen.
,,	3–10	In action outside Le Havre.
,,	10–12	Supported attack on Le Havre.
,,	14	In rest near Bolbec.
,,	17	In rest near Dieppe.
,,	22	Moved to Zoerle-Parys.
,,	24	Moved to West of Turnhout.
,,	26	Supported 146 Brigade crossing of Turnhout Canal.
,,	29	Supported Leicesters at Depot de Mendicite.
Oct.	5	Supported Polish Armoured Division attack towards Baale-Nassau.
,,	7	Supported Lincolns during counter-attack at Poppel.
,,	12	Moved to South West of Poppel.
,,	19	Moved to St. Leonards.
Oct.	21–23	Moved to Wustwezel. Supported Leicesters and R.S.F. during enemy counter-attacks.
,,	24	Moved to Wildert.
,,	26	Supported attack on Nispen.
,,	27	Moved to Esschen.
,,	28	Moved to Den Henvel. Supported attack on Wouw.
,,	29	Supported attack by 146 and 147 Brigades towards Roosendaal.
,,	30	Roosendaal liberated.
,,	31	Moved to Oud Gastel.
Nov.	2–3	Supported 56 Brigade in clearing up to Mass.

Nov.	6	Moved to Fijnart. Supported attack by S.W.B. and Lincolns on Willemstad.
,,	8	Moved up to Budel.
,,	13	Moved up to Weert.
,,	14	Supported attacks by 51st and 53rd Divisions towards Venlo.
,,	19	Moved to Zelen.
,,	22	Moved to Zandberg.
,,	26	Moved to Rooth.
,,	29	Moved to the "Island" and took over from Arty. of 50th Division at Lent.
Dec.	4	Supported 7 D.W.R. during enemy attack at Halderen.

1945
Jan.	18	Supported Leicesters during counter-attack at Zetten.
,,	19–21	Supported 56 Brigade at Zetten.
Feb.	8	Fired in support of Op. "Veritable".
,,	19	190 Battery moved to Druiten to support Recce regiment for Op. "Jock".
Mar.	30	Moved to Cleve supported 3rd Canadian Division.
Apr.	1	Moved to Bemmel.
,,	2–3	Supported clearing of the "Island".
,,	5	Moved to Elst.
,,	9	Moved to Eldern.
,,	12–14	Supported attack on Arnhem Op. "Anger".
,,	16	Moved to Arnhem.
,,	17	Supported R.S.F. at Ede. Moved to positions East of Ede.
,,	18–21	507 Battery supported Recce Regiment in clearing area north of Appledoorn.
,,	24	Moved to Lunteren. Supported 147 Brigade's advance towards Renswourde.
,,	25	Supported 1st Leicesters during enemy counter-attack at Renswourde.
May	7	Assisted in disarming Dutch SS Division near Doorn.

APPENDICES

APPENDIX H

HISTORY OF ROYAL EAST KENT MOUNTED RIFLES, 1914–1918[1]

The R.E.K.M.R. which formed part of the South East Mounted Brigade, was commanded by Lieut.-Col. The Earl of Guildford when orders to mobilize were received on 4th August, 1914, and to concentrate in the Broad Oak area, some two miles N.E. of Canterbury on 5th August.

On the outbreak of war the sole equipment of the East Kent Yeomanry was saddles, rifles, and two machine guns. Horses started to arrive in the middle of August, but it was not until the end of October, 1914, that the Regiment was fully equipped with weapons and transport.

By this time many of the men who had mobilized had left the regiment to form the 2nd Line and to take up commissions. The regiment, however, had quickly filled up to strength with raw recruits and had settled down to intensive training.

In the beginning of 1915 the regiment moved into hutments on the old polo ground at Canterbury, and despite many "alarums and excursions" remained there till 22nd September, 1915.

On that date the regiment, 513 strong, entrained at Canterbury for Liverpool, embarking on the *Olympic* on 23rd September, 1915, for an "unknown destination" which turned out to be Lemnos, via Alexandria. Three days after the regiment arrived at Lemnos, it was transshipped and landed on Gallipoli at Cape Helles, where it was continuously in action from October, 1915, till January, 1916, when it was evacuated to Lemnos en route for Egypt, arriving at Sidi Bishr on 11th February, 1916.

From the day the regiment left Canterbury it had been

---

[1] NOTE.—The above account by Lieut.-Colonel H. W. Lucy, O.B.E., T.D., unfortunately arrived too late to form part of the Introduction as the book had already gone to the printers. It is therefore inserted as an Appendix.

dismounted, and on arrival in Egypt hopes were running high at the prospect of being re-mounted. It was a very bitter disappointment therefore to all ranks to learn that the South East Mounted Brigade was to be amalgamated with the Eastern Mounted Brigade (Norfolk Yeo., Suffolk Yeo., and Welsh Horse) to form the 3rd Dismounted Yeomanry Brigade.

It was about this time that the regiment suffered the loss of Lieut.-Col. The Earl of Guildford, who was evacuated sick to England, Lieut.-Col. O. Moseley Leigh taking over command.

After service in the Canal Zone, the Regiment moved to Sollum on the Western border of Egypt in July, 1916, and shortly afterwards the three squadrons were formed into two companies of infantry, Chatham, Dover, Gillingham, Rochester, Thanet, and Waldershire Troops forming No. 1 Company, and Ashford, Canterbury, Faversham, Folkestone, London, and Sittingbourne Troops forming No. 2 Company.

In the beginning of 1917 the R.E.K.M.R. with the West Kent Yeomanry was formed into the 10th (Yeo.) Bn. The Buffs, and became part of the 74th (Yeo.) Div. on its formation in March, 1917. The Bn. left Sollum in March, 1917, travelling by sea to Alexandria where it disembarked for Sidi Bishr.

Early in April, 1917, the regiment left Egypt for Palestine, marching via Kantara, Sheik Zâwieh, and Belah to the vicinity of Gaza, the 74th (Yeo.) Div. being in reserve at the second battle of Gaza.

From April to October, 1917, the Bn. had a strenuous time with little fighting, but much digging, and even greater discomfort. Wadi Ghuzzi, Wadi Nukabir, Wadi Levi, Tel-el-Fara and Khan Yunis are names which the Yeomen of those days will never forget. They will always bring back memories of intense heat by day, extreme cold by night, shortage of water, and a superabundance of dust, flies, and every form of torment.

At the end of October, 1917, the Bn. took part in the battle for Beersheba, after which it was withdrawn to Karem for rest and re-equipment.

APPENDICES

Then began the big job of pushing "Johnnie Turk" northward, through the Plain of Sharon, Esdud (the ancient Ashdod), Hamsukerieh, Kutrah, Latron, and Beit Nuba, till on 7th December the Bn. reached Kubeibeh and took part in the battle for Jerusalem, which was captured on 9th December, 1917. Northwards again to Beit Manana and Ramillah, after which the Bn. was withdrawn to rest in the Moiya Wadi, near Bethlehem, where the Bn. spent Christmas.

Christmas Day was heralded in by a cloudburst. Christmas dinner proved to be a "feast"; hot tea, half a tin of bully beef per man, half a mug of small biscuits, and a very small ration of cheese and jam. Christmas parcels commenced to arrive in the middle of February, 1918.

In the meantime the Bn. had been employed on road-making, a strenuous and back-breaking job, so that it was with joy that the Bn. went back into the line at the beginning of March to relieve the 231 Bde. in front of Yebrouk. The following day the Bn. attacked and captured Yebrouk and advanced to the ridge overlooking the Nablus road. Pushing on, Et Tell was reached, after which the Bn. was withdrawn to reserve. This was the last action the Bn. took part in in the Palestine campaign.

On 13th April, 1918, the Bn. marched to railhead at Ludd where it entrained for Kantarah via Gaza. From Kantarah the Bn. marched to Alexandria where it embarked on the P. & O. liner SS. *Malwa* for France, reaching Marseilles on 6th May, 1918.

END

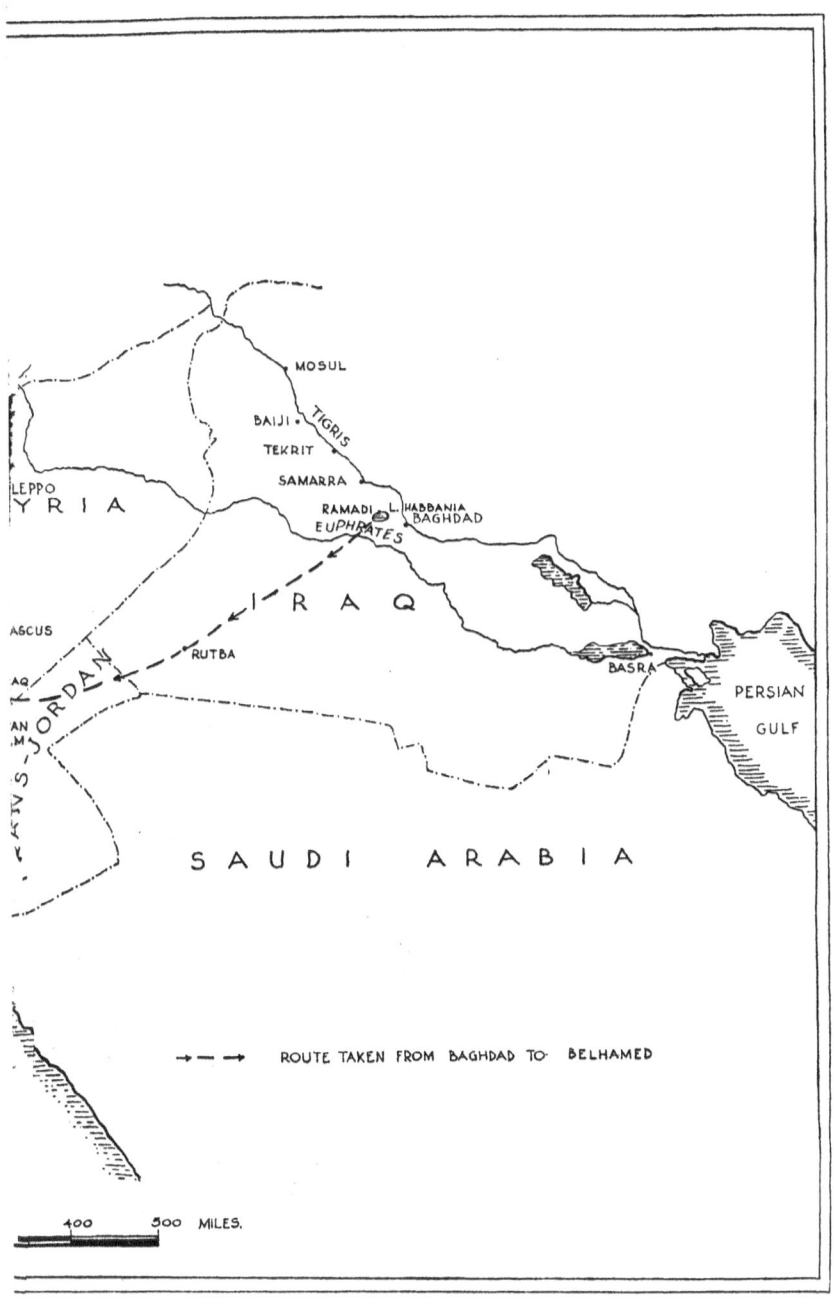

www.ingramcontent.com/pod-product-compliance
Lightning Source LLC
Chambersburg PA
CBHW030853170426
43193CB00009BA/590